— BAKE IT BETTER —

CLASSIC CAKES & BISCUITS

HODDER &
STOUGHTON

Classic Cakes and Biscuits first published in Great Britain in 2015
by Hodder & Stoughton
An Hachette UK company

This edition published in 2016

1

Hardback ISBN 978 1 473 64732 9

Editorial Director: Nicky Ross
Editor: Sarah Hammond
Project Editor: Laura Herring
Series Editor: Linda Collister
Art Director: James Edgar
Layouts: Nicky Barneby, Andrew Barker
Photographer: David Munns, Amanda Heywood
Food Stylist: Natalie Thomson, Lizzie Harris, Annie Rigg
Props Stylist: Victoria Allen, Linda Berlin

Typeset in Dear Joe, Mostra, Kings Caslon and Gill Sans

Printed and bound in China by C&C Offset Printing Co Ltd

Hodder & Stoughton policy is to use papers that are natural, renewable and recyclable products and made from wood grown in sustainable forests. The logging and manufacturing processes are expected to conform to the environmental regulations of the country of origin.

Hodder & Stoughton Ltd
Carmelite House
50 Victoria Embankment
London EC4Y 0DZ
www.hodder.co.uk

→ BAKE IT BETTER ←

Would you like to learn to be a better baker?

We know that so many people watch *The Great British Bake Off* for the tips and techniques you pick up – not only from the judges, but from watching the bakers too. We wanted to distil that knowledge into a library of cookbooks that are specifically designed to take you from novice to expert baker. Individually, each book covers the skills you will want to perfect so that you can master a particular area of baking – everything from cakes to bread, sweet pastries to pies.

We have chosen recipes that are classics of each type, and grouped them together so that they take you on a progression from 'Easy does it' through 'Needs a little skill' to 'Up for a challenge'. Put together, the full series of books will give you a comprehensive collection of the best recipes, along with all the advice you need to become a better baker.

The triumphs and lessons of the bakers in the tent show us that not everything works every time. But I hope that with these books as your guide, we have given you a head start towards baking it better every time!

Linda Collister
Series Editor

- BAKE IT BETTER -
CLASSIC
CAKES

Linda Collister

HODDER &
STOUGHTON

Contents

Needs a little skill 100

Up for a challenge 148

Welcome bakers!

When you're learning to bake, there's no better place to start than with a cake, and there are 40 absolute classics in this book.

As well as being great bakes, the recipes have been carefully chosen to introduce you to all the key techniques, such as creaming, whisking, rubbing in and folding that not only set you up to bake better cakes, but which you will find invaluable for all baking.

Start with the 'Easy does it' section and master the basics with recipes like Quick Berry Muffins, Sticky Gingerbread or Apple and Maple Syrup Traybake. As you grow in confidence you will feel ready to move to the recipes that 'Need a little skill' – a Bitter Chocolate Roulade perhaps, a perfect Dundee Cake or a sumptuous Devil's Food Cake. The more you bake, the sooner you will be 'Up for a challenge', testing your decorating skills with the Mile-high Chocolate Cake or whipping up a light-as-air sponge for the classic Fraisier.

The colour strip on the right-hand side of the page tells you at a glance the level of the recipe (from one spoon for easy to three spoons for a challenge), and gives you a helpful checklist of the skills and special equipment you will use.

Before you begin, have a look at the Baker's Guide at the beginning of the book. That will tell you what equipment you need to get started (just a bowl, a spoon and a cake tin will do!), introduce you to the most important ingredients, and explain some terms and techniques in more detail.

We have chosen Classic Cakes as the subject of our first book in the Bake It Better series because even the simplest of cake recipes gives impressive results. It's amazing what you can do with just flour, butter, sugar and eggs when you know how. So dive in, and get baking!

HOW TO USE THIS BOOK

SECTION 1: BAKER'S GUIDE

Read this section before you start baking.

The Baker's Guide contains key information on ingredients (pages 10–15), equipment (pages 16–21) and techniques (pages 22–35) relevant to the recipes in the book.

Refer back the Baker's Guide when you're baking if you want a refresher on a particular skill. In the recipes the first mention of each skill is highlighted in bold.

SECTION 2: RECIPES

Colour strips on the right-hand side and 1, 2 or 3 spoons show the level of the recipe.

Within the colour strips you'll find helpful information to help you decide what to bake: Hands-on time; Baking time; Makes; Special equipment; Sponge used and Storage.

Refer back to the Baker's Guide when a skill is highlighted in bold in the recipe if you need a reminder.

Try Something Different options are given where the recipe lends itself to experimenting with ingredients or decorations.

BAKE IT BETTER

Baker's Guide

Ingredients

The most important piece of advice we can give when you're checking the ingredients list of a recipe is don't be tempted to substitute. This is particularly true if you're new to baking, or it's a new recipe for you.

Below are the most frequently used cake ingredients, with advice on buying, storing and using them – the more you understand your ingredients, the easier it will be to avoid problems and get consistently good bakes.

BAKING POWDER, BICARBONATE OF SODA AND CREAM OF TARTAR

Some bakes need the help of a chemical raising agent to increase their lightness. The two most common are **bicarbonate of soda** (an alkali) and **cream of tartar** (an acid). **Baking powder** is a mixture of both.

Raising agents work by reacting together with moisture and heat to release small bubbles of carbon dioxide, which lighten the crumb of your bake. Some recipes use a slightly acidic ingredient, such as buttermilk or yoghurt, in combination with bicarbonate of soda to produce the bubbles of gas. Make sure you use the exact amount stated, and discard out-of-date or damp raising agents as they won't give you the best bake. To check if baking powder is still active mix a teaspoonful into a glass of warm water – if it bubbles up nicely it's fine to use, otherwise, throw it out.

If you want to you can make your own by combining 1 teaspoon bicarbonate of soda with 2 teaspoons cream of tartar, but baking powder is easy to come by so it's not really necessary. More useful to know is that you can make your own self-raising flour by adding 4 teaspoons baking powder to every 225g plain flour.

BUTTER

Most bakers use **unsalted butter**, which has a lovely rich flavour and gives a more evenly coloured bake because it contains less whey than salted butters. Some **salted butters** also have a strong taste that can be overpowering in a sweet bake, but if the urge to bake takes you and you only have salted butter, it's really not a big problem; just remember not to add any additional salt to sweet recipes.

Wrap butter well and store it in the fridge away from strong flavours, or freeze it for up to a month. Remove from the fridge in plenty of time so that it's the right consistency for your recipe. Creamed and all-in-one sponges (see page 24) use butter at room temperature so that it's easier to smoothly incorporate into dry ingredients; chilled and diced butter is needed for rubbed-in sponges (see page 22). In an emergency you can soften diced butter cubes for a few seconds in the microwave, but it takes much longer to firm up over-softened butter.

CHOCOLATE

The flavour of chocolate cakes and ganaches, toppings, fillings and frostings really depends on the chocolate you use. Good-quality chocolate is widely available in supermarkets these days and you can get chips in larger bags from online suppliers. Store bars of chocolate well wrapped in a cool, dry, dark cupboard, and away from strong-flavoured ingredients.

Take care when melting chocolate (see page 34) as it easily scorches if it gets too warm and then becomes unusable. Chocolate chunks and chocolate chips are useful for adding to sponge mixes and for toppings/decorations, but you can also use bars chopped into similar-sized pieces.

Dark chocolate is most widely used in this book. One with around 70 per cent cocoa solids will give the best flavour. Anything over 75 per cent can be too dry and bitter for general baking.

Milk chocolate has a much lower cocoa content and a milder, sweeter taste that can be slightly greasy. Good-quality milk chocolate has a higher percentage of cocoa solids, giving better flavour and a slightly firmer set when used as a coating, or decoration.

White chocolate doesn't contain any cocoa solids, so cocoa butter content is what you're looking for here: 30 per cent or more (children's bars usually have hardly any actual cocoa butter). Because there is more fat in white chocolate it sets less firmly than dark or milk chocolates.

COCOA POWDER
A dark, unsweetened powder made from pure cocoa with nearly all the cocoa butter removed – it is very bitter and powerfully flavoured, and adds an excellent chocolate taste to lightly textured sponges and butter icings. Don't use drinking chocolate, which has had sugar and dried milk powder added to it, as a substitute.

CREAM
Always use the cream recommended in the recipe – the fat content varies significantly and can have a huge effect on your bake.

Single cream has at least 18 per cent butterfat and is good for pouring and adding richness to rubbed-in mixtures (see page 22), but it is not suitable for whipping.

Double cream has at least 48 per cent butterfat and whips well (see page 35) when thoroughly chilled. Don't use the extra-thick double cream labelled 'for spooning' as you won't be able to whip it; nor is it suitable for making ganache.

Whipping cream does exactly what it says on the tub. It has at least 35 per cent butterfat. For best results, chill it thoroughly before whipping (see page 35).

Buttermilk, often found in supermarkets as 'cultured buttermilk', is low-fat or non-fat milk plus another lactic acid-producing culture to give it an acidic 'tang'. It is often used, along with bicarbonate of soda, to add lightness and flavour to cakes.

Clotted cream has at least 55 per cent butterfat and is best for serving on the side with a slice of cake, not for whipping or ganache-making.

Sour cream has only around 18 per cent butterfat and is made by introducing a bacterial culture to give it a naturally 'soured' tang.

Crème fraîche is cream that has been soured in a similar way to sour cream, but with a richer, milder flavour.

DRIED FRUIT
Vine fruits, such as raisins, sultanas and currants, are preserved but still soft. They add sweetness and moisture, as well as a fruity flavour, to cakes and, soaked overnight in alcohol, tea or fruit juice, plump up deliciously. Soft-dried apricots, prunes, figs, cranberries, blueberries, sour cherries and dates are also useful additions and can

replace vine fruits in many recipes. Candied peel is widely available ready chopped, but can also be found in boxes as whole pieces of orange, lemon or citrus peel, allowing you to cut the pieces into a size and mix that you prefer. Store opened packets in a screw-top jar to stop the fruit getting hard.

EGGS

All the recipes in this book use medium-sized eggs (about 62–65g each). Eggs help your cake rise. Their size is important as they work in ratio with other ingredients (fats, sugar and flour). Using a different-sized egg might affect results – you might need more liquid, or it may not bind together well, rise properly or cook all the way through.

Store eggs in the fridge, pointed-side down, to protect the yolk from drying out and spoiling. Keep them in the box they came in and in the cooler body of the fridge, not the door, and use by the best before date. Spare egg whites freeze well for up to a month – mark the quantity and date on the container and defrost thoroughly before use.

Eggs should be used at room temperature as they give a greater volume when beaten, so always try to bring them out of the fridge 30–60 minutes before using. If you've left it to the last minute you can gently warm up eggs by placing them in a bowl of lukewarm water for 10 minutes.

EXTRACTS AND FLAVOURINGS

Try to avoid synthetic flavourings as they can give your bake a rather unpleasant 'fake' taste.

Vanilla extract and **almond extract** are concentrated liquids, so use them in tiny quantities. You'll find 'essences' and 'flavours' in the shops, but these won't have the same effect so try not to use them.

Vanilla paste is made from the seeds of vanilla pods and provides an even more concentrated flavour than vanilla extract.

Coffee flavour can come from bottled coffee essence, although some people find it a rather strange flavour so you can instead use instant espresso powder or granules dissolved in boiling water.

Ground spices should be measured carefully and kept in screw-topped jars rather than open packs. Try to use them when they are still fresh, preferably within a few months of opening; it's probably best to buy them in small quantities.

Alcohol in the form of liqueurs or brandies is used in cake-making. Génoise sponges are often brushed with sugar syrup mixed with a dash of liqueur or brandy. When making a rich fruitcake, dried fruit is usually soaked in alcohol to balance the sweetness and help the cake keep for longer.

FLOUR

Use flour when it's still fresh and store it correctly – keep opened packs either in storage jars, plastic food boxes or plastic food bags to stop the flour getting damp. Don't add new flour to old in storage jars, and aim to use it within a month of opening or by its best before date.

Wheat flours are the most frequently used flours in cake-making. **Plain flour** is just that: flour with nothing added. **Self-raising flour** is made from plain flour with baking powder added so that the mixture expands and rises in the oven. Make your own self-raising flour by adding 4 teaspoons baking powder to every 225g plain flour.

The flours used for cake making are known as 'soft' flours, as they have a relatively low proportion of protein to starch – usually 8–10 per cent protein (protein is the gluten-forming part of the flour which is necessary for bread-making, but is too much for making cakes). Finely milled **wholemeal** and **spelt flours** labelled 'plain' or 'self-raising' are great for more robust cakes as they add a slightly richer and nutty flavour, but they are too heavy for finer bakes like creamed sandwich cakes (see page 24).

Gluten-free flours are now readily available and inexpensive. They are usually made from a combination of rice, potato, tapioca, maize, chickpea, broad bean, white sorghum or buckwheat flours, and vary in taste and texture from brand to brand, so it's worth trying a few out. A few are specially made for cake-making and can be substituted fairly easily, although some suggest adding xanthum gum (which comes in powder form) to help the structure of the bake and allow it to rise. Others recommend adding more liquid to your recipe, so make sure you follow the advice on the packet. (It's also worth checking whether your baking powder is gluten-free.)

HONEY

Look out for honey that comes from the nectar of a single variety of flower or plant (such as orange blossom), as the flavour should be more distinct, but be careful that it doesn't overpower the flavours in your bake. As a general rule, the paler the honey, the milder the flavour. Soft-set honey (but not honeycomb) is easiest to blend in, but solid honey can be used if it is softened first (by gentle warming in the microwave or in a small dish set in a bowl of hot water). Honey also adds moisture to cake mixtures, but too much can make it dense, so make sure you follow the recipe.

ICING SUGAR

Icing sugar comes as either a very finely powdered white sugar or a lightly golden unrefined sugar, which dissolves readily and can be used for piped or spreadable icings, frostings and toppings. Refined white will give you pure white icing, while unrefined will give a hint of gold. Sift icing sugar well to remove any lumps before use (see page 30). **Fondant icing sugar** is a combination of icing sugar and dried glucose syrup that you mix with water or juice to make a glossy, satiny icing that's slightly more substantial, or to make a dough-like modelling paste for edible decorations. **Royal icing sugar** is a mixture of icing sugar and dried egg white that can be mixed with water to make a stiff white icing. **Ready-made ready-to-roll** and **rolled icing** can be used to cover and decorate cakes and cupcakes.

MARGARINE AND SPREADS

Margarines are based on vegetable oils, with added salt and flavourings. Some are made specifically for baking and can be used straight from the fridge; they give good results but won't taste quite the same as bakes made with butter. Spreads designed for use on breads and crackers are not meant for baking and won't give a good bake as they contain too much water and not enough fat. Check the pack as most say whether they're suitable for baking or not.

MARZIPAN

Made from a sweet paste of ground almonds, this can be rolled out to cover and decorate, or used as a filling ingredient.

NUTS

With distinct and varied flavours and textures, the type of nut you use is very important to your bake. Some nuts are oilier than others, which will alter the crumb and can make it heavier than expected. Their consistency, whether whole, chopped or ground, is also crucial to baking success, so check the recipe to make sure you are using what is needed. Toasting nuts increases flavour, but they burn easily, so watch them carefully. Nuts can quickly turn rancid and bitter, so store them in a screw-topped jar or airtight container in a cool, dark spot and use before they hit their best before date.

OILS

American-style cake recipes, like Apple and Maple Syrup Traybake (page 66), often use **vegetable oil** instead of butter. The advantage is that it speeds up the method because you don't have to cream butter; plus it is a handy store-cupboard ingredient. **Sunflower oil** gives the best results as it has very little flavour, but a light, mild **olive oil** can also work very well. Don't use vegetable frying oil, which will give a distinctive, unpleasant 'savoury' flavour to your baking.

SUGAR

It's important to use the type of sugar specified in the recipe. They all combine with other ingredients in slightly different ways and this affects the end result.

Caster sugar is best for most sponges as the grains are fine and quickly break down when beaten with butter. **Golden caster sugar** is less refined than caster sugar, which gives it a pale golden colour and very slightly richer flavour. **Granulated sugar** takes much longer to dissolve and often gives a speckled finish to the tops of cakes.

Brown muscovado sugars are available in both light and dark; they add a toffee-ish flavour and colour to cake mixes, but they also tend to make them slightly more moist and heavy. They will form into lumps during storage, so you'll need to sift/press out the lumps before use.

SYRUP AND TREACLE

As with sugar, it's important to use the syrup or treacle specified, as they have quite different flavours. **Golden syrup** is a sticky, pale gold syrup made from sugar cane sap. It's sweeter than sugar and gives cakes a moist, dense texture. **Black treacle** is much darker brown, thicker and stickier than golden syrup and has a very strong, almost bitter, flavour. It gives the characteristic flavour and dark colour to gingerbreads (see page 62). **Maple syrup** is the boiled-down sap of sugar maple trees and has a wonderful red-gold colour and unsurpassed flavour. It is expensive, and do beware of cheaper 'maple-flavour' syrups that won't produce the same results.

Syrup and treacle can be awkward and messy to measure and weigh, but if you sit the whole tin in a bowl of just-boiled water, or warm the measuring spoon in a mug of boiled water beforehand, you will find it much easier and less messy by far.

Equipment

The beauty of baking is that you don't need huge amounts of kit to get started; in fact you can probably produce your first bake with items you already have – a bowl, a cake tin or two, scales for weighing your ingredients accurately and a wooden spoon should just about cover it. The other bits of kit you get will depend as much on the size of your kitchen as your enthusiasm for cake-making. Bear in mind that for more complex recipes you may need more than one tin or baking sheet, although you may be able to re-use what you already have. Read the equipment list alongside each recipe carefully before you start to make sure you have everything you need.

BAKING PAPER AND LINERS

Lining papers make it easier to remove your bake from the tin once it's cooked (see page 29). Some recipes require a double layer of lining paper to give extra protection from the heat of the oven. **Non-stick baking paper** or **baking parchment** is suitable for most purposes and both are good for delicate mixtures. **Parchment-lined foil** is heavier and can be folded to make a sturdy cake case – useful for making Battenberg Cake (see page 100).

Ready-made cake tin liners and discs for lining the bases of tins will save you time and effort if you bake dozens of cakes, and are available from most supermarkets. **Re-usable silicone liners** are excellent for lining baking sheets and can be cut to fit other tins you use regularly.

Greaseproof paper is best kept for wrapping cooked food as it is water resistant, but its waxy coating doesn't stand up well to heating and your cakes will just stick to it.

BOWLS

You'll probably end up with a variety of bowls. It's useful to have more than one and some different sizes, and there are pros and cons to the different types. **Heatproof glass** bowls are probably the best all-purpose choice for mixing, whisking and melting chocolate over hot water (see page 34). **Stainless steel** bowls are unbreakable and dishwasher-proof, but they won't go in the microwave. **Ceramic** bowls are pretty, but can break quite easily and can be heavy. **Plastic** are all-purpose and cheap, and ones with rubber bases are non-slip. (You can solve the non-slip issue by placing a damp cloth underneath any bowl.) **Anodised aluminium** bowls are very durable and will last a lifetime but, again, they're no good for the microwave.

CAKE BOARD

A cake board isn't essential when you're starting out – you can use a plate or the base of a cake box in most cases – but it is useful for more advanced cake recipes as it will protect the delicate sponge while you decorate. You can get disposable and re-usable cake boards.

CAKE TINS

It is very important to use the tin that's specified in the recipe. The quantities and baking time have been calculated to work with that particular cake tin and your bake won't turn out the way it's supposed to if you use a different one.

A really solid, heavy-duty tin will last forever, withstand repeated baking without scorching or warping, and stay rust-free if you take care of it, which means washing and drying it thoroughly after use.

Heavy-duty metal cake tins are probably

the most reliable and durable, but other options are non-stick metal tins, heavy aluminium, glass, ceramic or silicone. Avoid flimsy non-stick tins as they will quickly lose their coating. Never use a tin that has started to shed its coating as bits of it could end up in your bake. If you opt for silicone moulds, a baking sheet underneath will help stabilise the mould before you pour in the mixture, and when you're transferring it to the oven.

When you're starting out you'll get the most use out of a couple of 20.5cm straight-sided deep sandwich tins, a 450g loaf tin and maybe a square 20–20.5cm traybake tin. With these you'll be able to make most of the Easy Does It recipes. Unless you buy a tin with the size stamped on the base it's a good idea to mark the size underneath with an indelible marker to save getting out a tape measure each time you bake.

Deep round/square cake tins are good for richer cakes and fruitcakes, such as the Cherry Cake or the Porter Cake (see pages 112 or 152) and are available with fixed or loose bases. You can get 'push-up' loose-based tins with a watertight silicone seal for easy release.

Loaf tins can be used for cakes like Lemon Drizzle Loaf Cake or Double Marble Cake (see page 44 or 86), as well as for bread-making. The 450g (about 19 × 12.5 × 7.5cm) and 900g (about 26 × 12.5 × 7.5cm) tins are the most commonly used sizes.

Sandwich tins are the ones to start with. A pair of round, deep, straight-sided sandwich tins 20.5cm across, with sides 4–5cm high, will allow you to make most classic cakes. A third tin makes for quicker baking when making American-style layer cakes, such as the Three-layer Banana Cake (page 98), but you can always just re-use your other tin while the first layer is cooling.

Specialist tins are useful if you want to bake recipes such as the Lemon-scented Madeleines (page 64), for which you'll need a madeleine mould tray. Recipes such as the Battenberg Cake (page 100) and Bitter Chocolate Roulade (page 128) also use specialist tins, although you can use standard tins instead (see the recipe methods for instructions on adapting regular tins).

Springclip tins have a spring release, a base that clamps in place when the clip is fastened and a deep metal ring which lifts off when unfastened. These are really helpful when making cheesecakes and cakes that are not inverted, or are particularly fragile, such as the Apple and Ginger Crumble Cake (page 54). They come in many sizes, but 20.5cm and 22–23cm tins are the most useful.

Swiss roll tins are rectangular with shallow sides about 2cm high. The most useful sizes are 20 × 30cm and 23 × 33cm.

Traybake tins are square or rectangular with sides that are about 4cm high. They are endlessly versatile and are used in this book for making Chocolate Brownies (page 60) as well as basic sheet cakes like the Vanilla Traybake (page 42). The most useful ones are loose-based, or slide apart for the easy removal of your bake. A 20–20.5cm square tin and a 20.5 × 25.5cm rectangular tin will come in handy most often for the bakes in this book.

6- or 12-hole deep muffin tins/cupcake tins are what you need for small bakes, muffins and cupcakes. You can get non-stick or silicone versions (choose wire-framed for stability), which may not need lining with paper cases.

COOLING RACKS

A large wire cooling rack with legs allows air to circulate underneath your cooling cakes, preventing condensation (and the dreaded 'soggy bottom'). If needs be, you can improvise with a clean grill-pan rack, but the finer wires on a collog rack are more effective.

FOOD-PROCESSOR

A food-processor makes light work of chopping and blending. Some will also make cake mixtures with a plastic blade or paddle, but results vary, so go on personal recommendation if you wish to use the machine for cake-making. Generally, they'll work better for some of the wetter mixtures than for recipes where you need to incorporate a lot of air.

ICING TURNTABLE

This is a non-essential but useful bit of equipment that enables rotation of the cake while you're decorating. Pick one with a non-slip base.

KNIVES

A **large sharp knife** for chopping nuts and neat slicing is vital (as is a **knife sharpener**). A **long-bladed serrated bread knife** is good for slicing cakes into layers (see page 34). A **palette knife** is good for spreading, and an **off-set palette knife** (one with a kink in the blade) is essential for more advanced cake-decorating.

Knives are made from different materials. The main ones to consider are stainless steel, which is cheaper but needs to be sharpened regularly; carbon steel, which is more expensive, harder and easier to keep sharp; and ceramic, which is far harder than carbon steel ones, much lighter and don't require sharpening – but can chip easily.

LARGE METAL SPOON

A large metal spoon with a long handle is useful for folding in (see page 33) and for transferring your cake mixtures.

MEASURING JUG

Pick a heat-resistant and microwave-safe jug that has both metric and imperial measures, starting from 50ml if you can find one, otherwise 100ml, and going up to 2 litres. A small jug or cup that measures from 1 teaspoon (5ml) up to 4 tablespoons (60ml) is a very useful extra. You can also get measuring jugs with cup measurements – useful if you bake a lot of North American recipes.

MEASURING SPOONS

Everyday teaspoons, dessertspoons and tablespoons vary enormously in size so you shouldn't use them to measure ingredients. Baking is such an exact science that it's worth investing in proper measuring spoons for small amounts of liquids and dry ingredients (such as baking powder, spices, salt and sugar), ranging from ⅛ teaspoon to 1½ tablespoons. Go for spoons with narrow ends that will fit into fiddly spice jars. Unless the recipe says otherwise, all spoon measures in these recipes are level – skim off the excess with a finger or the back of a knife.

OVEN THERMOMETER

Baking requires accuracy and ovens vary; their internal thermostats can be notoriously unreliable. If you really get the baking bug you might want to invest in an oven thermometer to double-check it's the correct temperature and to work out where in your oven the hotter and cooler spots are located.

PASTRY BRUSH

Available in a variety of widths and bristles, pick a brush in a medium width for brushing on melted butter, beaten egg, glaze or sugar syrup. Make sure whatever type you buy is heat resistant and dishwasher-proof.

PIPING BAGS

Disposable plastic piping bags in various sizes are available from most supermarkets. Generally the ones with the non-slip exteriors are easiest to use. You can also find reusable **nylon piping bags** from specialist shops and cake-decorating suppliers. They have a little more weight and strength to them and don't have seams for the mixtures to leak through. Most can be rinsed and then washed inside out in very hot water. Always make sure they are completely dry before putting them away. (See page 35.)

PIPING NOZZLES

These conical tubes fit into the end of piping bags and are available in scores of shapes and sizes from the finest writing tip to large, sharp-toothed star nozzles for piping buttercream. The best value are the sets that provide a reusable bag plus a set of stainless steel nozzles, either just the small size for decorating or an all-round set that includes large (1.5cm/2cm), plain and star nozzles.

ROLLING PIN

In cake making a rolling pin is used for rolling out marzipan and icing. Choose a long, fairly heavy one that is about 6–7cm in diameter – ones without handles are generally easier to use.

SCALES

Baking is really a science, so it pays to be accurate if you want perfect results every time. As you'll be dealing with some quite small quantities, **digital** scales are preferable to **spring** or **balance** scales as they are much more precise and can weigh ingredients that are as little as 1 gram. You can see the weight easily at a glance and add multiple items to one bowl simply by resetting the balance to zero after adding each ingredient. Always keep a spare battery on standby.

SIEVE

Essential for removing lumps from icing sugar and other ingredients, and to bring air into mixtures. A stainless steel wire sieve with a large bowl is the most versatile and should last longer than plastic. A smaller tea-strainer sized sieve is also a good piece of kit to have, for dusting cakes and bakes with icing sugar and cocoa powder.

SPATULA

Flexibility is key here. You want a good-sized rubber or plastic spatula that's heat resistant for mixing ingredients together, cleaning out bowls and spreading mixtures. A smaller one is perfect for fiddly amounts. A metal spatula is good for spreading.

STORAGE CONTAINERS

It's not essential to go to the expense of buying a special container to store your bakes, but if you find yourself trying to transport your cakes a lot it's probably worth investing in a cake carrier, which makes transportation a breeze. Choose one that has secure locking clips and can go in the dishwasher. Otherwise, use a good stainless steel tin with a tight-fitting lid, or a heavy-duty plastic container with a secure lid. Store your bake well away from any heat sources (radiators, sunlight, kitchen light fittings, your fridge or cooker) and mark on a sticker the day of baking so you know when your bake is still good to eat.

TIMER

A digital kitchen timer, with seconds as well as minutes, is another good purchase for achieving that all-important accuracy. Get one with a loud ring and set it for 1 minute less than the suggested time in the recipe, especially if you are unsure of your oven temperature – you can always increase the cooking time if needed.

WHISKS AND MIXERS

These range from the most basic, which means the baker has to do the energetic whisking, to free-standing food mixers that do all the hard work for you.

Wire whisks can be balloon-shaped or flat. A sturdy hand-held wire whisk with an easy-grip handle that fits your hand is ideal for whisking mixtures on and off the heat.

Hand-held rotary whisks have two beaters in a metal frame, which are turned by hand. They're perfect for whisking egg whites (see page 31), whisking mixtures over heat (no trailing leads) and whisking out lumps in batters.

Hand-held electric whisks are more expensive, but much more powerful and can also be used for creamed cake mixtures (see page 24) and more general mixing. Look for models with a set of attachments and a retractable cord for easy storage.

Free-standing mixers really do save time and energy if you do a lot of baking. A large free-standing model with attachments for beating, whisking and making dough is a great investment. If possible, buy an extra bowl too, as it helps when making cakes with multiple elements; a bowl with a snap-on lid is very useful too. Large mixers do all the beating and whisking for you, so you will get more volume into your meringues and whisked egg mixtures in a much shorter time, and are great for batch-baking. They do take up space though, so they're not ideal for a small kitchen – an electric hand whisk is probably the best choice here.

WOODEN SPOONS

You can never have enough wooden spoons – they're heat-resistant, won't scratch non-stick pans and are ideal for beating mixtures (see page 31). It's a good idea to keep ones for baking separate from those that are used for savoury cooking, as wooden spoons are porous and will absorb strong flavours.

ZESTER

The zest of lemons, limes and oranges is full of flavour and often used in baking recipes. A zester is the best way to remove the zest so you don't end up with lots of bitter pith as well. A long zester with a sturdy, easy-grip handle is easiest to use and clean. If you can, go for one of the new types with a ceramic-coated stainless steel surface and slide-on zest catcher.

Skills

Once your ingredients are lined up and equipment sorted, you're ready to get baking. This section covers everything from lining your tin to mixing and folding, and it's worth reading at least once. Follow this advice and you can enjoy your baking safe in the knowledge that you'll be happy with the end results.

All the recipes in the book tell you exactly what you need to do step-by-step, but you'll notice that some of the baking terms are highlighted in bold, which means you can refer back to this section if you want a bit more detail, or to refresh your memory.

THE 5 CAKE-MAKING METHODS

The key to any good cake is the texture of the sponge. Whether it's the delicate crumb of a Victoria sponge, a denser fruitcake or light-as-air Swiss roll, it's all down to the way the ingredients are combined. Once you've got to grips with these techniques the world of cakes will be there for the baking.

Below each method are some examples of recipes in the book that use them. Try these and in no time you'll be an expert in each method.

RUBBED-IN METHOD

This refers to the action of combining fat and flour to add air to the mix, making the final bake lighter. It's used for fairly robust, lower-fat cakes like rock cakes and simple fruitcakes, and is quick to do, either with your hands and a bowl, or using a mixer or food-processer. Rubbed-in mixtures use cold butter, straight from the fridge; try to keep your palms clean while you combine the ingredients as your fingertips are cooler and won't melt the butter.

Because these mixtures use about half fat to flour they lose their freshness quickly, so cakes should be eaten on the same day. *Learn with: Spicy Scottish Rock Cakes (page 40), Simple and Pretty Fruitcake (page 46)*

How to rub in by hand
1. **Sift** the flour (and any spices or raising agents) into a mixing bowl.
2. Make sure the butter is cool and firm and cut it into small cubes. It helps to have floury hands to do this to stop it melting and sticking as soon as you touch it.
3. Add the butter pieces to the flour and quickly toss them around in the flour with your fingertips.

4. Once the butter pieces are coated, pinch them into the flour using just your fingertips and thumbs. Lift your hands to the top of the bowl and gently rub more of the mixture between your fingers and thumbs so that it combines as it falls back into the bowl.

5. Keep doing this until the mixture has a finer, crumb-like consistency (*see photo, right*). To check if you've missed any clumps, give the bowl a shake – you'll see them come to the surface.

6. Once you're happy with the consistency, quickly stir, or mix in, any other flavourings with a spoon or fork, plus eggs and/or milk, to make a fairly stiff cake mixture, but don't over-beat it as you don't want to develop the gluten in the flour and toughen the crumb.

....

How to rub in using a food-processor
1. Tip the flour into your food-processor bowl, add the chilled, diced butter and pulse in short bursts until there are no visible butter pieces remaining.

2. Add the sugar and pulse again until combined, then slowly pour the liquid through the feeder tube, pulsing until the dough starts to clump together.

3. Tip into a bowl and use your hands to very gently knead and gather the mixture into a ball.

....

How to rub in using a free-standing mixer
1. Fit the machine with the creamer/ paddle attachment and slowly mix your dry ingredients with the chilled, diced butter until the butter is no longer visible.

2. Add the sugar and mix again. You can then add the liquid and gently mix until starting to clump together.

3. Gather the mixture into a smooth ball.

ALL-IN-ONE METHOD

The recipes that use this method are the heroes of the cake world, offering speed, simplicity and reliability. All the ingredients are combined in one go by beating with a wooden spoon, electric beater or whisk. Make sure the ingredients are at room temperature so they can be smoothly combined and air can be easily incorporated into the mix. Take the butter and eggs from the fridge a good hour before you need them.

1. Sift the flour and any spices, cocoa powder or raising agents (a little baking powder is usually included even with self-raising flour to help the mixture rise well) into a large bowl, then add the sugar, butter (or oil), beaten eggs and any liquid (milk, coffee, fruit juice) and start **beating** everything together fairly slowly.

2. Once all the dry ingredients have been incorporated, scrape down the sides of the bowl and beat for a couple of minutes at a fast speed until it is smooth and creamy (*see photo, left*).

Learn with: Apple and Ginger Crumble Cake (page 54), Fudgy Chocolate Birthday Cake (page 82)

CREAMED METHOD

This is the method used for most of our best-loved cakes. As with the all-in-one mixtures, make sure the ingredients are at room temperature so they quickly combine and take up as much air as possible. You should always use the type of sugar specified in the recipe, but with creamed mixtures this is particularly important.

1. Put the softened butter into a large bowl and **beat** with a wooden spoon, whisk or electric mixer until the butter is very creamy – almost like mayonnaise (*see photo, right*).

2. Gradually beat in the sugar, scraping

down the sides of the bowl every minute or so, until fully combined, then add any small amounts of flavouring, if using. (Save larger amounts of flavouring, such as coffee or alcohol, until later). Keep on beating and scraping down the sides of the bowl, until the mixture is very pale in colour and the texture is fluffy and lump-free.

3. Beat the eggs with a fork until well broken up, then beat them into the mixture with a wooden spoon, a tablespoon at a time. Take your time to beat in thoroughly after each addition as you're incorporating air into the mixture, which will make your finished cake much lighter. Add 1 tablespoon of the weighed flour from your recipe with each of the last two portions of egg to prevent the mixture from curdling. If it does start to separate a little it's not a disaster – the cake will taste just the same, but it might not rise quite so well (see page 36).

4. Sift the remaining flour and salt into the bowl (plus any spices) and gently **fold** in using a large metal spoon, until you can no longer see any specks or streaks of flour.

5. At this point you can add any additional flavours (such as coffee, juice or alcohol), edible food colouring, fruit, nuts, milk or melted chocolate, as per the recipe. Again, for best results, make sure all additions are at room temperature.

6. Make sure all your ingredients are combined and you have a soft mixture; a good test for a creamed sponge mixture is that it should be just soft enough to drop off a wooden spoon when lightly shaken.

7. Transfer to the prepared tin and the oven immediately, as the raising agents will be getting to work already.

Learn with: Victoria Sandwich Cake (page 74), Whisky Dundee Cake (page 104) and Porter Fruitcake (page 152)

MELTED METHOD

Sponges that use the melted method are usually pretty straightforward to make and are good for hard-to-combine ingredients with a high moisture content, like treacle or fruit juice. They are usually runnier mixtures than those on previous pages and make cakes with a soft, moist crumb.

You will need a medium to large-sized pan (large enough to hold all the ingredients) and a wooden spoon.

1. Dice the fat (usually butter) and put it into the pan with the sugar(s) and golden syrup or black treacle, or a liquid like tea or fruit juice. Stir over a low heat until the butter has melted and the mixture is very smooth and lump-free. Some mixtures then need to be boiled or simmered for a few minutes.

2. To avoid scrambling the eggs, leave the mixture to cool until barely warm before adding the beaten eggs, flour and any other ingredients, then pouring the mixture into your tin (*see photo, left*).

Learn with: Malted Tea-loaf Cake (page 56), Sticky Gingerbread (page 62) and Chocolate Brownies (page 60)

WHISKED METHOD

Whisked sponges rely on whisked eggs, rather than the addition of raising agents, to make them light and fluffy. It's a very versatile method used to produce cakes of varying levels of complexity, from the fairly simple Classic Swiss Roll (page 94) to the challenging Gâteau de l'Opéra (page 168).

Cake mixtures where whole eggs and sugar are whisked together are also known as 'génoise' sponges and may, or may not, have a small quantity (around 15g per egg) of melted, cooled (or very creamy and pourable) butter folded into the mixture right at the end, after the flour. This makes the sponge softer and richer.

'Biscuit' sponges like the Fraisier (page 162) are also whisked, but the yolks and whites are whisked separately with sugar, and combined later. These sponges are slightly drier and are often used for multi-layered creations because they are a bit more robust.

The key to success with whisked sponges is good technique (see page 31). Also make sure your eggs are at room temperature to aid expansion. Ideally, you should use an electric hand whisk or a large free-standing mixer fitted with a whisk attachment for the task. If you only have a rotary whisk, it's best to stand the mixing bowl over a pan of steaming hot water (but don't let the base of the bowl touch the hot water), as the gentle warmth increases the expansion of the eggs (be very careful!).

For a simple whisked sponge

1. Whisk the eggs and sugar at high speed for at least 5 minutes, until the colour changes from bright yellow to a very pale, creamy colour and the volume increases about five-fold. You should have a thick, mousse-like foam consistency. You can tell that the mixture is ready when it passes the 'ribbon test'. To do this, lift the whisk out of the mixture – if a very distinct ribbon-like trail of mixture falls back into the bowl, you can stop whisking (*see photo, right*).

2. At this point the carefully **sifted** flour is added to the bowl and gently **folded** into the foamy mixture. This very light sponge is raised entirely by the air bubbles, so the folding in of the flour must be done with care and a light hand.

Learn with: Classic Swiss Roll (page 94), Lemon Curd Layer Cake (page 144)

For a 'biscuit' sponge

1. Carefully separate the egg whites from the yolks and melt the butter.

2. Whisk the whites to soft peaks (*see photo, left*), then gradually whisk in half the sugar, a couple of teaspoons at a time, to make a light meringue.

3. Add the remaining caster sugar to the yolks, along with any other ingredients, and whisk until you have a mousse-like mixture that falls in thick ribbons form the whisk.

4. Fold the meringue into the mousse mixture in batches.

5. Sift the flour on top and gently **fold** it into the mixture.

6. Drizzle the melted butter over the top and fold that in, too.

Use for: Fraisier (page 162), Gâteau de l'Opéra (page 168)

EXPERT ADVICE FROM START TO FINISH

This section takes you through every stage of the cake-making process, explaining the how, what and why behind the key techniques.

HOW TO LINE CAKE TINS

Most recipes ask you to prepare your cake tin, which usually involves greasing and lining it in some shape or form. This stops the cake sticking to the tin. If you double-line your tin, the paper will also act as protection from the oven's heat. Prepare your tin before you start so that your mixture doesn't have to sit and wait later.

When you're getting ready to bake, always make sure your tin is clean and dry.

Shallow tins like a sandwich tin or a traybake tin should be greased and base-lined. Lightly brush melted butter inside the base, sides and rim (the butter makes a better barrier than oil and tastes nicer than lard or vegetable fat). Set the tin on a sheet of baking paper and draw around it (*see photo, above right*), then cut out the shape and press it onto the base, taking care that there are no creases (you can also buy ready-cut discs – see page 17).

Loaf tins should first be lightly brushed inside with melted butter. Then cut a long strip of baking paper that is the same width as the tin base and twice its length (the extra paper each end will help you lift the baked loaf from the tin to save damaging it). Press the paper onto the base and up the short sides to line it (*see photo, right*) – the long sides will not be covered by paper (they are well-greased and once you loosen the cake after baking it will lift out easily).

Circular deep tins should be greased and lined on the base and sides. First brush with melted butter then cut out two rounds of baking paper very slightly smaller than the base of the tin (see instructions above). Next cut a strip of baking paper that's long enough to go all round the sides, and high enough to stand about 5cm above the rim.

Make a fold 3cm deep along one long edge of the strip and open it back out so that you have a crease. Snip all the way along the folded edge up to the crease, at 1cm intervals, to create a fringe. Press one of the paper rounds into the base of the tin, then press the long strip around the sides up to the crease, so that the paper fringes fold inside the tin (*see photo, left*), slightly overlapping; be careful to avoid creases.

Brush a little melted butter onto the first base round, then put the second round onto it, covering the fringe. Lightly brush a little more melted butter on the sides and base lining to hold them in place (you can also buy cake tin liners that need no extra preparation, rather like huge cupcake cases – see page 17).

HOW TO SIFT DRY INGREDIENTS

It might often seem unnecessary, but sifting dry ingredients like flour, raising agents, cocoa powder, icing sugar and spices, not only removes any large lumps, but also introduces air and disperses the ingredients throughout the mixture, which can make a big difference to the evenness of your bake.

Tip your ingredients into a large dry sieve over a large bowl and gently tap the sieve with your hand so the ingredients settle into the bowl.

You can also use a food-processor to combine dry ingredients effectively – this is great for mixtures using muscovado sugar, which tends to form hard lumps. The machine will add air automatically, so you won't need to sift ingredients into it.

HOW TO BEAT A MIXTURE

Recipes often tell you to beat an ingredient or mixture and what this usually means is to add air by vigorous mixing. You can beat individual ingredients like butter or eggs, or whole cake mixtures as you do in the all-in-one method (see page 24).

There are various kit options available for beating, ranging from the most basic wooden spoon, to a food-processor. An electric whisk or mixer will add air into the mixture for you, but to do this by hand, angle the bowl slightly away from you and beat in small circles, rotating the spoon or whisk away from you, lifting it slightly out of the mixture in the upward movement to trap the air that will then be incorporated into the mixture in the downward movement (*see photo, right*).

HOW TO WHISK EGGS

Whether you're whisking whole eggs or just their whites, eggs should always be at room temperature to help them expand to their maximum volume.

Whisking egg whites needs a large, spotlessly clean and grease-free bowl (any trace of fat or yolk stuck to the bowl or whisk will prevent the whites from being beaten successfully – you can cut a lemon in half and run the cut side around the inside of the bowl and over the whisk to be really sure).

Put the egg whites in the bowl and whisk on a low speed (or slowly by hand) for about 30 seconds so they become frothy and the structure starts to develop.

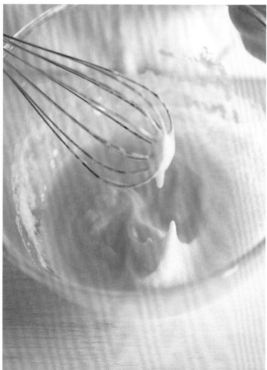

If you add a pinch of cream of tartar or a drop of lemon juice at this point the slight acidity will help the structure to stiffen, which helps you achieve the maximum volume. Increase the speed and continue whisking until the mixture is a mass of tiny bubbles with a very smooth and fine texture. To tell if the whites have reached **soft peak stage**, lift the whisk out of the mixture – you should get a peak of egg whites that slightly droops down (*see photo, left*).

The next stage, after a little more whisking, is **stiff peak**, when the peak should stand upright, with no droop (*see photo, below left*). At this stage you should be able to turn the bowl upside down and hold it over your head (or the worktop, if you're not feeling quite so adventurous) without the whites falling out.

Whisking egg whites for meringues involves adding sugar, which you do when the whites reach soft peak stage. If you add the sugar too early it will dissolve quickly and make the mixture soft and damp. But don't wait until stiff peak stage because the structure won't be elastic enough to hold the sugar, resulting in a lumpy, bobbly meringue instead of a shiny, glossy, smooth one.

Whisking to the 'ribbon stage' is used for delicate sponges where eggs and sugar are whisked at high speed to build up a thick, mousse-like mix. Use a large bowl to allow for increased volume and whisk on a high speed for 4–5 minutes until the mixture becomes so thick that when the whisk is lifted out of the bowl the mixture falls back into it to leave a thick, ribbon-like trail on the surface. (See page 26 for more on this and for photograph.)

HOW TO FOLD IN

This is the way to delicately combine two or more ingredients – for example adding sifted flour to a creamed cake mixture or incorporating beaten egg whites – so that you don't knock out all the air you've carefully beaten or whisked in. Use the edge of a large spoon or plastic spatula to cut down cleanly through the centre of the mixture until you touch the bottom of the bowl, then turn the spoon right-way up and bring it up through the mixture to the top. Turn the spoon over so that the contents flop gently onto the rest of the mixture (*see photo, right*). Give the bowl a quarter turn so that you start from a different place, then cut down again through the mixture, lift it and flop it over again. Keep doing this folding action, using the least number of movements possible, until you can't see any more unmixed streaks.

HOW TO CHECK IF YOUR CAKE IS COOKED

The most reliable way to test delicate cakes and most sponges is the fingertip test: gently press the top of the sponge in the centre with your fingertip – the sponge is ready if it springs back into place and has started to shrink back from the sides of the tin. If a slight dent remains in the sponge after you press it (or it starts to sink), then keep it in the oven for a few more minutes.

The cocktail stick or skewer test is used for heavier and richer cakes, all fruitcakes and dense chocolate cakes. Simply stick a fine metal or wooden skewer or a wooden cocktail stick, into the centre of the cake. If it comes out clean rather than damp with cake mixture, the cake is ready, although in some exceptions (Brownies are a good example) the skewer should come out still slightly sticky.

HOW TO TURN OUT A SPONGE

Carefully run a round-bladed knife around the inside of the tin to loosen the sponge, and leave it to firm up for 30–60 seconds. To avoid your wire rack leaving marks on the top of a delicate sponge, cover a clean board with a clean, dry tea towel and turn the sponge out upside down onto it. Peel off the lining paper from the base, then set the wire rack on top and turn the whole thing over again. Carefully remove the board and towel. You can leave the sponge to cool, right-side up, on the wire rack.

HOW TO CUT A SPONGE INTO LAYERS

This sounds tricky but is actually very easy once you get the hang of it. First, make a small vertical nick or cut up the side of the sponge with the tip of a small knife – this will help you align the layers in the right place when sandwiching them back together. Gently but firmly press down on top of the sponge with the flat of your hand, and, using a long serrated knife (a bread knife is ideal), carefully saw the sponge horizontally in half to make two even layers (*see photo, above left*). If possible keep the cake still and let the knife do the work.

HOW TO MELT CHOCOLATE

Break the chocolate into even-sized pieces so that it all melts at the same rate. Put it into a heatproof bowl set over a saucepan of steaming hot (but not boiling) water; be careful not to let the base of the bowl touch the water as it will burn the chocolate (*see photo, left*). As the chocolate softens, stir it gently so it melts evenly. You can use the chocolate as soon as it is liquid and smooth, around 30°C (86°F). If it overheats and reaches 50°C (122°F) it will 'seize' and become grainy, hard and unusable, so you'll have to start again. White chocolate is very easy to overheat and the pieces may keep their shape, even when the chocolate is melted, because of the high fat and sugar content. Some recipes advise to take the bowl off the heat once the chocolate is half melted to continue melting off the heat.

HOW TO WHIP WHIPPING CREAM

Make sure the cream is thoroughly chilled before you start to stop it curdling (in warm weather, chill the whisk and bowl, too). Use a hand-held wire whisk (balloon is best), hand-held rotary whisk, electric whisk, or free-standing mixer. If you need the cream for folding in, whip on a medium speed to a **soft peak**. If you are going to pipe the cream, whisk for a couple more seconds again until it holds a **firm peak** (*see photo, above right*).

HOW TO FILL A PIPING BAG

Drop the piping nozzle, if you are using one, into the piping bag, then snip off enough of the tip so that the nozzle fits snugly and just peeps out. Twist the bag right above the nozzle (so the mixture doesn't ooze out while you're filling it), then put the bag in a tall glass or jug and fold the top of the bag over the rim (the container will support the bag so that it's easier to fill). Spoon the mixture into the bag until about two-thirds full (*see photo, right*). Unfold the bag from the rim and twist the top to push the icing down to the (still twisted) nozzle end, pushing out any air pockets, then twist it again to compact the mixture and prevent it escaping. Untwist the nozzle end and squeeze the bag so that the mixture fills the nozzle. Practise the flow and shape of the piping before you begin.

Help!

No matter how experienced you are in the kitchen, sometimes things just go wrong. Here are the most frequently encountered baking issues, and how to resolve them.

MY CREAMED MIXTURE HAS CURDLED!

Don't panic, all is not lost! First work out why this has happened, then try to fix it.

The butter and egg emulsion 'splits' (looks curdled) for three reasons: the butter was too cold and not sufficiently beaten (see page 31) before and after the sugar was added; the eggs were too cold, making it difficult to make the emulsion work; or the eggs were added too quickly, without enough beating in between each addition. As well as the tips on page 24, to prevent it happening next time, use a warmed mixing bowl if the kitchen is chilly, make sure the butter is properly softened and that the eggs are removed from the fridge in plenty of time. You can often save the mixture by beating in a tablespoon of hot water, or by adding another egg yolk.

If you haven't been able to rescue it, bake the cake anyway – it may be smaller and heavier, but it will taste just as good.

WHY DIDN'T MY CAKE RISE?

Check your ingredients: did you use the correct flour, or did you accidentally leave out the raising agents? If baking powder was an ingredient, check it's still active; if it's stale or damp it will have lost the power to produce carbon dioxide, which is what raises the sponge (see page 11).

It may be that your oven wasn't heated to the correct temperature before baking. Most cake mixtures need to be cooked fairly quickly, making the fat melt as the starch expands to form the structure of the cake. An oven thermometer will tell you if your oven's thermostat is out by a few degrees and you can also check if there are any hot or cool spots; if you're baking more than one cake at a time this can alter the bake, so they may need rotating around, or given a little longer in the oven.

WHY ARE THERE CRACKS ON THE TOP OF MY CAKE?

Cracks are usually caused by the oven being too hot, or the cake was on too high a shelf. The cake forms a crust too quickly but the rest of the mixture continues to rise, causing the surface to crack. Don't worry too much though, it will still taste good.

WHY DID MY CAKE SINK IN THE MIDDLE?

Your cake wasn't baked enough. This is another reason to get an oven thermometer to double-check your oven's thermostat. If the centre of the cake mixture doesn't get hot enough (around $100\,^\circ$C$/212\,^\circ$F), then the structure won't become set and firm, and the middle of the cake will collapse as it cools. Use a kitchen timer and test for doneness (see page 33) before pulling the cake out of the oven to cool. And if you open the oven door too soon after putting the cake in it's likely to sink, so don't be tempted to take a peek until time is up.

Disguise the dip with whipped cream and fresh fruit, or cover it up with icing.

WHY IS THERE A PEAK IN THE MIDDLE OF MY CAKE?

A slight dome is usual, a mountain isn't! If your cake tin is too small for the mixture the outside edges will set and form a crust while the middle keeps on rising, as this is the last part of the cake mixture to get hot. Or maybe the cake mixture was too dry and stiff: check the egg sizes (see page 13) and always weigh everything accurately.

You can trim the cool dome away neatly and cover the surface of your cake with a dusting of icing sugar or a layer of icing.

WHY HAS MY CAKE OVERFLOWED ITS TIN?

It's likely that the tin was too small for the cake mixture, so check the recipe for the tin you need to use. Sandwich cakes usually call for 'deep' sandwich tins, with sides 4–5cm high – these are not the same as layer-cake tins or pans, which are shallower.

To make it ready for the table, just cut off the excess and neaten up the top and sides. Again, finish with a dusting of icing sugar or cover with a layer of icing.

WHY HAS MY SPONGE CAKE STUCK TO THE TIN?

Sponge cakes are sweet, sticky mixtures, so you really need to spend a little time on preparation. Non-stick tins are great but you still need to brush the inside and rim with melted butter and cover the base with baking paper (see page 29). To be really careful you can sprinkle a little extra of the flour used to make the cake into the tin, then shake and twirl the tin so that the flour coats the sides evenly before tapping out the excess. Rich fruitcakes and some deep sponge cake recipes call for the sides to be lined too, as this helps the edges set firm as well as helping the cake bake evenly – if you skip this step you risk the edges becoming scorched and dry, so it's worth taking the extra time to do it.

To get a truly stuck-in cake out of its tin, run a round-bladed knife all the way around the inside of the tin and then leave it for about 5 minutes so it firms up a bit. It will shrink slightly as it cools, so hopefully you'll be able to get it out. If it's still not budging, leave it to cool and set firm, place a plate on top, then turn it upside down and shake it out onto the plate.

WHY IS MY CAKE RATHER TOUGH?

Over-working an all-in-one or rubbed-in cake mixture (see pages 24 and 22) can develop the gluten in the flour, causing a tougher, bread-like bake, so be careful not to over-beat these mixtures (see page 31): stop as soon as everything has been incorporated and looks smoothly amalgamated.

There's not a great deal you can do if your cake is heavy like this, but try using it in a trifle, moistened with sherry.

WHY IS MY CAKE SOGGY?

Check your recipe to see whether your cake needs to be turned out onto a wire rack as soon as it comes out of the oven (see page 34) – this will prevent the steam inside it condensing and making the base soggy. Sponge cakes are usually unmoulded fairly rapidly, but larger cakes and fruitcakes are best left to cool in the tin to prevent them cracking or splitting, and only unmoulded once they have firmed up. A few cakes, often those baked in springclip tins, need a few minutes for the edges to firm up before the sides of the tin are unclipped. Always run a round-bladed knife around the inside of the tin to loosen the cake unless the recipe says otherwise. And if you do have a cake with the dreaded soggy bottom, you can always just cut off the base.

BAKE IT
BETTER
Recipes

Spicy Scottish Rock Cakes

A great starter cake for getting to grips with the **rubbed-in method**. No fancy equipment here – just grab a spoon and mixing bowl to make a batch of these little foolproof cakes.

225g self-raising flour
½ teaspoon ground mixed spice
¼ teaspoon ground ginger
couple of good pinches of salt
85g unsalted butter, chilled and diced
85g golden caster sugar

100g luxury dried fruit mix
1 medium egg
2 tablespoons milk
1 tablespoon demerara or coarse sugar crystals, for sprinkling

Easy does it

HANDS-ON TIME:
10 minutes

BAKING TIME:
12–15 minutes

MAKES:
10 cakes

SPECIAL EQUIPMENT:
None

METHOD USED:
Rubbed-in method, see page 22

STORAGE:
Eaten the day you make them

1. Preheat the oven to 200°C (180°C fan), 400°F, Gas 6. Line the baking sheet with baking paper.

2. **Sift** the flour, mixed spice, ground ginger and salt into a mixing bowl, then drop in the butter pieces, tossing them in the flour to lightly coat. Using the very tips of your fingers and thumbs, **rub in** the butter with the flour so that the mixture looks like fine crumbs. Add the golden caster sugar and luxury dried fruit mix to the bowl and stir with a wooden spoon or plastic spatula.

3. Break the egg into a separate bowl, pour in the milk and beat them with a fork until just combined.

4. Pour the mixture into the dry ingredients and stir together until you have a very firm, stiff dough. The dough should hold its shape, but if it refuses to come together or there are stray dry crumbs at the bottom of the bowl, stir in a little more milk, a teaspoon at a time. Don't add too much milk, though – if the mixture is too soft it will collapse into scones in the oven!

5. Use a spoon to scoop out the mixture and make 10 heaped peaky mounds on the prepared baking sheet. Space them well apart so that they can spread out. Sprinkle over the demerara or coarse sugar crystals.

6. Bake for 12–15 minutes until a good golden colour and firm to the touch. If they look like they are not baking evenly after the first 8 minutes, rotate the baking sheet.

7. Put the rock cakes on a wire rack and leave them to cool. Eat warm or at room temperature, preferably on the day you baked them.

Try Something Different

To make Fat Rascals (a richer version of Rock Cakes), replace the ground ginger with ½ tsp ground cinnamon and a few gratings of nutmeg, and use single cream instead of milk. Top each cake with 3 blanched almonds before you bake them. Eat warm, smothered with melting butter.

Vanilla Traybake

A traybake is a simple no-fuss **all-in-one** mixture. It uses just a few ingredients you probably already have, but can be glammed up with anything from glittery sprinkles to silver balls.

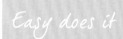

HANDS-ON TIME:
10 minutes

BAKING TIME:
20–25 minutes

MAKES:
20 squares

SPECIAL
EQUIPMENT:
25.5 × 20.5 × 5cm
traybake tin, cake
tin or roasting tin

METHOD USED:
All-in-one method,
see page 24

STORAGE:
Keep for up to
4 days in an airtight
container

For the sponge

125g unsalted butter, softened
125g caster sugar
1 teaspoon vanilla extract
2 medium eggs, at room temperature, beaten
1 tablespoon milk, at room temperature
150g self-raising flour

For the frosting

250g icing sugar
100g unsalted butter, softened
1 tablespoon milk
½ teaspoon vanilla extract, or to taste
decorations of your choice

1. Preheat the oven to 180°C (160°C fan), 350°F, Gas 4. Grease and **line** the tin with butter and baking paper.

2. To make the sponge, put the butter, sugar, vanilla, eggs, milk and flour into a large bowl or the bowl of a food-mixer. **Beat** everything together with a spoon or the whisk attachment. Start slowly – otherwise the mixture could fly out of the bowl – and scrape down the sides of the bowl every now and then with a spatula. After about 2 minutes the mixture should look very smooth and light. If you are adding any flavourings or other ingredients, stir them in now.

3. Scrape the mixture into the prepared tin and spread it out right into the corners, making sure it is nice and even. Bake for 20–25 minutes until the top is a good golden brown. You can **check** your cake is cooked by gently pressing the centre lightly with your fingertips; it should spring back.

4. Stand the tin on a wire rack and run a round-bladed knife around the inside to loosen the sponge. Leave it to cool and firm up in the tin and it will be easier to remove. When cooled, **turn out** the cake and peel off the paper.

5. While the sponge is cooling, make the frosting. **Sift** the icing sugar into a mixing bowl then add the butter, milk and vanilla extract and beat well with a spoon or electric whisk on a low speed until the frosting is smooth and light.

6. Swirl the icing over the top of the cold sponge with a palette knife. If you want to decorate the top, do it now before the icing firms up. Cut into squares to serve.

Try Something Different

Stir in 5 tbsp chocolate chips, dried fruit, fudge chunks or chopped mixed nuts at the end of Step 3.

Lemon Drizzle
Loaf Cake

This lemon drizzle is made using the same speedy **all-in-one** technique as the Vanilla Traybake (page 42), but with a little baking powder added to achieve a good rise.

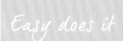

For the sponge
175g unsalted butter, very soft (but not runny)
250g caster sugar
3 medium eggs, at room temperature, beaten
100ml milk, at room temperature
finely grated zest of 2 medium unwaxed lemons
250g self-raising flour
½ teaspoon baking powder
good pinch of salt

For the drizzle
finely grated zest of 1 medium unwaxed lemon
juice of 2 medium lemons
100g caster sugar

HANDS-ON TIME:
15 minutes

BAKING TIME:
55–60 minutes

MAKES:
1 large cake

SPECIAL EQUIPMENT:
900g loaf tin (about 26 × 12.5 × 7.5cm)

METHOD USED:
All-in-one method, see page 24

STORAGE:
Keep for up to 5 days in an airtight container

1. Preheat the oven to 180°C (160°C fan), 350°F, Gas 4. Grease the tin with butter and **line** the base and two short sides with a long strip of baking paper.

2. To make the sponge, put the butter into a large mixing bowl or the bowl of a food-mixer. Add the sugar, eggs, milk and finely grated lemon zest and **sift** over the flour, baking powder and salt.

3. **Beat** everything together using a wooden spoon or the whisk attachment. Start slowly so that the ingredients don't fly out of the bowl, then increase the speed to medium–high and beat for a minute or so until you have a very smooth and creamy cake mixture.

4. Scrape the mixture out of the bowl and into the prepared tin and spread it out evenly, working the cake mixture into the corners and making sure the surface is level.

5. Bake for 55–60 minutes until the top is a good golden brown. **Check** your cake is cooked by inserting a cocktail stick or skewer into the centre; if it comes out clean, it is ready.

6. While the cake is in the oven, make the drizzle. Put the lemon zest, juice and sugar into a small bowl and stir well until you have a thick, sticky glaze.

7. Stand the cake in its tin on a wire rack and prick the sponge all over with a cocktail stick. Quickly pour the drizzle over the sponge, using the back of the spoon to push it into the holes.

8. Leave the cake, still in its tin, on the rack until cold. When it is cold, run a round-bladed knife around the inside of the tin to loosen the cake, then use the ends of the lining paper to lift it out. Peel off the lining paper, cut it into slices and serve.

Simple and Pretty Fruitcake

A moist and light 'cut and come again' fruitcake that uses the very forgiving **rubbed-in** method, which makes it a perfect fruitcake for first-time bakers to make.

HANDS-ON TIME:
20 minutes

BAKING TIME:
70 minutes

MAKES:
1 large cake

SPECIAL EQUIPMENT:
20.5cm springclip tin or deep round cake tin

METHOD USED:
Rubbed-in method, see page 22

STORAGE:
Keep for up to 4 days in an airtight container

For the sponge
350g self-raising flour
good pinch of salt
175g unsalted butter, cold and firm (but not hard), diced
175g golden caster sugar
finely grated zest of 1 unwaxed lemon
275g luxury mixed fruit
150g marzipan, cut into 1.5cm cubes

3 medium eggs, at room temperature
4 tablespoons milk, at room temperature

For the topping
2 tablespoons apricot jam, sifted, or apricot glaze
2 teaspoons boiling water
2 tablespoons toasted flaked almonds

1. Preheat the oven to 180°C (160°C fan), 350°F, Gas 4. Grease and **line** the tin with baking paper.

2. To make the sponge, **sift** the flour and salt into a mixing bowl, then add the butter, tossing it in the flour to coat. Using the very tips of your fingers, **rub in** the butter with the flour until the mixture looks like fine crumbs. Stir in the golden caster sugar and lemon zest with a wooden spoon. When everything is combined, add the mixed fruit and marzipan and mix well.

3. Beat the eggs and milk in a small bowl with a fork until just combined, then tip them into the mixing bowl and stir well with the spoon until you have a stiff mixture. Scrape the mixture into the prepared tin and spread evenly.

4. Bake for 70 minutes until golden brown. **Check** your cake is cooked by inserting a cocktail stick or skewer into the centre; if it comes out clean, it is ready. You might need to test in several places to avoid hitting a lump of marzipan, though!

5. Set the tin on a wire rack, run a round-bladed knife around the inside of the tin to loosen the cake, then unclip the sides. Leave on the rack until cold.

6. To make the topping, mix the jam with the boiling water until smooth, then brush it over the cake. Scatter over the almonds and leave to set for 20 minutes.

Try Something Different

Add a simple icing: sift 50g icing sugar into a bowl and stir in 2½ tsp lemon juice until smooth. Taste, adding a few more drops of lemon juice if needed, then pour the icing over the cake, letting it gently run down the sides.

Double Chocolate Cupcakes

Using oil instead of butter in this super-speedy cupcake recipe means you don't have to cream the mixture.

For the sponge
140g self-raising flour
40g cocoa powder
good pinch of salt
200g caster sugar
125ml sunflower oil
1 medium egg, at room temperature
175ml milk, at room temperature
1 teaspoon vanilla extract
100g white chocolate chips (or milk or dark)

For the frosting
75g icing sugar
25g cocoa powder
50g unsalted butter
50g caster sugar
2 tablespoons milk
extra chocolate chips, to decorate

HANDS-ON TIME:
10 minutes

BAKING TIME:
18–20 minutes

MAKES:
12 cupcakes

SPECIAL EQUIPMENT:
12-hole cupcake tray, Food-processor (optional)

METHOD USED:
All-in-one method, see page 24

STORAGE:
Keep for up to 2 days in an airtight container

1. Preheat the oven to 190°C (170°C fan), 375°F, Gas 5. Line the cupcake tray with paper cases.

2. Put the flour, cocoa powder, salt and sugar into the food-processor bowl fitted with the blade. Pulse 3–4 times until everything is thoroughly mixed. (If you don't have a food-processor make the cakes using the traditional all-in-one whisking method, it just takes a bit longer.)

3. Pour the sunflower oil into a jug with the egg, milk and vanilla extract and beat everything together with a fork until the egg is broken up.

4. Switch on the food-processor and pour the liquid through the feed tube with the machine running. Once it is all added, stop the machine, scrape down the bowl, then pulse again for 10 seconds, until the mixture is smooth, creamy and streak-free.

5. Remove the blade and stir the chocolate chips into the cake mix using a plastic spatula. Divide the mixture between the paper cases so they are half filled.

6. Bake for 18–20 minutes. **Check** the cakes after 15 minutes and if they aren't cooking evenly, rotate the tray. They are ready when they spring back when you gently press them in the centre. Carefully remove from the tray and cool on a wire rack.

7. To make the frosting, **sift** the icing sugar and cocoa into a heatproof bowl. Melt the butter with the sugar and milk in a small pan over a low heat, stir well, then bring to the boil. Once boiling, immediately pour the mixture over the icing sugar and cocoa. Mix until smooth. Leave for 10 minutes until thickened and spreadable.

8. Swirl the frosting over the cooled cupcakes using a round-bladed knife or an offset palette knife. Scatter over the extra chocolate chips before the frosting sets.

Old-fashioned Banana Bread

Banana bread is another classic **all-in-one** cake. This one has a lovely dense texture, so there is no need for baking powder. Dark brown bananas add intense flavour and sweetness.

100g unsalted butter
250g self-raising flour
good pinch of salt
150g light muscovado sugar
100g pecan or walnut pieces
50g dark chocolate chips

250g peeled very ripe bananas
(2–3 depending on size)
2 medium eggs, at room temperature, beaten

1. Preheat the oven to 180°C (160°C fan), 350°F, Gas 4. Grease the tin with butter and **line** the base and two short sides with a long strip of baking paper.

2. Gently melt the butter in a small pan over a low heat, or in the microwave. Leave to cool.

3. Put the flour, salt, muscovado sugar, pecan or walnut pieces and dark chocolate chips into a mixing bowl and mix thoroughly with a wooden spoon, crushing any big lumps of sugar.

4. Put the peeled bananas onto a large plate and mash them fairly roughly with a fork – you don't want a smooth purée, it's better to have some small lumps left in to give a little texture to the cake. Add the bananas to the bowl with the eggs and the cooled melted butter, then mix together for 1 minute, using a wooden spoon, until everything is well combined.

5. Scrape the mixture into the prepared tin and spread it around evenly, getting it right into the corners of the tin.

6. Bake for 55 minutes until the top of the cake is a good golden brown. **Check** your cake is cooked by inserting a cocktail stick or skewer into the centre; if it comes out clean, it is ready. Test it in a few other spots, too, in case you hit a lump of molten chocolate.

7. Stand the tin on a wire rack and leave to cool for 5 minutes. Run a round-bladed knife around the inside of the tin to loosen the cake, then carefully lift it out using the ends of the lining paper. Leave it on the wire rack until it is completely cold, then peel off the lining paper.

HANDS-ON TIME:
15 minutes

BAKING TIME:
55 minutes

MAKES:
1 large loaf cake

SPECIAL EQUIPMENT:
900g loaf tin (about 26 × 12.5 × 7cm)

METHOD USED:
All-in-one method, see page 24

STORAGE:
Eat the same day or keep for up to 4 days in an airtight container

Quick Berry Muffins

These lovely and easy fresh fruit muffins are a great way to practise making a **creamed** cake mixture. It's a simple way to add lightness to a bake that you'll use again and again.

60g unsalted butter, softened
150g caster sugar
1 medium unwaxed lemon
2 medium eggs, at room temperature
275g self-raising flour
½ teaspoon bicarbonate of soda

125ml natural yoghurt (unsweetened, not Greek-style)
200g fresh blueberries or raspberries
2 tablespoons coarse sugar crystals, for sprinkling

1. Preheat the oven to 200°C (180°C fan), 400°F, Gas 6. Line the cupcake tray with paper cases.

2. Put the butter into a mixing bowl or the bowl of a food-mixer and beat well with a wooden spoon or the whisk attachment until the mixture is creamy. Gradually beat in the caster sugar, scraping down the bowl every now and then. Finely grate the zest of the lemon into the bowl and beat it in.

3. Break the eggs into a separate bowl and beat them with a fork until broken up, then beat into the mixing bowl, a tablespoon at a time, until the mixture is quite soft.

4. **Sift** the flour and bicarbonate of soda into the bowl and stir in with a plastic spatula or wooden spoon.

5. Squeeze 1 tablespoon of juice from the lemon and stir this into the yoghurt, then stir this into the muffin mixture. As soon as it is thoroughly combined, add the fresh blueberries or raspberries to the bowl and gently **fold** in so the fruit does not break up.

6. Spoon the mixture into the paper cases, dividing it equally so that they are equally filled, then sprinkle over the coarse sugar crystals.

7. Bake for 20–25 minutes until golden brown. **Check** that the centres of the muffins feel firm when gently pressed. Set the tray on a wire rack and leave the muffins to cool in the tray for 5 minutes, then lift them out of the tray and onto the wire rack to cool. Eat warm or at room temperature on the day you baked them.

Try Something Different

For a slightly healthier bake, replace the white flour with wholemeal self-raising flour, add an extra tablespoon of yoghurt, and replace the sugar crystals with granola for a healthy crunchy topping.

Easy does it

HANDS-ON TIME:
10 minutes

BAKING TIME:
20–25 minutes

MAKES:
12 muffins

SPECIAL EQUIPMENT:
12-hole cupcake tray, deep-hole bun tray or muffin tray

METHOD USED:
Creamed method, see page 24

STORAGE:
Eaten the day you make them

Apple and Ginger
Crumble Cake

This delicious apple and ginger cake shows you how to add flavour to a basic **all-in-one** mixture.

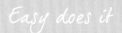

For the sponge

175g unsalted butter, softened
175g golden caster sugar
3 medium eggs, at room temperature, beaten
200g self-raising flour
good pinch of salt
2 teaspoons ground ginger
3 lumps (about 60g) stem ginger, drained and finely chopped
3 tablespoons ginger syrup from the stem ginger jar
3 Braeburn apples (about 400g)

For the topping

150g plain flour
½ teaspoon ground ginger
75g golden caster sugar
75g unsalted butter, chilled and diced
icing sugar, for dusting
whipped cream flavoured with sugar and vanilla, to serve

HANDS-ON TIME:
25 minutes

BAKING TIME:
60–70 minutes

MAKES:
1 large cake

SPECIAL EQUIPMENT:
20.5cm springclip tin or loose-based deep round cake tin

METHOD USED:
All-in-one method, see page 24

STORAGE:
Keep for up to 2 days in an airtight container

1. Preheat the oven to 180°C (160°C fan), 350°F, Gas 4. Grease and **line** the tin with butter and baking paper.

2. To make the sponge, put the butter, sugar and eggs into a large mixing bowl or the bowl of a mixer and **sift** over the flour, salt and ground ginger.

3. Add the ginger and syrup. Beat with a spoon or the whisk attachment (start slowly so you don't make a mess), for 2 minutes until you have a streak-free creamy batter. Spread the mixture into the prepared tin.

4. Peel, quarter and core the apples, then thinly slice them. Arrange in an even layer on top of the mixture.

5. To make the crumble topping, **sift** the flour and ground ginger into a small bowl. Stir in the sugar, then add the butter pieces and toss them in the flour until coated. Using the tips of your fingers, **rub** in the butter with the flour until the mixture looks like fine crumbs.

6. Sprinkle the topping evenly over the apples, then press down gently but firmly with the flat of your hand – this will make the cake easier to slice. Then dip your fingers in cold water and lightly flick it over the crumble topping to just dampen it – another clever trick to make slicing easier!

7. Bake for 60–70 minutes until well risen and lightly golden. **Check** your cake is cooked by inserting a cocktail stick or skewer into the centre; if it comes out clean, it is ready.

8. Set the tin on a wire rack and run a round-bladed knife around the inside of the tin to loosen the cake, then carefully unclip the sides or gently take the cake out of the tin. Leave until cold on the wire rack, then dust with icing sugar. Serve with whipped cream flavoured with a little sugar and vanilla extract.

Malted Tea-loaf Cake

You only need a pan, wooden spoon and tin for this **melted** mixture – the perfect method for making moisture-rich cakes. Here the tea-soaked fruit produces a deliciously sticky cake.

350g mixed dried vine fruits (raisins, sultanas and currants)
250ml strong 'builders" tea (without milk)
100g unsalted butter, diced
100g dark muscovado sugar

2 teaspoons ground mixed spice
225g wholemeal plain flour
good pinch of salt
2½ teaspoons baking powder
2 medium eggs, at room temperature, lightly beaten

1. Put the dried fruits, tea, butter, dark muscovado sugar and ground mixed spice into a large pan. Set over a low heat and stir gently with a wooden spoon until the butter has melted, then increase the heat to medium and let the mixture simmer for 5 minutes, stirring now and then. Turn off the heat and leave to cool for 15–20 minutes until you can comfortably dip your little finger into it.

2. While the mixture is cooling down, preheat the oven to 180°C (160°C fan), 350°F, Gas 4. Grease the tin with butter and **line** the base and two short sides with a long strip of baking paper.

3. Set a sieve over the pan of barely warm mixture and **sift** in the wholemeal plain flour, salt and baking powder (tip any bran that's left in the sieve into the pan). Pour in the beaten eggs, then mix well with the wooden spoon until combined. Scrape the mixture into the prepared tin and spread it out evenly.

4. Bake for 45 minutes until the cake is well risen and a good golden brown. **Check** your cake is cooked by inserting a cocktail stick or skewer into the centre; if it comes out clean, it is ready.

5. Stand the tin on a wire rack and leave until cold, then use the ends of the lining paper to help lift the cake out.

Try Something Different

For a slightly different, citrusy flavour, use mixed fruit that includes chopped orange and lemon peel.

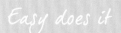

Easy does it

HANDS-ON TIME:
15 minutes

BAKING TIME:
45 minutes

MAKES:
1 medium loaf cake

SPECIAL EQUIPMENT:
450g loaf tin (about 19 × 12.5 × 7.5cm)

METHOD USED:
Melted method, see page 26

STORAGE:
Wrap in baking or greaseproof paper, store in an airtight container and eat within 4 days. The cake will deepen in flavour as it matures and is even better the day after baking

Blackberry Cinnamon Streusel

Tangy blackberries add a jam-like layer between the moist **all-in-one** sponge and crunchy streusel topping – a crumbly combination of flour, butter, sugar and, in this case, cinnamon.

For the sponge
125g self-raising flour
1½ teaspoons ground cinnamon
125g unsalted butter, softened
125g golden caster sugar
½ teaspoon vanilla essence
2 medium eggs, at room temperature
175g fresh blackberries

For the streusel topping
75g self-raising flour
50g demerara sugar
1 teaspoon ground cinnamon
50g unsalted butter, at room temperature, diced
2 tablespoons flaked almonds (optional), for sprinkling
icing sugar, for dusting

HANDS-ON TIME:
20 minutes

BAKING TIME:
55 minutes

MAKES:
1 medium cake

SPECIAL EQUIPMENT:
20.5cm springclip tin or loose-based deep round cake tin

METHOD USED:
All-in-one method, see page 24

STORAGE:
Store in an airtight container in the fridge and eat within 3 days. The cake tastes best if you let it come back up to room temperature or gently warm it before serving

1. Preheat the oven to 180°C (160°C fan), 350°F, Gas 4. Grease and **line** the tin with butter and baking paper.

2. To make the sponge, **sift** the flour and ground cinnamon into a mixing bowl or the bowl of a food-mixer, then add the butter and golden caster sugar.

3. In a separate bowl, beat together the vanilla essence and eggs with a fork for a few seconds, just until the eggs are broken up. Tip these into the mixing bowl. Beat everything together with a wooden spoon or the whisk attachment, starting slowly so that the mixture doesn't fly out of the bowl. After a minute or so, scrape down the sides of the bowl, then beat again until the ingredients are combined and the mixture is very smooth and streak-free.

4. Scrape the mixture into the prepared tin and spread it out evenly, then scatter the fresh blackberries over the top nice and evenly.

5. To make the streusel topping, put the flour, demerara sugar and ground cinnamon into a bowl and mix them together. Add the butter and toss the pieces in the flour until coated. Using the tips of your fingers and thumbs, **rub** in the butter and flour until you have small pea-sized lumps.

6. Scatter the streusel topping over the fruit in an even layer, then top with the flaked almonds (if using). Bake for about 55 minutes, until the topping is a good golden brown. If you think the top is browning too quickly, cover it loosely with a sheet of baking or greaseproof paper. **Check** your cake is cooked by inserting a cocktail stick or skewer into the centre (avoiding the berries); if it comes out clean, it is ready.

7. Set the tin on a wire rack and run a round-bladed knife around the inside to loosen the cake, then leave for 5 minutes to firm up before unclipping the tin. Cool on the rack and dust with icing sugar to serve.

Chocolate Brownies

Who can resist a brownie? This rich brownie is made from high-quality dark chocolate and uses a combination of the **melted** and **whisked methods** to create that signature squishy texture.

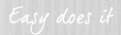

HANDS-ON TIME:
20 minutes

BAKING TIME:
25 minutes

MAKES:
36 squares

SPECIAL EQUIPMENT:
20.5cm square brownie tin or shallow cake tin

METHOD USED:
Melted method, see page 26
Whisked method, see page 26

STORAGE:
Keep in an airtight container and eat within a week

225g unsalted butter, diced
100g good-quality dark chocolate (about 70 per cent cocoa solids), broken or chopped into even-sized pieces
200g caster sugar

4 medium eggs, at room temperature
½ teaspoon vanilla extract
50g plain flour
50g cocoa powder
good pinch of salt
75g walnut pieces

1. Preheat the oven to 180°C (160°C fan), 350°F, Gas 4. Grease and **line** the tin with butter and baking paper.

2. Put the butter into a small heavy-based pan and drop in the chocolate pieces. Set the pan over the lowest possible heat and melt gently, stirring frequently with a wooden spoon, until the mixture is smooth but not hot. Remove the pan from the heat and leave the mixture to cool until needed.

3. Put the caster sugar, eggs and vanilla extract into a large mixing bowl and **whisk** with a wire hand whisk until thoroughly combined, then whisk in the cooled melted chocolate mixture.

4. **Sift** the plain flour, cocoa powder and salt into the bowl, and mix thoroughly with a wooden spoon or plastic spatula. Stir in the walnuts, then scrape the mixture into the prepared tin and spread it out evenly. Bang the tin on the worktop to settle the mixture and knock out any pockets of air.

5. Bake for about 25 minutes. **Check** your brownies are cooked by inserting a cocktail stick or skewer halfway between the sides of the tin and the centre of the cake. Don't test the centre because you want that to be slightly soft as the cake will continue cooking for few minutes once it's out of the oven, and you want a squidgy, not a dry, brownie! The mixture will puff up in the oven but don't be alarmed if it starts to sink as it cools – that's normal and will give you a dense, fudgy brownie.

6. Stand the tin on a wire rack then run a round-bladed knife around the inside of the tin to loosen the cake. Leave the cake to cool completely in the tin before cutting it into squares.

Sticky Gingerbread

Rich, moist gingerbread is made using the **melted** method. This one is made with spices and thick black treacle.

225g self-raising flour
good pinch of salt
1 teaspoon bicarbonate of soda
1 tablespoon ground ginger
1 teaspoon ground cinnamon
1 teaspoon ground mixed spice
115g unsalted butter, chilled and diced
60g glacé ginger, or crystallised or drained stem ginger, very finely chopped

115g golden syrup
115g black treacle
115g dark brown muscovado sugar
275ml milk (not skimmed)
1 medium egg, at room temperature, beaten

1. Preheat the oven to 180°C (160°C fan), 350°F, Gas 4. Grease the tin with butter and **line** the base and two short sides with a long strip of baking paper.

2. **Sift** the flour, salt, bicarbonate of soda, ginger, cinnamon and mixed spice into a large mixing bowl then add the butter pieces, tossing them in the flour until coated. Using your fingertips, **rub** in the butter until the mixture looks like fine crumbs. Stir in the ginger with a wooden spoon, then put the bowl to one side.

3. Weigh the golden syrup and black treacle directly into a pan then warm gently until melted and runny but not hot. Leave to cool until barely warm.

4. Put the muscovado sugar and milk into a separate pan over a low heat and stir until the sugar dissolves. Let it cool until barely warm, then pour it into the flour mixture, followed by the melted syrup mixture and egg. Mix together with a wire hand whisk or a spoon until it's a thick but runny batter the consistency of double cream.

5. Transfer the mixture to the prepared tin and bake for 45–50 minutes until well risen and firm to the touch. **Check** your cake is cooked by inserting a cocktail stick or skewer into the centre; if it comes out clean, it is ready.

6. Stand the tin on a wire rack. Run a round-bladed knife around the inside of the tin to loosen the cake. Leave it in the tin until completely cold, then turn it out.

Try Something Different

Top the gingerbread with a simple zesty lemon glacé icing. Sift 65g icing sugar into a bowl and mix in 1 tbsp lemon juice until you have a smooth, runny, thin icing. Spoon this over the loaf while it is still in the tin, gently spreading it and letting it trickle down the sides. Scatter over small chunks of the same ginger you used for the cake. Leave to set before slicing.

HANDS-ON TIME:
20 minutes

BAKING TIME:
45–50 minutes

MAKES:
1 large loaf cake

SPECIAL EQUIPMENT:
900g loaf tin (about 26 × 12.5 × 7cm)

METHOD USED:
Melted method, see page 26

STORAGE:
Wrap the loaf in fresh baking paper or foil and store in an airtight container. Keep for up to 1 week

Lemon-scented Madeleines

These little lemony cakes are made from a **whisked sponge,** giving them their light texture – no baking powder required. A fab way to get the hang of whisking eggs to the right consistency.

140g unsalted butter, diced
155g plain flour
good pinch of salt
finely grated zest of 1 large
unwaxed lemon
4 medium eggs, at room temperature
140g caster sugar
icing sugar, for dusting

1. Preheat the oven to 190°C (170°C fan), 375°F, Gas 5. Carefully brush the tray with melted butter, chill, then brush the tray a second time.

2. Gently melt the butter in a pan and leave to cool until needed.

3. **Sift** the flour and salt into a bowl and stir in the lemon zest until thoroughly combined. Put to one side for now.

4. Put the eggs and caster sugar into a large mixing bowl or the bowl of a mixer and **whisk** for about 4 minutes, until the mixture is very thick, pale and mousse-like. The whisk should leave a thick, ribbon-like trail when lifted.

5. Sprinkle the flour mixture over the egg and sugar mousse and gently but thoroughly **fold** it in using a large metal spoon. Drizzle the melted butter over the top and gently fold in in the same way until there are no more streaks.

6. Spoon about a heaped teaspoon of the mixture into each of the prepared moulds – they should be about two-

thirds to three-quarters full, so adjust as needed as moulds vary. You will need to bake these in two batches.

7. Bake for 10–12 minutes until golden and the sponge springs back when gently pressed in the middle.

8. Stand the tray on a wire rack and leave to cool and firm up for a couple of minutes, then tip out the Madeleines onto the wire rack and leave to cool.

9. To bake the next batch, wipe out the warm moulds with kitchen paper, then brush them with melted butter, chill for 2 minutes, and re-butter as before. Then fill them again with more mixture.

10. Dust with icing sugar just before serving.

Try Something Different

Lemon zest adds a delicate flavour, but you could use 1 tsp orange flower water or the zest of 1 small orange instead, or 2 or 3 drops of almond extract.

HANDS-ON TIME:
15 minutes

BAKING TIME:
10–12 minutes

MAKES:
12 Madeleines

SPECIAL EQUIPMENT:
Metal or silicone Madeleine mould tray

METHOD USED:
Whisked method, see page 26

STORAGE:
Keep for up to 5 days in an airtight container

Apple and Maple Syrup Traybake

Once you've mastered a basic traybake you can make this extra-light Bramley apple and maple syrup version using the **whisked** method.

For the sponge

400g Bramley cooking apples
¼ teaspoon ground cinnamon
2 tablespoons maple syrup
2 medium egg whites, at room temperature
2 medium whole eggs, at room temperature
finely grated zest of ½ unwaxed lemon
150g light brown muscovado sugar
125ml sunflower oil

50g pecan or walnut pieces, plus extra for topping (optional)
275g plain flour
(white or wholemeal)
½ teaspoon baking powder
1 teaspoon bicarbonate of soda

For the topping

3 tablespoons maple syrup
75g unsalted butter, softened
75g light brown muscovado sugar
175g full-fat cream cheese

1. Preheat the oven to 180°C (160°C fan), 350°F, Gas 4. Grease and **line** the tin with butter and baking paper.

2. Peel, quarter and core the apples, then cut into 1cm chunks. Put them in a bowl with the ground cinnamon and the maple syrup, and toss them together until thoroughly coated. Put the apple to one side until needed.

3. Put the egg whites into a mixing bowl or the bowl of a food-mixer and **whisk** with an electric hand whisk or the whisk attachment, until it makes stiff peaks when you lift the whisk. Put to one side or scoop into a smaller bowl.

4. Break the whole eggs into a separate larger mixing bowl or the empty food-mixer bowl. Add the lemon zest and the sugar, and whisk until the mixture is thick and very frothy and the whisk leaves a distinct ribbon-like trail when lifted. There's no need to wash the whisk before the next step.

Continued

HANDS-ON TIME:
25 minutes

BAKING TIME:
30–35 minutes

MAKES:
20 squares

SPECIAL EQUIPMENT:
25.5 × 20.5 × 5cm traybake tin, cake tin or roasting tin

METHOD USED:
Whisked method, see page 26

STORAGE:
Keep for up to 3 days in an airtight container

5. Now keep whisking the mixture and at the same time pour in the 125ml sunflower oil in a thin, steady stream.

6. Stir in the apple mixture and the 50g pecan or walnut pieces (if using) with a large metal spoon or plastic spatula. **Sift** the 275g flour, ½ teaspoon baking powder and 1 teaspoon bicarbonate of soda into the bowl (if you are using wholemeal flour, tip the bran left in the sieve into the bowl), and gently stir in. **Fold in** the beaten egg whites in three batches.

7. Gently scrape the mixture into the prepared tin and spread it out evenly. Bake in the centre of the oven for 30–35 minutes until the sponge is golden brown. **Check** your cake is cooked by inserting a cocktail stick or skewer into the centre; if it comes out clean, it is ready.

8. Set the tin on a wire rack and run a round-bladed knife around the inside of the tin to loosen the sponge. Leave until cold then **turn out** the cake and peel off the baking paper.

9. While the sponge is cooling, make the topping. Put the 3 tablespoons maple syrup, 75g butter, 75g muscovado sugar and 175g cream cheese into a mixing bowl and **beat** with a wooden spoon or electric whisk until creamy and smooth.

10. Turn out the cooled sponge onto a serving plate or cake board and spread the topping over the traybake using a palette knife. If you want to add some chopped nuts, sprinkle them over now. Leave in a cool spot to firm up, then cut into 20 pieces.

Carrot Spice Cake

Always popular, this classic carrot cake is quick to put together using the **all-in-one method** and has a delightful combination of creamy and crunchy textures.

HANDS-ON TIME:
25 minutes

BAKING TIME:
25–30 minutes

MAKES:
1 large cake

SPECIAL EQUIPMENT:
2 × 20.5cm round sandwich cake tins

METHOD USED:
All-in-one method, see page 24

STORAGE:
Keep for up to 4 days in an airtight container

For the sponge
230g self-raising flour
1 teaspoon baking powder
1½ teaspoons ground cinnamon
¼ teaspoon grated nutmeg
½ teaspoon ground ginger
½ teaspoon ground mixed spice
200g caster sugar
100g walnut pieces, plus 1 tablespoon finely chopped for topping

3 medium eggs
150ml sunflower oil
500g carrots, coarsely grated

For the cream cheese frosting
1 large unwaxed lime
200g full-fat cream cheese
50g unsalted butter, softened
150g icing sugar

1. Preheat the oven to 180°C (160°C fan), 350°F, Gas 4. Grease and **line** the cake tins with butter and baking paper.

2. To make the sponge, **sift** the self-raising flour, baking powder, ground cinnamon, grated nutmeg, ground ginger and ground mixed spice into a large bowl. Add the caster sugar and walnuts and mix with a wooden spoon.

3. In a separate bowl, add the eggs to the sunflower oil and beat lightly with a fork. Pour into the dry ingredients, tip in the grated carrots and mix again. Divide the carrot mixture equally between the two prepared cake tins – if you want to be really accurate, use your scales, or you can just do it by eye.

4. Bake for 25–30 minutes until the cakes are golden and a cocktail stick or skewer inserted into the centre comes out clean. **Turn out** the cakes onto a wire rack, carefully peeling off the lining paper, then leave them until cold.

5. While the cakes are cooling, make the cream cheese frosting. Finely grate the lime zest into a mixing bowl, squeeze in 1½ teaspoons of the lime juice and add the cream cheese and butter. Sift the icing sugar over the top then beat everything together with an electric whisk until the mixture is smooth, creamy and spreadable. If it is a warm day or your kitchen is hot, cover the bowl at this point and pop it in the fridge to chill for a couple of minutes to thicken up the frosting.

6. Now put your cake together. Flip one sponge so it's top-side down on a serving plate and spread it with half the cream cheese frosting. Pop the second sponge on top and spread it with the rest of the frosting using a round-bladed or palette knife. You don't need to make a perfectly neat finish, but it looks nice with a little swirl made with a flick of the knife at the end. Finally, scatter the finely chopped walnuts around the edge.

Gluten-free Sticky Orange Polenta Cake

This rich gluten-free sponge is made from a standard **creamed** mixture, but polenta and almonds replace the flour.

For the sponge
250g unsalted butter, softened
1 large navel orange, organic/unwaxed
225g golden caster sugar
4 medium eggs, at room temperature
60g medium/fine polenta
250g ground almonds
2 teaspoons gluten-free baking powder

For the syrup
3 tablespoons golden caster sugar
1 tablespoon orange liqueur, orange brandy or orange juice

To decorate
2 tablespoons toasted flaked almonds
extra orange zest (optional)

HANDS-ON TIME:
20 minutes

BAKING TIME:
50 minutes

MAKES:
1 medium cake

SPECIAL EQUIPMENT:
20.5cm springclip tin

METHOD USED:
Creamed method, see page 24

STORAGE:
Eat the same day or the next day. Keep in an airtight container

1. Preheat the oven to 180°C (160°C fan), 350°F, Gas 4. Grease and **line** the cake tin with butter and baking paper.

2. To make the sponge, put the butter into a large mixing bowl or the bowl of a mixer. Finely grate the zest of the orange onto the butter (putting the fruit to one side for now) and **beat** well with a spoon or whisk attachment until creamy and mayonnaise-like. Gradually beat in the sugar, a couple of tablespoons at a time, scraping down the sides of the bowl every now and then. When all the sugar is in, beat for another couple of minutes, until the mixture is light and fluffy. Scrape down the sides of the bowl once more.

3. Break the eggs into a separate bowl and beat with a fork until broken up. Gradually beat the eggs into the butter mixture, a tablespoon at a time, beating well each time. Don't worry if the mixture looks slightly runny or curdled once the last bit of egg has been added.

4. **Sift** the polenta, almonds and baking powder into the bowl. Cut the orange in half, squeeze out the juice and add 1 tablespoon to the bowl, keeping the rest for the syrup. Gently **fold** everything together using a large metal spoon or plastic spatula until thoroughly combined and streak-free.

5. Scrape the mixture into the tin and spread it out evenly. Bake for about 50 minutes until the sponge is a good golden brown and **check** that the middle springs back when gently pressed.

6. While the sponge is baking, make the syrup. Put the sugar, 5 tablespoons of the reserved juice and the liqueur (if using) into a small pan and heat gently, stirring, until the sugar dissolves. Bring to the boil, simmer for 2–3 minutes to make a light syrup, then lower the heat to keep it warm.

7. As soon as the cake is ready, put it on a wire rack still in its tin. Prick the hot sponge all over with a cocktail stick, then quickly spoon the hot syrup over – the cake will sink in the middle. Scatter with the almonds and zest (if using), then cool completely.

8. Run a round-bladed knife around the inside of the tin to loosen the cake, then unclip the sides and take it out of the tin.

Victoria Sandwich Cake

The nation's favourite cake, traditionally the ingredients are calculated by weighing the eggs in their shells and using this weight for the butter, sugar and flour.

Easy does it

HANDS-ON TIME:
20–25 minutes

BAKING TIME:
20 minutes

MAKES:
1 medium cake

SPECIAL
EQUIPMENT:
2 × 20.5cm round
deep sandwich cake
tins

METHOD USED:
Creamed method,
see page 24

STORAGE:
Eat immediately or
keep in an airtight
container for a
jam-filled cake, or in
the fridge if you've
used cream, for up
to 3 days. (Take
it out of the fridge
20 minutes before
serving.)

For the sponge
3 medium eggs, at room temperature
about 175g unsalted butter, softened
about 175g caster sugar
¾ teaspoon vanilla extract
about 175g self-raising flour
1 tablespoon water from the warm water tap

For the filling
6 tablespoons good-quality raspberry jam
150ml double or whipping cream, well chilled (optional)
icing sugar, for dusting

1. Preheat the oven to 180°C (160°C fan), 350°F, Gas 4. Grease and **line** the cake tins with butter and baking paper.

2. Weigh the eggs – 3 medium eggs in their shells weigh around 175g – then use this same weight for the butter, sugar and flour.

3. Put the soft (but not oily) butter into a large mixing bowl or the bowl of a food-mixer and **beat** well with a wooden spoon or the whisk attachment until very creamy and mayonnaise-like. Scrape down any butter mixture from the sides of the bowl with a plastic spatula, then gradually beat in the sugar a couple of tablespoons at a time. Scrape the mixture off the sides of the bowl again and beat well for 1 minute or until the mixture looks very light and fluffy. Scrape down the mixture again.

4. Break the 3 eggs into a small jug, add the ¾ teaspoon vanilla extract and beat with a fork just until the eggs are broken up. Gradually add to the butter mixture a tablespoon at a time, beating well after each addition and scraping down the sides of the bowl from time to time. If the mixture looks like it might be 'splitting' or curdling, rather than appearing smooth and creamy, stir in a tablespoon of the flour with each of the last two additions of egg.

5. **Sift** the rest of the flour onto the mixture. Start to gently **fold** in the flour with a large metal spoon or plastic spatula and after two or three movements add the warm water. Keep folding in until the flour is well mixed in and there are no streaks.

Continued

75

6. Divide the mixture between the two prepared tins – if you want to be really precise, use your scales, or just do it by eye, then spread it evenly.

7. Bake for 20–25 minutes until the sponges are a light golden brown, starting to shrink back from the sides of the tin. Check the sponges after 15 minutes and if they aren't baking evenly, rotate the trays. **Check** that the sponge springs back when lightly pressed in the middle.

8. When cooked, take them out of the oven and run a round-bladed knife around the outside of each tin to loosen the sponge. Leave for a minute to firm up, then carefully **turn out** the cakes onto a wire rack. Leave until they are completely cooled.

9. If you are using cream, put a bowl and whisk (or whisk attachment) in the fridge to chill.

10. To assemble the cake, set one sponge crust-side down on a serving plate. Using the back of a tablespoon, evenly spread the sponge with the 6 tablespoons raspberry jam.

11. Pour the cream, if using, into the chilled bowl and **whip** with the chilled whisk or attachment until it thickens and soft peaks form when you lift out the whisk. Spoon the cream onto the cake and then gently smooth it evenly over the jam. Top with the second sponge, crust-side up, and dust with icing sugar.

11

Try Something Different

To make a Chocolate Sponge Cake, replace the flour in the recipe above with 150g self-raising flour and 30g cocoa powder, sifting the cocoa powder into the bowl with the flour and replacing the warm water with 2 tbsp room-temperature milk. Sandwich the sponges with chocolate spread instead of jam, or make up a classic chocolate butter icing using 125g soft unsalted butter creamed with 400g sifted icing sugar and flavoured with 3 tbsp cocoa powder plus 3–4 tbsp milk or cold coffee. This will make enough to fill and top the cake.

Rich Lemon Cupcakes

Take your cupcakes to the next level by adding buttermilk to the classic **creamed** mixture. The buttermilk is mildly acidic, giving your bake a lovely fine and light texture.

125g unsalted butter, softened
200g golden caster sugar
I large unwaxed lemon
2 medium eggs, at room temperature
200g self-raising flour
100ml buttermilk

For the frosting
75g unsalted butter, softened
250g icing sugar, sifted
3 tablespoons Lemon Curd (see page 145)

1. Preheat the oven to 180°C (160°C fan), 350°F, Gas 4. Line the cupcake tray with paper cases.

2. Put the butter into a mixing bowl or the bowl of a food-mixer and **beat** for 1 minute with a wooden spoon or the whisk attachment until the mixture is very creamy and mayonnaise-like.

3. Sprinkle the caster sugar into the bowl. Finely grate the zest of the lemon on top, then halve the lemon, squeeze the juice into a small bowl and put to one side. Beat the mixture until very light and fluffy, scraping down any mixture that has splattered onto the sides of the bowl every now and then.

4. Break the eggs into a small bowl and beat with a fork until broken up. Gradually beat the eggs into the mixture a tablespoon at a time, beating well after every time and scraping down the sides of the bowl as before.

5. **Sift** one-third of the flour into the bowl and **fold** in with a large metal spoon, then add one-third of the buttermilk and fold in. Repeat twice more until all the flour and buttermilk have been well mixed in. Lastly, fold in 2 teaspoons of the reserved lemon juice (you won't need the rest).
Continued

Easy does it

HANDS-ON TIME:
15 minutes

BAKING TIME:
20–25 minutes

MAKES:
12 cupcakes

SPECIAL EQUIPMENT:
12-hole cupcake tray or deep-hole bun tray

METHOD USED:
Creamed method, see page 24

STORAGE:
Keep for up to 4 days in an airtight container

6. Spoon the mixture into the paper cases so that they are evenly filled. Bake for 20–25 minutes until the cakes are a light golden brown and feel just firm to the touch. Check the cakes after 15 minutes and if they aren't baking evenly, turn the tray around.

7. To make the frosting, beat the 75g butter in a large bowl or mixer bowl until creamy using a wooden spoon or electric whisk attachment.

8. At a slow speed, gradually beat in the 250g sifted icing sugar. Once all the sugar has been incorporated, beat in the 3 tablespoons lemon curd to make a smooth and light icing. The frosting should be firm enough to spread, pipe or swirl on top of your cupcakes; if it seems soft or slightly runny, cover the bowl and pop it in the fridge until it is firm but spreadable.

9. Remove the tray of cupcakes from the oven and set it on a wire rack. Leave to cool for 2 minutes, then transfer the cupcakes to the rack and leave until cold.

10. Swirl the frosting over the cooled cupcakes using a round-bladed knife or offset palette knife.

11. Sprinkle over any decorations immediately before the frosting firms up.

Try Something Different

For vanilla cupcakes, replace the lemon zest and juice with ¾ tsp vanilla extract. Top with vanilla frosting, replacing the lemon curd with 4 tbsp milk and 1 tsp vanilla extract. Or replace the lemon zest and juice with the finely grated zest of 1 medium orange and 2 tsp of the squeezed juice and flavour the topping with 2 tbsp orange juice instead of the lemon curd.

Fudgy Chocolate
Birthday Cake

This is a really good chocolate cake that should be in everyone's repertoire, quickly made using the no-fuss **all-in-one** method. Its glossy frosting is easy to apply yet gives a great finish.

HANDS-ON TIME:
25 minutes

BAKING TIME:
60–70 minutes

MAKES:
1 large cake

SPECIAL
EQUIPMENT:
22cm springclip tin

METHOD USED:
All-in-one method,
see page 24

STORAGE:
Tastes best the day
after you make it.
Keep in an airtight
container for up to
5 days

For the sponge
200g self-raising flour
75g cocoa powder
large pinch of salt
1 teaspoon baking powder
250g light brown muscovado sugar
250g unsalted butter, very soft
6 medium eggs, at room temperature, beaten
100g chocolate chips (milk, dark or white chocolate)

For the frosting
100g good-quality milk chocolate
100g unsalted butter, at room temperature, diced
100g icing sugar
2 tablespoons cocoa powder

1. Preheat the oven to 180°C (160°C fan), 350°F, Gas 4. Grease and **line** the tin with butter and baking paper.

2. To make the sponge, **sift** the self-raising flour, cocoa powder, salt and baking powder into a large mixing bowl or the bowl of a food-mixer. Add the muscovado sugar, breaking up any lumps, the butter and the eggs.

3. Using a wooden spoon or the whisk attachment, start **beating** everything together, slowly at first so that the mixture doesn't fly everywhere, then a little faster until the mixture is silky smooth and light. Scrape down any mixture splattered on the sides of the bowl from time to time so that the batter is evenly mixed with no streaks.

4. Stir in the chocolate chips using the wooden spoon or a plastic spatula, then scrape the mixture into the prepared tin. Spread the mixture evenly, then make a saucer-like hollow in the middle of the cake, about 2cm deep. This helps the sponge rise evenly; you may still get a little cracked dome, but it will avoid a large volcanic peak.

5. Bake the cake in the centre of the oven for 50–60 minutes until the top is firm to the touch. **Check** your cake is cooked by inserting a cocktail stick or skewer into the centre; if it comes out clean, it is ready.
Continued

6. Set the tin on a wire rack, then run a round-bladed knife around the inside of the tin to loosen the sponge, and gently unclip the tin. Leave until completely cold before icing.

7. To make the frosting, break up the 100g milk chocolate into even-sized pieces and put it into a heatproof bowl large enough to hold all the frosting ingredients. Set the bowl over a pan of steaming hot but not boiling water – don't let the base of the bowl touch the water – and leave to **melt** gently, or melt the chocolate carefully in the microwave in 10-second bursts.

8. Remove the bowl from the pan and stir in the 100g unsalted butter. When melted and smooth, sift the 100g icing sugar and 2 tablespoons cocoa powder into the bowl and mix with a wooden spoon to make a smooth and thick but spreadable icing.

9. Spread and swirl the frosting evenly over the top of the cooled cake using a round-bladed knife or an off-set palette knife.

10. Now carefully spread and smooth the frosting evenly around the sides of the cake. If you want to add any decorations or candles pop them on now while the frosting is still soft.

Try Something Different

For a darker and less sweet topping, use 50g good-quality milk chocolate and 50g good-quality dark chocolate (around 70 per cent cocoa solids).

Double Marble Cake

This impressive cake cuts into pretty chocolate brown and golden marbled slices – made by dividing the **creamed** mixture and adding cocoa to half of it. Rich icing makes it even more special.

For the sponge

225g unsalted butter, softened
225g caster sugar
½ teaspoon vanilla essence
4 medium eggs, at room temperature, beaten
225g self-raising flour
good pinch of salt
3 tablespoons cocoa powder
2 tablespoons milk, at room temperature

For the topping

100g good-quality dark chocolate (around 70 per cent cocoa solids), broken up
40g unsalted butter, very soft
50g white chocolate, broken up

HANDS-ON TIME:
30 minutes

BAKING TIME:
60 minutes

MAKES:
1 large loaf cake

SPECIAL EQUIPMENT:
900g loaf tin (about 26 × 12.5 × 7cm)

METHOD USED:
Creamed method, see page 24

STORAGE:
Keep for up to 5 days in an airtight container

1. Preheat the oven to 180°C (160°C fan), 350°F, Gas 4. Grease the tin with butter and **line** the base and two short sides with a long strip of baking paper.

2. To make the sponge, put the butter into a large mixing bowl or the bowl of a food-mixer and **beat** thoroughly with a wooden spoon or the whisk attachment until the mixture is creamy and mayonnaise-like.

3. Gradually beat in the caster sugar, scraping down any mixture on the sides of the bowl now and then, then beat until the mixture becomes light and fluffy. Beat in the vanilla essence.

4. Gradually beat in the eggs, a tablespoon at a time, beating well after each addition and adding a tablespoon of the flour with the last two additions.

5. **Sift** the rest of the flour and the salt onto the mixture and gently **fold in** using a large metal spoon.

6. Scoop out half the mixture into a separate bowl and put it to one side.

7. Sift the cocoa powder into one bowl of cake mixture, add the milk and very gently stir everything together using a large metal spoon or plastic spatula until all the cocoa is mixed in.

Continued

8. Using soup spoons, put alternate spoonfuls of the two mixtures into the prepared tin until you have used them both up. Bang the tin on the worktop several times to level the contents and knock out any pockets of air. Now carefully swirl the two mixtures together with the handle of a teaspoon or a table knife.

9. Bake the cake for 60 minutes until the top is lightly golden and firm. **Check** your cake is cooked by inserting a cocktail stick or skewer into the centre; if it comes out clean, it is ready.

10. Set the tin on a wire rack, run a round-bladed knife around the inside of the tin to loosen the cake, then leave for 5 minutes to firm up. Gently remove the cake from the tin – use the ends of the lining paper to help lift the cake out – and leave on the wire rack until cold.

11. While the cake is cooling, make the topping. Put the 100g dark chocolate into a heatproof bowl and set over a pan of steaming hot but not boiling water – don't let the base of the bowl touch the water – and leave to **melt** gently, then remove the bowl from the pan (the chocolate can also be melted in the microwave in 10-second bursts). Stir until smooth, then stir in 25g of the soft butter.

12. Melt the 50g white chocolate in a separate bowl in the same way, but take extra care as white chocolate melts at a lower temperature and can seize and become grainy. Stir the remaining butter into the melted white chocolate.

13. Spread the dark chocolate mixture over the top of the cake – don't worry if it drips down the sides. Using a teaspoon, drizzle the melted white chocolate mixture randomly over the top of the cake and marble and swirl it into the dark chocolate using the handle of a teaspoon or a table knife. Leave the cake until it is set and firm before you slice it.

13

Try Something Different

For an even more chocolatey indulgence, sprinkle 1½ tbsp dark chocolate chips over the sponge mixtures once they are in the loaf tin but before you bang the tin on the worktop (step 8).

Coffee and Walnut Cake

Just like the Victoria Sandwich Cake on page 74, this rich-tasting classic coffee sponge is made by the **creamed** method, but a little added baking powder keeps it nice and light.

For the sponge

100g walnut pieces
175g unsalted butter, softened
175g golden caster sugar
3 medium eggs, at room temperature
175g self-raising flour
good pinch of salt
½ teaspoon baking powder
1 tablespoon instant coffee powder or granules
1 tablespoon boiling water

For the filling and frosting

125g unsalted butter, diced
3 tablespoons instant coffee powder or granules
2 tablespoons boiling water
300g icing sugar
4 tablespoons single, double or whipping cream, at room temperature
walnut halves, to decorate

1. Preheat the oven to 180°C (160°C fan), 350°F, Gas 4. Grease and **line** the tins with butter and baking paper.

2. To make the sponge, first put the walnut pieces in an ovenproof dish or roasting tin and toast in the oven for 5–6 minutes until lightly coloured. Leave to cool, then chop slightly smaller. Set aside 25g for the filling and frosting and keep the remaining 75g for the sponge.

3. Put the butter into a mixing bowl or the bowl of a food-mixer and **beat** well with a wooden spoon or the whisk attachment until creamy and mayonnaise-like. Gradually beat in the golden caster sugar, a couple of spoonfuls at a time, scraping down the sides of the bowl from time to time where the mixture has splattered. Once all the sugar has been mixed in, scrape down the sides of the bowl again to get the last bits of mixture and beat for another minute or so until the mixture is light and fluffy.

4. Break the eggs into a separate bowl and beat with a fork just until broken up. Gradually beat the eggs into the butter mixture, beating well after each addition. Add 1 tablespoon of the flour with each of the last two bits of egg to help prevent the mixture curdling.

5. Add the reserved 75g toasted walnut pieces to the bowl, then **sift** the remaining flour, salt and baking powder into the bowl. In a small bowl, dissolve the instant coffee in the boiling water and pour it into the mixing bowl. Using a large metal spoon or plastic spatula, gently **fold** these ingredients into the butter mixture until thoroughly combined and there are no streaks.

6. Divide the mixture equally between the two prepared tins and spread evenly.
Continued

Easy does it

HANDS-ON TIME:
30 minutes

BAKING TIME:
20–25 minutes

MAKES:
1 medium cake

SPECIAL EQUIPMENT:
2 × 20.5cm round deep sandwich cake tins

METHOD USED:
Creamed method, see page 24

STORAGE:
Keep for up to 4 days in an airtight container

7. Bake for 20–25 minutes until the sponges are a good golden brown. **Check** your cake is cooked by lightly pressing in the centre – the cake will spring back if it's done. Run a round-bladed knife around the inside of the tins to loosen the sponges, leave them to firm up for 2 minutes, then **turn out** onto a wire rack and leave them to cool completely.

8. While the sponges are cooling, make the coffee filling and frosting. Put the 125g unsalted butter into a small pan and melt over a low heat.

9. In a small bowl, dissolve the 3 tablespoons instant coffee in the 2 tablespoons boiling water and sift the 300g icing sugar into a large heatproof mixing bowl.

12

10. Bring the butter to a boil, then quickly take it off the heat and pour it straight onto the icing sugar, swiftly followed by the warm coffee and the 4 tablespoons cream. Beat well with a wooden spoon until the mixture is very smooth, then stir in the reserved 25g toasted walnut pieces. Leave the frosting until it is thick enough to spread (you can speed this up by covering the bowl and putting it in the fridge for a few minutes).

11. To assemble the cake, set one sponge crust-side down on a serving plate and spread with half the coffee icing mixture. Cover with the second sponge, crust-side up, and spread and swirl the rest of the frosting on top.

12. To finish the cake, decorate with the walnut halves.

Classic Swiss Roll

Mastering the **whisked** sponge in this light and traditional Swiss roll is a great way to prepare for trying more challenging bakes like the Lemon Curd Layer Cake on page 144.

HANDS-ON TIME:
20 minutes

BAKING TIME:
9–10 minutes

MAKES:
1 medium cake

SPECIAL
EQUIPMENT:
20 × 30cm Swiss
roll tin

METHOD USED:
Whisked method,
see page 26

STORAGE:
Eat the day you
make it or the next
day. Keep in an
airtight container

For the sponge

3 medium eggs, at room temperature
75g caster sugar
75g plain flour
pinch of salt

For the filling

extra caster sugar, for sprinkling
200ml whipping or double cream
½ teaspoon vanilla extract
6 rounded tablespoons raspberry
or strawberry jam

1. Preheat the oven to 220°C (200°C fan), 425°F, Gas 7. Grease and **line** the tin with butter and baking paper.

2. To make the sponge, break the eggs into a large mixing bowl or the bowl of a food-mixer and **whisk** with an electric mixer on a high speed for a few seconds just until slightly frothy.

3. Add the caster sugar to the bowl and whisk on a high speed for about 5 minutes or until the mixture becomes very thick, pale and mousse-like, and the whisk leaves a ribbon-like trail when it is lifted.

4. **Sift** the flour and pinch of salt onto a sheet of greaseproof paper, then sift half of it again, straight onto the egg mousse. Using a large metal spoon, very gently **fold** in the flour. Sift the rest of the flour onto the mixture and fold in until you can no longer see any streaks or specks. Gently scrape any splattered mixture down the sides of the bowl and check the bottom of the bowl for any unmixed flour, stirring it in as you go.

5. Carefully transfer the mixture to the prepared tin and spread it out evenly, making sure the corners are well filled. Bake for 9–10 minutes until the sponge is golden brown. You can **check** your cake is cooked by lightly pressing it in the centre – the cake will spring back when done.
Continued

Try Something Different

For a Gingerbread Swiss Roll, make the sponge as in the main recipe, replacing the caster sugar with light brown muscovado sugar and adding 1 tsp ground ginger and ½ tsp each ground cinnamon and ground mixed spice. Bake, roll and cool, spread with ginger conserve instead of the jam and then spread with 200ml whipping or double cream, whipped to **soft peaks,** as before and roll up.

6. While the sponge is baking, lay a sheet of baking paper (about 30 × 40cm) on the worktop and sprinkle it with a little caster sugar.

7. As soon as the sponge is ready, flip it out onto the baking paper and carefully lift off the tin. Peel off the lining paper.

8. Using a large, sharp knife make a shallow cut about 2cm in from one short end – this will help give the roll a neat spiral when it is sliced.

9. Now, starting from the end with the cut, gently roll up the warm sponge with the paper so that the paper is rolled inside it. Set the roll on a wire rack and leave until cold.

10. When ready to fill, **whip** 200ml whipping or double cream with ½ teaspoon vanilla extract to soft peaks. Gently unroll the sponge and trim off the edges with a sharp knife. Spread with about 6 rounded tablespoons raspberry or strawberry jam, leaving a 2.5cm border round the edge.

11. Cover the jam with a layer of the whipped cream, again leaving a 2.5cm border. Now gently re-roll the sponge, starting once more from the end with the cut. Sprinkle with a little more caster sugar to finish.

Three-layer Banana Cake

Light muscovado sugar adds a lovely toffee flavour to a simple **all-in-one** vanilla sponge mixture.

For the sponge
175g unsalted butter, softened
150g golden caster sugar
25g light brown muscovado sugar
175g self-raising flour
3 medium eggs, at room temperature
½ teaspoon vanilla extract
1 tablespoon milk, at room temperature

For the filling and topping
300ml whipping cream, well chilled
100g vanilla fudge, cut into 5mm chunks
2 ripe medium bananas, thinly sliced

To decorate
extra fudge or grated chocolate (or both)

HANDS-ON TIME:
25 minutes

BAKING TIME:
18–20 minutes

MAKES:
1 large cake

SPECIAL EQUIPMENT:
3 × 20.5cm round sandwich cake tins

METHOD USED:
All-in-one method, see page 24

STORAGE:
Eat the day you make it or the next day. Keep in an airtight container

1. Preheat the oven to 180°C (160°C fan), 350°F, Gas 4. Grease and **line** the cake tins with butter and baking paper. If you only have one tin, bake in batches. Rinse the hot tin under cold running water to quickly cool it, then dry, re-grease and line it again.

2. To make the sponge, put the butter, two sugars and flour into a large bowl or the bowl of a food-mixer.

3. Break the eggs into a smaller bowl, add the vanilla extract and milk, and beat with a fork until just mixed. Pour into the larger bowl, then **beat** with a wooden spoon or the whisk attachment until smooth and blended with no streaks. Divide the mixture into the three tins, either by eye or, if you want to be more accurate, by weight. Spread the mixture evenly into the prepared tin or tins.

4. Bake for 18–20 minutes until the cakes are a light golden brown. Have a look at the cakes after 15 minutes, if they aren't baking evenly, turn the tins around. **Check** your cake is cooked by pressing it – it should be just firm to the touch.

5. Run a round-bladed knife around the inside of the tins to loosen the sponges, then **turn out** onto a wire rack. Leave until cold. Put a bowl and whisk (or whisk attachment) in the fridge to chill.

6. When you are ready to assemble the cake, make the filling and topping. Pour the cream into the chilled bowl and **whip** with the chilled whisk or attachment, until it thickens and soft peaks form when you lift the whisk out of the cream.

7. Set one layer of sponge crust-side down on a serving plate. Spread with one-third of the whipped cream, then scatter over half the fudge. Top with half the banana slices, then cover with a second sponge. Spread half the remaining cream over this sponge and scatter over the rest of the fudge, then cover with the remaining banana slices. Finally, set the last layer of sponge on top, crust-side uppermost, and spread with the remaining cream. Decorate with fudge, grated chocolate, or both.

Battenberg
Cake

A step up from the free-and-easy Double Marble Cake (page 86), the Battenberg uses colouring in a more precise way to make a pretty cake that looks impressive.

For the sponge
125g unsalted butter, softened
125g caster sugar
2 medium eggs, at room temperature
2 drops of almond extract
100g self-raising flour
good pinch of salt
50g ground almonds
2 teaspoons milk
a few drops pink or red food colouring

To finish
icing sugar or cornflour, for dusting
350g white marzipan
8 tablespoons apricot jam

Needs a little skill

HANDS-ON TIME:
50 minutes

BAKING TIME:
20–25 minutes

MAKES:
1 medium cake

SPECIAL EQUIPMENT:
Battenberg tin (20 × 15cm) or 20cm square shallow cake tin

METHOD USED:
Creamed method

STORAGE:
Keep for up to 5 days in an airtight container

1. If you are using a special Battenberg tin that comes with dividers to make four strips of sponge, grease and **line** the tin with butter and baking paper. Alternatively, you can make your own: cut a 20 × 28cm rectangle of parchment-lined foil, set it paper-side up on the worktop and fold it in half widthways. Open it out, then push the centrefold upwards to make a pleat 4cm high. Crease it firmly, then press the parchment-lined foil sheet with the centre pleat onto the base of greased tin to line it – the pleat will run down the centre of the tin to divide it into two separate sections each 20 × 10cm. Preheat the oven to 180°C (160°C fan), 350°F, Gas 4.

2. To make the sponge, put the butter into a mixing bowl or the bowl of a food-mixer and **beat** until creamy with a wooden spoon or the whisk attachment. Scrape down the sides of the bowl and whisk in the sugar a couple of tablespoons at a time. Scrape down the sides of the bowl where any mixture has splattered up, then beat really well for a couple of minutes until the mixture is light and fluffy. Scrape down the sides of the bowl again to get any stray mixture.

Continued

3. Break the 2 medium eggs into a separate bowl, add the 2 drops of almond extract and beat with a fork until broken up, then gradually beat into the butter mixture a tablespoon at a time, beating well after each addition. Add a tablespoon of the 100g self-raising flour with each of the last two additions of egg to prevent the mixture from curdling.

4. Sift the remaining flour, good pinch of salt and 50g ground almonds into the bowl. Add the 2 teaspoons milk and carefully **fold** everything together with a large metal spoon. Transfer half the mixture (for this cake it is best to do this by weight, to be really accurate) into a clean bowl. Add the pink or red food colouring a few drops at a time to one portion, mixing it in really well so that it turns pink with no coloured streaks.

5. Spoon the uncoloured pale yellow cake mixture into two sections of the prepared Battenberg tin or into one side of the prepared square tin (check the pleated divider is still straight and dead centre). Spoon the pink cake mixture into the other two sections of the Battenberg tin or the other section of the prepared square tin. Carefully spread each portion so that the surface is level and the corners are evenly filled.

6. Bake for 20–25 minutes until the sponges are well risen. **Check** the cake is cooked – it should be springy when gently pressed. Set the tin on a wire rack, run a round-bladed knife around the inside of the tin to loosen the sponges, then leave to cool until barely warm. Carefully **turn out** onto the wire rack and peel off the lining paper – the cakes will still be fragile so handle them gently – then leave until cold.

7. To assemble the cake, set the sponges on a chopping board. If you used the square tin to bake two sponges, cut each sponge in half lengthways using a serrated bread knife to make four strips of cake – two pink and two yellow. Trim all the strips so that the short sides are exactly square as they may have risen unevenly.

8. Make sure the worktop is spotlessly clean and crumb-free, then dust it lightly with icing sugar or cornflour. Knead the 350g white marzipan for a minute so that it is supple, then roll it out to a neat 20 × 30cm rectangle.

9. Heat the 8 tablespoons apricot jam with 1 tablespoon cold water, then push it through a sieve to make a smooth purée. Brush one long side of one pink strip very lightly with jam and set it jam-side down on one short side of the marzipan rectangle, lined up next to the edge. Brush the three other long sides of this piece of cake lightly with jam.

10. Now brush one long side of a yellow cake strip with jam and set it jam-side down onto the marzipan next to the pink strip and touching it. Brush the top of this strip with jam.

11. Set the other yellow strip on top of the pink strip that is in place on the marzipan.

12. Lightly brush one long side of the second pink strip with jam and set it next to this second yellow strip, so that it sits on top of the yellow strip that's on the marzipan. You will now have created the familiar checkerboard pattern.

13. To finish the cake, brush the top and long sides of the assembled cake with the apricot jam (gently re-warmed), then roll the cake or wrap the marzipan neatly around and over the cake, leaving the checkerboard ends visible. Press the marzipan join to seal it (it should be along one bottom edge). Gently smooth the marzipan with your hands to neaten it up and press out any air pockets, then trim the ends and crimp the top edges of marzipan by pinching it gently, at regular intervals, between your index finger and thumb.

14. Dust lightly with icing sugar just before serving.

Whisky
Dundee
Cake

This may seem straightforward, but the mark of a good Dundee cake is a rich and moist firm sponge mixture evenly peppered with fruit, carefully baked with a not-too-dark crust.

Needs a little skill

HANDS-ON TIME:
30 minutes

BAKING TIME:
2½ hours

MAKES:
1 large cake

SPECIAL EQUIPMENT:
20cm round deep cake tin

METHOD USED:
Creamed method page 24

STORAGE:
Once matured, keep for up to 3 weeks in an airtight container

For the sponge
550g mixed dried fruit (raisins, sultanas, currants) and chopped mixed peel
5 tablespoons whisky
275g plain flour
couple of good pinches of salt
1 teaspoon baking powder
65g ground almonds
225g unsalted butter, softened

finely grated zest of 1 large unwaxed lemon
225g golden caster sugar
4 medium eggs, at room temperature
18 blanched almond halves

For the glaze
2 tablespoons milk
4 teaspoons golden caster sugar

1. To make the fruitcake, put the mixed dried fruit and mixed peel into a bowl, spoon over the whisky, stir well, then cover with clingfilm and leave to macerate overnight.

2. Next day, preheat the oven to 180°C (160°C fan), 350°F, Gas 4. Grease and **line** the tin with butter and baking paper.

3. **Sift** the flour, salt, baking powder and ground almonds into a bowl and put to one side until needed.

4. Put the butter and lemon zest into a large mixing bowl or the bowl of a food-mixer and **beat** with a wooden spoon or the whisk attachment until the mixture is very creamy and mayonnaise-like. Scrape down the sides of the bowl where any mixture has splattered and gradually beat in the golden caster sugar, scraping down the sides of the bowl from time to time.

5. Break the eggs into a separate bowl and beat with a fork until broken up, then beat into the butter mixture a tablespoon at a time, beating well each time. Add a tablespoon of the sifted flour mixture with each of the last two additions of egg to prevent the mixture from curdling.
Continued

Try Something Different

For a less traditional version, you could make this with a luxury bag of mixed fruit that contains glacé cherries, pineapple or chunks of dried apricot. It's well worth soaking the fruit in whisky for 12 hours for a really special flavour, but you could use brandy or dark rum instead.

6. Sift half the remaining flour mixture into the bowl – this helps to really lighten the cake mixture – and **fold in** with a large metal spoon or plastic spatula. Fold in half the fruit and whisky mixture into the bowl. Sift the rest of the flour on top, then fold in followed by the rest of the fruit and whisky. When everything is really well mixed, scrape the mixture into the prepared tin and spread evenly. Bang the tin on the worktop a couple of times to settle the mixture and knock out any air pockets.

7. Make a shallow hollow in the centre of the cake's surface so it will rise evenly. Dip your fingers in cold water and press them lightly over the top of the cake – this prevents the crust getting too hard.

8. Press the 18 blanched almond halves in a neat circle on top of the cake. Wrap a few sheets of newspaper around the outside of the tin and tie with kitchen string. Set the tin on top of another folded newspaper on the baking sheet. This stops the crust being over-baked.

9. Bake for 40 minutes, then reduce the oven temperature to 170°C (150°C fan), 325°F, Gas 3 and bake for a further 1¾ hours. **Check** your cake is cooked by inserting a cocktail stick or skewer into the centre; if it comes out clean, it is ready. Keep an eye on your cake from time to time while it is baking and if you think it is in danger of turning too dark on top, cover it with a sheet of baking paper or foil.

10. At the end of the baking time, make the glaze. Bring the 2 tablespoons milk to the boil and stir in the 4 teaspoons golden caster sugar until dissolved. When the cake is ready, pull it out of the oven and brush it with the hot glaze. Return the cake to the oven for another minute – this will add a nice sheen to the nuts. Set the cake, still in the tin, on a wire rack and leave overnight, then unmould the cake and peel off the lining paper. Wrap in fresh baking paper and foil and leave for 7–10 days before cutting.

Red Velvet Cupcakes

Eye-catching red velvet cupcakes seem to be everywhere these days. The perfect party piece, they are a great excuse, if you need one, to practise your piping skills.

For the sponge
175ml milk
100g good-quality dark chocolate (about 70 per cent cocoa solids), broken up
125g caster sugar
60g unsalted butter, softened
1 medium egg, at room temperature
½ teaspoon vanilla extract
150g self-raising flour
good pinch of salt
1–2 teaspoons red gel food colour

For the topping
150g good-quality white chocolate (around 25 per cent cocoa solids), broken up
110g full-fat cream cheese, brought to room temperature at least an hour beforehand
75g unsalted butter, softened
½ teaspoon vanilla extract

To finish
freeze-dried raspberry pieces or red sugar sprinkles

HANDS-ON TIME:
50 minutes

BAKING TIME:
15–18 minutes

MAKES:
12 cupcakes

SPECIAL EQUIPMENT:
12-hole cupcake tray or deep-hole bun tray; piping bag fitted with a star piping nozzle; paper cupcake cases

METHOD USED:
Creaming method page 24

STORAGE:
Keep for up to 3 days in an airtight container in the fridge. (Take them out of the fridge 30 minutes before serving)

1. Preheat the oven to 180°C (160°C fan), 350°F, Gas 4. Line the cupcake tray with paper cases.

2. To make the sponge, start by pouring the milk into a small pan. Add the dark chocolate pieces and 50g of the caster sugar. Stir gently with a wooden spoon over a very low heat until melted – be patient, and don't let the mixture get hot. Remove the pan from the heat and give it a quick whisk with a wire hand whisk to make sure the milk is blended and smooth. Leave it on one side to cool.

3. Put the butter into a mixing bowl and **beat** well with an electric whisk or the food-mixer whisk attachment until it goes pale and creamy. Stop the whisk and scrape any butter on the sides back down into the bowl. Add just a couple of tablespooons of the remaining 75g caster sugar, and beat again; repeat, stopping occasionally to add the rest of the sugar a couple of tablespoons at a time, and scrape down the sides as you go. When all the sugar has been added, beat well for another minute until all the ingredients are thoroughly combined and your mixture is nice and fluffy.
Continued

4. Break the egg into a small bowl, add the ½ teaspoon vanilla extract and lightly beat with a fork. Now turn on your whisk again and gradually pour the eggs into the butter mixture, whisking all the time. When all the egg has been added, keep whisking for another minute until light and airy.

5. Now you're ready to add the chocolatey milk. Mix the 150g self-raising flour and a pinch of salt together. Take one-third of this mix and **fold** it into the butter mixture with a large metal spoon or plastic spatula. Now fold in a third of the chocolate milk in the same way.

6. Add half of the remaining flour and fold that in, followed by half of the remaining chocolate milk. Continue to fold in alternate spoonfuls of flour and milk until all the ingredients are thoroughly combined and silky smooth.

7. Add your red gel food colouring. It's best to start with 1 teaspoon and fold it in until you can see no streaks. You can always add more after mixing, depending on how vibrant you'd like your red velvet sponge to be.

8. Using a metal spoon, half fill each paper case with the mixture, then bake for 15–18 minutes until the cakes spring back when you lightly press their tops. Stand the tray on a wire rack and cool for 2 minutes, then take them off the tray and pop them back on the wire rack to cool completely.

9. When the cakes are cold, make the frosting. First **melt** the chocolate. Break the 150g white chocolate into pieces and put them in a small heatproof bowl set over a pan of steaming hot (but not boiling) water. Be careful not to let the base of the bowl touch the hot water. White chocolate is quite sensitive and melts at a lower temperature than dark chocolate, so remove the bowl from the pan while there are still a few unmelted lumps and stir to melt, until smooth.

10. Put the 110g cream cheese in a separate bowl and beat until smooth and creamy, then beat in the 75g butter a little at a time. Add the melted chocolate and ½ teaspoon vanilla extract, and beat again for 2 minutes until the mixture is like whipped cream.

11. Now it's time to pipe the frosting on to your cakes. Fill a **piping** bag fitted with a star piping nozzle by spooning in the frosting mixture. Twist the bag, sealing the end to stop the buttercream from escaping.

12. Holding the top of the piping bag, firmly squeeze down the filling as you start to pipe the frosting on to your cake. Start at the edge, keeping the tip of the nozzle just above the cake.

13. Keep squeezing the icing out in a steady spiral until you have covered the whole cake.

14. To get the perfect finish, end the frosting in the very centre and just lift up the nozzle a fraction so that the icing forms a gentle swirling peak.

15. Decorate with the dried raspberry pieces or red sugar sprinkles and leave to firm up for at least half an hour on the worktop before serving.

Cherry Cake

This lovely **creamed** sponge's slightly firmer texture helps keep the delicious ruby red cherries in every mouthful of cake, rather than sunk down at the bottom.

....

200g glacé cherries
200g self-raising flour
good pinch of salt
good pinch of baking powder
175g unsalted butter, softened
175g caster sugar
3 medium eggs, at room temperature
50g ground almonds

....

1. Halve the glacé cherries, then put them into a colander or sieve and rinse well under hot running water to remove the sticky sugar coating. Drain thoroughly, then pat dry on kitchen paper and leave to dry on a fresh sheet of kitchen paper. It's really important to rinse and dry the cherries otherwise their sticky syrup drags them down through the cake mix to sit at the bottom; but you want the cherries scattered evenly throughout the cake.

2. Preheat the oven to 170°C (150°C fan), 325°F, Gas 3. Grease and **line** the tin with butter and baking paper.

3. **Sift** the flour, salt and baking powder onto a sheet of greaseproof paper and put to one side until needed.

4. Put the butter into a mixing bowl or the bowl of a mixer and **beat** with a wooden spoon or the whisk attachment until the mixture is creamy and mayonnaise-like.

5. Gradually beat in the sugar, a couple of tablespoons at a time. Once all the sugar has been added, scrape down the sides of the bowl, then beat the butter mixture well for 2 minutes until very light and fluffy.

Continued

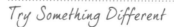

Try Something Different

....

Madeira cake is made in the same way as Cherry Cake but flavoured with lemon zest and juice rather than cherries and ground almonds. Follow the recipe above, adding the finely grated zest and squeezed juice of ½ unwaxed large lemon after the eggs have been beaten in, and mix thoroughly before folding in 250g plain flour, sifted, with a pinch of salt and 1 teaspoon baking powder.

Needs a little skill

HANDS-ON TIME:
25 minutes

BAKING TIME:
60–70 minutes

MAKES:
1 medium cake

SPECIAL EQUIPMENT:
20.5cm round deep cake tin (preferably loose-based) or a springclip tin

METHOD USED:
Creamed method page 24

STORAGE:
Keep for up to 6 days in an airtight container

6. Scrape down the sides of the bowl again. Break the 3 medium eggs into a small bowl and beat with a fork until just broken up. Gradually beat the eggs into the butter mixture a tablespoon at a time, beating well each time and scraping down the sides of the bowl from time to time.

7. Sprinkle the 50g ground almonds over the mixture and **fold** in with a large metal spoon.

8. Tip the cherries into a separate bowl, sprinkle over a tablespoon of the sifted flour and toss gently – the flour stops the cherries sinking to the bottom of the cake.

9. Sift the rest of the flour, once more, onto the cake mixture and gently but thoroughly fold in using a large metal spoon. Scatter the cherries and any remaining flour in the bowl on top and fold in until evenly distributed.

10. Scrape the mixture into the prepared tin and spread evenly. Make a slight hollow (about 1cm deep) in the centre of the mixture so that the cake rises evenly.

11. Bake for 60–70 minutes until the cake is a good golden brown and firm to the touch. **Check** your cake is cooked by inserting a cocktail stick or skewer into the centre; if it comes out clean, it is ready.

12. Set the tin on a wire rack and leave until completely cold. Carefully take out of the tin and peel off the lining paper.

Devil's Food Cake

This American cake is made with soured cream, giving the sponge a moist, light crumb. The marshmallow frosting requires patient whisking, but the luxurious result is worth the effort.

For the sponge
100g good-quality dark chocolate (around 70 per cent cocoa solids), chopped
175ml boiling water
4 tablespoons cocoa powder
1 teaspoon bicarbonate of soda
125g unsalted butter, softened
350g caster sugar
2 medium eggs, at room temperature
1 teaspoon vanilla essence
300g plain flour, sifted
125ml soured cream, at room temperature

For the filling and frosting
2 medium egg whites, at room temperature
350g white caster sugar
1½ tablespoons maple syrup
1 teaspoon vanilla extract
good pinch of salt

HANDS-ON TIME:
80 minutes

BAKING TIME:
20 minutes

MAKES:
1 large cake

SPECIAL EQUIPMENT:
3 × 20.5cm round deep sandwich cake tins

METHOD USED:
Creamed method page 24

STORAGE:
Keep for up to 2 days in an airtight container

1. Preheat the oven to 180°C (160°C fan), 350°F, Gas 4. Grease and **line** the tins with butter and baking paper.

2. To make the sponge, put the chocolate into a heatproof medium bowl set over a pan of steaming hot but not boiling water – don't let the base of the bowl touch the water – and **melt** the chocolate gently. Remove the pan from the heat.

3. While the chocolate is melting, pour the boiling water over the cocoa powder in a heatproof bowl and mix or whisk with a hand wire whisk thoroughly until smooth and lump-free. Stir in the bicarbonate of soda and leave to cool for 5 minutes. Pour this onto the melted chocolate and stir or whisk until smooth and thoroughly combined. Put to one side until needed.

4. Put the butter into a large mixing bowl or the bowl of a food-mixer and **beat** well with an electric whisk or the whisk attachment until creamy. Gradually add the sugar to the bowl and beat well, scraping down the mixture that has splattered on the sides of the bowl from time to time, until thoroughly combined. Don't worry about the texture of the mixture at this point, it won't be light and fluffy like a regular creamed mixture, and that's fine.

5. Beat the eggs with the vanilla, using a fork, just until broken up. Gradually beat into the butter mixture, beating well after each addition and scraping down the sides of the bowl as before.
Continued

6. On a very slow speed, mix in the 300g sifted plain flour in five batches, alternating with the 125ml soured cream. When thoroughly combined, scrape down the sides of the bowl and mix in the lukewarm chocolate mixture, again on a very slow speed. When thoroughly combined with no streaks, divide the mixture equally among the three prepared tins (for this cake it is best to do this by weight for accuracy), and then spread out evenly.

7. Bake for about 20 minutes. **Check** your cakes are cooked by inserting a cocktail stick or skewer into the centre of each cake; if it comes out clean, they are ready. After 14 minutes, check the cakes are cooking evenly, if they aren't, turn the tins round. Run a round-bladed knife around the inside of each tin to loosen the sponges, then leave for a minute to firm up. **Turn out** onto a wire rack and leave to cool completely.

8. Now make the marshmallow fluff filling and frosting. Put the 2 egg whites and 350g caster sugar into a large heatproof bowl and set it over a pan of gently simmering water – don't let the base of the bowl touch the water.

9. Using an electric hand whisk or a rotary hand whisk, **whisk** for 10 seconds, then whisk in the 1½ tablespoons maple syrup, 1 teaspoon vanilla extract, 125ml cold water and a good pinch of salt. Keep whisking on full speed for 12 minutes until the mixture has become thick and glossy and holds a soft peak when the whisk is lifted. Remove the bowl from the pan and whisk again for about 15 minutes until the mixture has cooled to room temperature and has turned snowy white, very thick and holds a stiff peak when the whisk is lifted. Spoon out one-third of the mixture for the filling, then cover the bowl as the rest will be used for the frosting (this stops dark cake crumbs sneaking in).

10. Before the mixture starts to set, quickly assemble the cake: set one sponge crust-side down on a serving platter and spread with half the filling mixture, top with a second sponge, crust-side up, and spread with the rest of the filling. Cover with the third sponge, crust-side up.

11. Divide the reserved frosting in half, then, using a clean round-bladed knife or off-set palette knife, quickly cover the top and sides of the cake with one portion of the frosting. This is the 'crumb catcher' layer – it doesn't need to be neat. Clean the knife and swirl the remaining frosting over the top of the first layer so that it is evenly covered. Leave uncovered on the worktop to firm up for about 5 hours or overnight before serving.

Try Something Different

To make **chocolate curls**, gently melt 50g dark chocolate (70 per cent cocoa solids) and pour it onto a clean marble slab (or onto your worktop). Quickly spread with a metal spatula to a rectangle 20 × 30cm and 2mm thick. When it is set and has turned dull, use a sharp knife at a 45-degree angle away from you to shave off delicate curls of chocolate.

Black Forest Gateau

The ultimate celebratory cake. Layers of light **whisked** sponge made with cocoa instead of flour will hone your whisking skills. You can really go to town on the decadent decorations.

Needs a little skill

HANDS-ON TIME:
55 minutes

BAKING TIME:
20–25 minutes

MAKES:
1 large cake

SPECIAL EQUIPMENT:
3 × 20.5cm round deep sandwich cake tins; Piping bag fitted with a star nozzle

METHOD USED:
Whisked method page 26

STORAGE:
Keep in the fridge in an airtight container and eat within 48 hours

For the sponge
9 medium eggs, at room temperature
large pinch of salt
200g caster sugar
90g cocoa powder

For the filling and topping
850g jar black cherries in light syrup flavoured with Kirsch (700g drained weight), or 850g jar black cherries in light syrup and 3 tablespoons Kirsch
475ml double or whipping cream, well chilled

1 teaspoon vanilla extract
3 tablespoons caster sugar
50g dark chocolate, grated

1. Preheat the oven to 180°C (160°C fan), 350°F, Gas 4. Grease and **line** the tins with butter and baking paper.

2. To make the sponge, separate the eggs, putting the whites into a large and spotlessly clean grease-free bowl or the bowl of a food-mixer, and the yolks into a separate bowl. Add the salt to the egg whites and **whisk** with an electric whisk or the whisk attachment until stiff peaks form when you lift the whisk from the bowl. Put the bowl to one side for now (or transfer the whites to another bowl if you need to reuse the mixer bowl).

3. Add the sugar to the egg yolks and whisk for 4–5 minutes until the mixture is very thick and mousse-like and the whisk leaves a thick ribbon-like trail when lifted out of the mixture.

4. Very gently **fold** the egg whites into the yolk mixture in three batches using a large metal spoon. **Sift** the cocoa powder over the mixture and fold in really well so that there are no streaks.

5. Divide the mixture equally among the three prepared tins (for this cake it is best to do this by weight for accuracy) and gently spread evenly.

6. Bake the sponges for 20–25 minutes. **Check** the cakes are cooked – they should spring back when gently pressed in the centre and start to shrink away from the sides of the tins. After 16 minutes, check the cakes, if they are not baking evenly, turn the tins round.

7. Set the tins on a wire rack and leave to cool completely then **turn out** and peel off the lining paper.
Continued

8. Thoroughly drain the 850g cherries, reserving the syrup. Pat the cherries dry on kitchen paper and reserve 12 for decoration.

9. To make the filling and topping, **whip** the 475ml well-chilled double or whipping cream with the 1 teaspoon vanilla until soft peaks form when you lift the whisk (the cream whips best if the bowl and whisk first have been chilled too). Sprinkle the 3 tablespoons caster sugar over the cream and whip for no more than 10 seconds until combined and the cream is slightly thicker. Set aside one-quarter of the cream for piping, covering and chilling it until needed. Divide the rest of the cream in half: one portion to sandwich the sponges, the other to cover the cake.

10. To assemble the cake, set one sponge crust-side down onto a serving plate. Brush well with some of the reserved cherry syrup (add the 3 tablespoons Kirsch to the 75ml light syrup). Leave to soak for 5 minutes, then spread half the 'sandwiching' cream. Arrange half the remaining cherries over the cream. Set another sponge on top, crust-side down, and brush with more of the syrup. Leave for 5 minutes, then gently spread with the rest of the 'sandwiching' cream and add the cherries as before. Set the last sponge on top, crust-side up, and lightly brush with cherry syrup.

11. Put the cake into the fridge (very lightly covered with a sheet of clingfilm) for about 30 minutes, just to firm it up, then cover the top and sides of the cake with the 'covering' cream using a clean round-bladed knife or offset palette knife. Chill as before for 15 minutes.

12. To decorate the cake, spoon the cream reserved for piping into the **piping** bag fitted with the star nozzle and decorate the top of the cake with piped swirls or a neat rope, then add the reserved cherries and the 50g grated dark chocolate. Cover lightly and chill until ready to serve. Store in the fridge in an airtight container and eat within 48 hours.

Flourless Rich Chocolate Torte

This dark chocolate delight is perfect for gluten-free bakers, because the rich sponge is made using ground almonds instead of flour. Get creative with chocolate shards for a dramatic look.

Needs a little skill

HANDS-ON TIME:
55 minutes

BAKING TIME:
25 minutes

MAKES:
1 medium cake

SPECIAL
EQUIPMENT:
20.5cm round
springclip tin or
deep round cake tin;
Non-stick baking
paper, or a re-usable
silicone sheet, or a
printed-chocolate
transfer sheet

METHOD USED:
Creamed method
page 24

STORAGE:
Bake the day before.
Keep for up to
5 days in an airtight
container

For the sponge
125g good-quality dark chocolate (about 70 per cent cocoa solids)
125g unsalted butter, at room temperature
100g caster sugar
4 medium eggs, at room temperature, separated
good pinch of salt
125g ground almonds

For the covering
125g good-quality dark chocolate (about 70 per cent cocoa solids)
1 tablespoon Amaretto liqueur
100g unsalted butter, softened

To decorate
75g good-quality dark chocolate (around 70 per cent cocoa solids)
cocoa powder or edible gold dust, for dusting (optional)

1. Preheat the oven to 180°C (160°C fan), 350°F, Gas 4. Grease and **line** the tin with butter and baking paper.

2. To make the sponge, break up the dark chocolate into even-sized pieces and put it into a heatproof bowl set over a pan of steaming but not boiling water – don't let the base of the bowl touch the water – and **melt** the chocolate very gently, stirring occasionally until smooth. Remove the bowl from the pan and leave to cool until needed.

3. Put the butter into a large mixing bowl or the bowl of a mixer and **beat** well with an electric whisk or the whisk attachment until the butter is creamy and mayonnaise-like. Set aside 1 tablespoon of the caster sugar for the egg whites, then gradually beat the remaining sugar into the butter, a couple of tablespoons at a time. Scrape down any mixture from the sides of the bowl and beat for a further 2 minutes until the mixture looks pale and fluffy. Scrape

down any mixture again and beat in the 4 egg yolks, one at a time, beating well after each addition.

4. Put the 4 egg whites and salt into a separate large spotlessly clean and grease-free mixing bowl and **whisk** until soft peaks form when the whisk is lifted. Sprinkle the reserved sugar over the whites, then whisk for another minute or so until the mixture stands in stiff peaks.

5. Pour the cooled melted chocolate into the butter and sugar mixture and gently **fold** in using a large metal spoon or plastic spatula. Add the ground almonds and fold in. Add one-quarter of the egg whites and gently stir them in with the metal spoon or spatula to loosen the mixture. Then very gently fold in the rest of the whites in three batches, taking care not to knock out all the air.
Continued

6. Spoon the mixture into the prepared tin and spread evenly then bake for about 25 minutes. **Check** your cake is cooked by inserting a cocktail stick or skewer halfway between the side of the tin and the centre; it should come out clean but the centre should still be moist – it's important not to overcook this cake.

7. Set the tin on the worktop on top of a wet tea towel, run a round-bladed knife around the inside of the tin to loosen the sponge and leave to cool.

8. When the cake is cold, **turn out** from the tin and make the covering. Break up the 125g dark chocolate, put it into a heatproof bowl with the 1 tablespoon Amaretto liqueur and **melt** gently as in Step 2. Remove the bowl from the pan and stir in the 100g soft unsalted butter a little at a time to make a smooth, glossy icing. If the chocolate starts to firm up before all the butter has been mixed in, set the bowl back over the hot water and stir until smooth again.

9. Set the cake upside down on a wire rack set over a baking sheet (to catch the drips) and, as soon as the chocolate is pourable but starting to thicken, pour it over the cake and let it drizzle down the sides. Use a round-bladed knife or an off-set palette knife to neaten up and smooth the sides. Transfer to a cake board or serving plate and leave until almost set.

10. Meanwhile, make the chocolate decoration. Break up the 75g dark chocolate and melt as in Step 2. Remove the bowl from the pan and stir until smooth, then pour the chocolate onto the baking paper/silicone sheet/chocolate transfer sheet and spread it out fairly thinly. Work quickly so that the chocolate doesn't firm up before it is evenly spread. Leave in a cool spot but not in the fridge (otherwise beads of moisture will appear on it when it is back at room temperature).

11. Once set, carefully break the chocolate into shards and arrange them on top of the cake – you can either gently press them into the icing so that the shards stand vertically like sails, or scatter them over the icing to cover.

12. Dust with cocoa powder or edible gold dust, using a clean brush to gently scatter it evenly.

13. To cut neat slices, use a warmed large, sharp knife. Keep a jug of very hot water and kitchen paper at hand so you can dip the knife in the water and wipe it clean and dry between each slice.

Try Something Different

For an even more intense flavour, replace the ground almonds with ground whole unblanched almonds. Lightly toast 125g whole unblanched almonds for 7 minutes in an oven preheated to 180°C (160°C fan), Gas 4. Leave to cool, then grind to a fine powder in a food processor.

Bitter Chocolate Roulade

This elaborate roulade is made from a butterless and flourless mix which produces a rich yet delicate sponge. It requires a little more skill than the Classic Swiss Roll (page 94).

For the sponge

175g good-quality dark chocolate (around 75 per cent cocoa solids), chopped or broken up
6 medium eggs, at room temperature
good pinch of salt
175g caster sugar
1 tablespoon cocoa powder
icing sugar, for dusting

For the filling

225ml double cream, well chilled
250g tin crème de marrons (sweetened chestnut purée)
1 teaspoon dark rum or brandy

To decorate

marrons glacés (candied chestnuts) or grated chocolate or chocolate shavings or curls

1. Preheat the oven to 180°C (160°C fan), 350°F, Gas 4. Grease and **line** the Swiss roll tin with butter and baking paper.

2. To make the sponge, put the dark chocolate into a heatproof bowl and set over a pan of steaming but not boiling water – don't let the base of the bowl touch the water – and **melt** the chocolate, gently stirring now and then.

3. Remove the bowl from the pan, stir gently until smooth, then leave to cool until needed.

4. Separate the eggs, putting the whites in one large mixing bowl or the bowl of a food-mixer, and the yolks into another.

5. Add the salt to the egg whites and **whisk** using an electric whisk or the whisk attachment, until the whites stand in stiff peaks when the whisk is lifted. Put to one side for now (or spoon the whites into another clean bowl if you need the mixer bowl).

6. Add the caster sugar to the egg yolks and whisk for about 3 minutes with the electric whisk or the whisk attachment (there's no need to wash the whisk) until the mixture is very thick and mousse-like and the mixture leaves a distinct ribbon-like trail when the whisk is lifted.

7. Pour the cooled melted chocolate into the bowl and gently **fold** in with a plastic spatula or large metal spoon. Add one-quarter of the stiffly whisked egg whites to the bowl and stir in to loosen the mixture, then gently fold in the rest of the whites in three batches using the plastic spatula or large metal spoon.

8. **Sift** the cocoa powder into the bowl and fold in very carefully – you want to make sure it is well mixed in with no streaks, but you don't want to knock out all the air.
Continued

9. Carefully scrape the mixture into the prepared tin (or the case set on a baking sheet) and gently ease it into the corners so that the tin is evenly filled (otherwise the sponge will rise unevenly). Again, be really careful not to knock out the air.

10. Bake for 20–25 minutes until well risen. **Check** the cake is cooked – the top should feel just firm when lightly pressed with a finger. Remove the tin or case from the oven and set it on a wire rack (carefully slide the case onto the rack from the baking tray). Leave the sponge to cool in the tin or case – don't worry if it sinks, that's fine.

11. While the sponge is cooling, make the filling. **Whip** the 225ml chilled double cream to soft peaks. Stir together the 250g chestnut purée and 1 teaspoon dark rum or brandy until smooth, then lightly stir through the whipped cream to give a marbled or swirled effect. Cover the bowl and chill until needed.

12. Set a large sheet of baking paper on the worktop and dust it lightly with icing sugar. **Turn out** the sponge onto the paper, then remove the tin and lining paper. Using a large sharp knife, make a shallow cut along one short edge about 2cm in. Gently spread the marbled chestnut cream over the sponge to within 2cm of all the edges.

13. Gently fold the cut edge over and then roll up the sponge fairly tightly using the sugar-dusted baking paper to help you pull the roll into a neat shape. Finish with the join at the far end underneath. The roll WILL crack so don't worry if it does, it's all part of the look! Trim off the ends with a large sharp knife to neaten.

14. Gently lift the roll onto a serving plate and decorate with marrons glacés or chocolate shavings or curls (see page 127 and above for how to do this).

Try Something Different

If you prefer a chocolate-based filling, omit the chestnut purée and fold in 50g finely grated dark chocolate (around 70 per cent cocoa solids) instead. Decorate with shavings of white chocolate or dust with cocoa powder or icing sugar, rather than use the marrons glacés as decoration.

Sachertorte

The legendary rich **whisked** chocolate cake from the Hotel Sacher in Vienna is a great way to practise writing with icing – have a few trial runs first before you go for it on the cake!

Needs a little skill

HANDS-ON TIME:
50 minutes

BAKING TIME:
35 minutes

MAKES:
1 medium cake

SPECIAL EQUIPMENT:
22cm springclip tin or deep round cake tin;
Small disposable piping bag

METHOD USED:
Whisked method page 26

STORAGE:
Keep for up to 1 week in an airtight container

For the sponge
175g good-quality dark chocolate (about 70 per cent cocoa solids), chopped or broken up
100g unsalted butter, diced
4 medium eggs, plus 1 egg white, at room temperature
good pinch of salt
115g caster sugar
½ teaspoon vanilla paste
100g plain flour

For the apricot glaze
175g apricot conserve
1 teaspoon lemon juice

For the chocolate glaze
165g good-quality dark chocolate (about 70 per cent cocoa solids)
20g unsalted butter
4 tablespoons double cream

To finish
30g dark chocolate, melted, for piping

1. Preheat the oven to 170°C (150°C fan), 325°F, Gas 3. Grease and **line** the tin with butter and baking paper.

2. To make the sponge, put the chocolate pieces into a heatproof bowl with the butter. Set the bowl over a pan of steaming hot but not boiling water – don't let the base of the bowl touch the water – and **melt** the chocolate gently, stirring occasionally. When melted and smooth, remove the bowl from the pan and put to one side until needed.

3. Separate the 4 eggs; put the 5 egg whites into a large mixing bowl or the bowl of a food-mixer, and the 4 yolks into a separate large bowl. Add the salt to the egg whites, then **whisk** with an electric whisk or the whisk attachment until soft peaks form. Whisk in 85g of the caster sugar a tablespoon at a time, then whisk briefly until it makes stiff peaks. Put the meringue to one side (or spoon it carefully into another bowl if you need the mixer bowl) until required.

4. Add the remaining 30g caster sugar and the vanilla paste to the yolks and whisk (there's no need to wash the whisk) on a high speed until very thick and the whisk leaves a ribbon-like trail when lifted from the mixture. Gently stir in the chocolate mixture with a plastic spatula – the mixture will be very thick.

5. **Sift** the flour onto the mixture, add one-quarter of the meringue and stir in with a large metal spoon or spatula – take your time as the mixture will be quite stiff. **Fold** in the rest of the meringue in three batches. When thoroughly combined – check there are no lumps of meringue or streaks of chocolate – transfer the mixture to the prepared tin and spread evenly.
Continued

9

6. Bake for about 35 minutes until just firm when gently pressed in the centre. **Check** your cake is cooked by inserting a cocktail stick or skewer into the centre; if it comes out clean, it is ready. Set the tin on a wire rack, run a round-bladed knife around the inside of the tin to loosen, then leave to cool for 5 minutes before unmoulding. Leave on the wire rack until completely cool.

7. To make the apricot glaze, gently heat the 175g apricot conserve in a small pan with the 1 tablespoon cold water and 1 teaspoon lemon juice, then press the mixture through a sieve into a small bowl. Set the cake upside down on a board and slice into two **layers** horizontally. Return the bottom layer (this was the top of the cake) to the wire rack, cut side up, and spread with half the apricot mixture. Cover with the second sponge layer so that the cut sides are together. Gently reheat the glaze and brush it over the top and sides of the sponge. Leave to cool on the wire rack.

8. To make the chocolate glaze, break or chop up the 165g dark chocolate and put it into a heatproof bowl with the 20g unsalted butter and gently melt, as in Step 2. Remove the bowl from the heat and stir until smooth. Heat the 4 tablespoons double cream until almost, but not quite, boiling, then leave for a minute before pouring onto the chocolate mixture in a thin, steady stream while stirring constantly. Pour the glaze over the cake and gently ease it down the sides to completely and smoothly coat the cake, using a palette knife to carefully smooth it if needed. Leave to set in a cool spot but not in the fridge. Transfer the cake to a board.

9. To decorate, melt the remaining 30g dark chocolate as in Step 2 and pour it into a small **piping** bag.

10. Snip off the tip of the piping bag to give a fine writing tip about 3mm across. Pipe 'Sacher' across the top of the cake for a professional finish!

Gâteau le Progrès

Circles of hazelnut meringue sandwiched between layers of rich buttercream and topped with praline. A mouthwatering tower of sweetness and a bake that is worth the challenge.

For the hazelnut meringue
6 medium egg whites, at room temperature
good pinch of salt
300g golden caster sugar
150g ground roasted hazelnuts
2 tablespoons cornflour

For the praline
200g whole unblanched hazelnuts
200g caster sugar

For the buttercream
100g caster sugar
4 medium egg yolks, at room temperature
250g slightly salted butter, softened (but not oily)

1. Preheat the oven to 120°C (100°C fan), 250°F, Gas ½. Lightly grease the baking sheets with butter.

2. Using a cake tin or plate as a guide, draw three 20cm circles on a sheet of baking paper the same size as your baking sheets. Don't cut out the circles but press the baking paper, marked-side down, onto the baking sheets.

3. To make the meringue, put the egg whites and salt into a large, spotlessly clean mixing bowl or the bowl of a food-mixer. Spoon 6 tablespoons of the golden caster sugar into a separate small bowl and put to one side until needed. Put the remaining sugar into a separate bowl and thoroughly mix in the ground roasted hazelnuts and cornflour.

4. Using an electric whisk or the whisk attachment, **whisk** the egg whites on a slow speed until frothy, then increase the speed until the mixture stands in soft peaks when the whisk is lifted out of the bowl. Sprinkle the reserved 6 tablespoons sugar over the whites, then whisk for a further 30 seconds until the mixture stands in stiff peaks and is glossy and smooth.

5. Sprinkle one-third of the hazelnut mixture over the meringue and fold in lightly using a large metal spoon. **Fold** in the rest of the hazelnut mixture in two batches.
Continued

HANDS-ON TIME:
2 hours

BAKING TIME:
1½ hours

MAKES:
1 medium cake

SPECIAL EQUIPMENT:
2 × baking sheets; Large piping bag fitted with a 1.5cm plain nozzle; Sugar thermometer

METHOD USED:
None of the traditional methods. This is a meringue cake.

STORAGE:
The cake is at its best after a night in the fridge, but will keep for up to 5 days in an airtight container in the fridge. (Remove 30 minutes before serving)

6. Transfer the mixture to the **piping** bag fitted with the plain nozzle. Pipe three discs of meringue inside the drawn circles. Start in the centre and pipe spirals. If necessary, go back and fill in any gaps. The trick with this cake is to pipe the meringue discs in neat rings and then get them nice and crisp in the oven.

7. Bake the meringue rounds for about 1½ hours until a very light golden colour and crisp and dry. For more even baking, you can rotate the sheets after 50 minutes. Remove the baking sheets from the oven, set them on a wire rack and leave the rounds until cold before peeling them off the lining paper.

8. While the rounds are cooling make the praline. Have an oiled baking sheet ready. Put the 200g whole unblanched hazelnuts and 200g caster sugar into a medium-sized heavy-based pan and set over a low heat. Stir occasionally with a metal spoon (the caramel will stick like glue to a wooden spoon) until the sugar starts to melt. When all the sugar has melted, increase the heat to medium and cook until the sugar starts to colour, giving the pan a gentle shake from time to time. Then stir gently to make sure the nuts brown evenly, taking care as the mixture will be very hot, until the mixture turns a chestnut-brown colour. Immediately — and carefully, it's very hot! — pour it onto the baking sheet and leave until cool and set.

9. Now make the buttercream. Put the 100g caster sugar and 6 tablespoons cold water into a small heavy-based pan and heat gently, without boiling, until the sugar dissolves. Bring to the boil until the syrup reaches 110°C/230°F on a sugar thermometer – this will take about 5 minutes. Watch the syrup carefully as you don't want it to start to caramelise.

10. Meanwhile, put the 4 medium egg yolks into a heatproof bowl set on top of a damp cloth (to prevent the bowl slipping) and whisk for a few seconds with an electric whisk just to combine. When the syrup reaches the required temperature, pour it into the bowl in a thin steady stream, whisking constantly at high speed. You can also do this in a large free-standing mixer but aim for the yolks and not the sides of the bowl or the syrup will harden before it is whisked in. Continue whisking for about 5 minutes until the mixture becomes very thick and mousse-like, pale in colour and the whisk leaves a distinct ribbon-like trail when lifted. Whisk until the mixture is completely cold, then gradually whisk in the 250g soft butter.

11. Break the praline into pieces, then put half into a food-processor and pulse to a fine powder. Don't overwork the praline, though, or it will turn oily and paste-like. Stir the powder into the buttercream, cover and, if necessary, chill until firm enough to spread.

12. Select 12 large chunks of the reserved hazelnut praline for the decoration and set aside, then roughly chop the rest using a large sharp knife. Keep this for decorating the sides of the cake.

13. Set one meringue round on a serving plate. Divide the buttercream into four equal portions. Spread one portion over the meringue round and set a second one on top. Spread with a second portion of buttercream and add the last round of meringue. Spread one portion of buttercream over the top and use the remaining portion to cover the sides. Press the chopped praline around the bottom of the sides of the cake. Pop it in the fridge to chill for 15 minutes.

14. Decorate the top of the cake with the reserved praline chunks before serving.

Try Something Different

Swap the hazelnuts for unblanched almonds for a different flavour. Lightly toast 150g whole unblanched almonds for 7 minutes in an oven preheated to 180°C (160°C fan), Gas 4. Leave to cool then grind to a fine powder in a food processor and use for the meringue layers instead of the ground almonds. You could also replace the hazelnuts in the praline with 200g whole unblanched almonds.

Sea Salt
Caramel Cake

This classic **creamed** sponge has a lovely light crumb thanks to the addition of buttermilk. The feathered salty caramel topping looks simple but takes a little skill to master.

For the sponge
250g unsalted butter, softened
300g golden caster sugar
4 medium eggs
1 teaspoon vanilla extract
300g self-raising flour
good pinch of salt
5 tablespoons buttermilk, at room temperature

For the filling and frosting
250g unsalted butter, softened
450g dark muscovado sugar
175ml double cream
250g icing sugar, sifted
¼–½ teaspoon sea salt flakes
100g good-quality dark chocolate (about 70 per cent cocoa solids), chopped

HANDS-ON TIME:
90 minutes

BAKING TIME:
22–25 minutes

MAKES:
1 large cake

SPECIAL EQUIPMENT:
3 × 20.5cm deep round sandwich cake tins; Small disposable piping bag

METHOD USED:
Creamed method page 24

STORAGE:
Bake the the day before. Keep for up to 4 days in an airtight container

1. Preheat the oven to 180°C (160°C fan), 350°F, Gas 4. Grease and **line** the tins with butter and baking paper.

2. To make the sponge, put the butter into a large mixing bowl or the bowl of a food-mixer and **beat** well with a wooden spoon or the whisk attachment until creamy. Gradually beat in the caster sugar, then scrape down any mixture that has splattered on the sides of the bowl and beat for a further 2 minutes or until well mixed and lighter (although the mixture will be slightly heavier than the usual creamed mixture).

3. Break the eggs into a separate bowl, add the vanilla extract and beat with a fork just until broken up, then gradually beat into the butter mixture, beating well after each addition and scraping down the sides of the bowl every now and then. Add a tablespoon of the self-raising flour with each of the last two additions of egg to prevent the mixture curdling.

4. **Sift** the remaining flour and salt into the bowl, then add the buttermilk and gently **fold** everything together using a large metal spoon.

5. When thoroughly combined, divide the mixture among the three prepared tins (for this cake it is best to do this by weight for accuracy) and spread evenly.

6. Bake the cakes for 22–25 minutes until the sponges are golden. **Check** the cakes are cooked – they should start to shrink away from the sides of the tins and spring back when lightly pressed in the centre with your fingertip. Check the cakes after 20 minutes, and if they are not baking evenly, turn the tins round.
Continued

7. Run a round-bladed knife around the inside of the tins to loosen the sponges, then leave to cool and firm up for 2 minutes before **turning out** onto a wire rack. Leave to cool completely.

8. While the sponges are cooling, make the filling and frosting. Put 175g of the butter into a heavy-based medium pan with the 450g dark muscovado sugar and 175ml double cream. Set over a low heat and stir with a wooden spoon until melted and lump-free, then increase the heat and bring the mixture to a boil, stirring constantly. As soon as it boils, turn down the heat so that the mixture gently simmers and simmer for 5 minutes, stirring frequently so that it doesn't catch around the base.

9. Carefully pour into a heatproof mixing bowl and immediately start to whisk with an electric whisk while slowly and gradually beating in the 250g sifted icing sugar. Continue beating after all the sugar has been added, for about 8 minutes or until the mixture is fluffy and cooled to barely warm. Gradually beat in the remaining 75g soft butter (if the mixture is too warm it will melt the butter and the mixture will be too soft). Sprinkle over ¼ teaspoon of the salt and stir in with a plastic spatula – taste and add a little more salt as needed. Cover the bowl and leave on the worktop for now.

10. Put the 100g chopped dark chocolate into a small heatproof bowl and set over a pan of steaming hot but not boiling water – don't let the base of the bowl touch the water – and **melt** the chocolate gently, stirring occasionally. Remove the bowl from the heat, stir again, then spoon two-thirds into a separate bowl and fold in 250g of the caramel mixture. Put to one side until spreadable. Cover the rest of the caramel and put to one side for now.

11. Set one sponge crust-side down on a serving platter and spread with half the chocolate caramel. Cover with another sponge, crust-side up, and spread with the rest of the chocolate caramel. Using a round-bladed knife or off-set palette knife, thickly spread the caramel over the top and sides of the cake to completely cover. If the caramel mixture has become too firm to spread easily, gently warm it over a pan of steaming water, and stir it until it is smooth and spreadable.

12. If necessary, gently reheat the remaining chocolate in the same way until smooth and melted. Spoon into the **piping** bag and snip off the end to make a writing tip about 3mm across. Hold the bag vertically over the cake and, starting in the centre, pipe a spiral of chocolate on top of the cake without touching the surface with the tip. Try to keep an even, gentle pressure on the bag so that the lines are equally thick and evenly spaced. Work quickly and don't worry about the odd wobble.

13. Now gently draw the tip of a cocktail stick through both the chocolate spiral and the caramel frosting, from the centre to the sides at six regular intervals, to make the first set of lines. Then draw the cocktail stick back from the edge towards the centre to make lines in between the first set of lines.

14. Leave the cake to firm up for about 3 hours, uncovered on the worktop, before serving.

Lemon Curd Layer Cake

Home-made lemon curd is well worth the effort as nothing tastes as sublime, and it really lifts the flavours of this light genoise sponge. Layers of luscious loveliness.

Needs a little skill

HANDS-ON TIME:
2 hours

BAKING TIME:
20 minutes

MAKES:
1 large cake

SPECIAL
EQUIPMENT:
2 × 20.5cm round
deep sandwich
cake tins; Small
disposable piping
bag

METHOD USED:
Whisked method
page 26

STORAGE:
Put the cake into an
airtight container
and chill in the
fridge for 8 hours or
overnight so that it
can firm up and the
flavours can develop.
(Remove from the
fridge 30 minutes
before serving.)
Keep for up to 3 days
in the fridge

For the sponge
6 medium eggs, at room temperature
175g caster sugar
175g plain flour
good pinch of salt
extra caster sugar, for sprinkling

For the syrup
100g caster sugar
2 large unwaxed lemons

For the lemon curd
125g unsalted butter, diced
225g caster sugar
finely grated zest and juice of 3
medium unwaxed lemons
3 medium eggs, at room temperature

For the filling and covering
250ml double cream, well chilled
2 tablespoons caster sugar
400g ricotta
2–3 teaspoons limoncello, to taste
(optional)

To decorate
50g toasted flaked almonds
3 tablespoons Lemon Curd

1. Preheat the oven to 180°C (160°C fan), 350°F, Gas 4. Grease and **line** the tins with butter and baking paper.

2. To make the sponge, put the eggs into a large mixing bowl or the bowl of a food-mixer and **whisk** using an electric whisk or the whisk attachment for 30 seconds so that the eggs are frothy, then whisk in the caster sugar. Whisk on a high speed for about 5 minutes until the mixture is very thick, pale and mousse-like, and the whisk leaves a thick ribbon-like trail when lifted.

3. **Sift** the flour and salt into a separate bowl, then sift one-third of that again onto the whisked mixture. Very gently **fold** in using a large metal spoon, taking care not to knock out the air you've whisked in. Repeat, adding the remaining flour in two batches. When there are no streaks of flour visible, divide the mixture equally between the two prepared tins (for this cake it is best to do this by weight for better accuracy) and gently spread evenly.

4. Bake the sponges for 20 minutes, or until well risen and a light golden brown. **Check** the cakes are cooked – they should be just firm when gently pressed in the centre. Run a round-bladed knife around the inside of the tins to loosen the sponges. Cover a wire rack with a sheet of baking paper and sprinkle with a little caster sugar. Carefully **turn out** the sponges onto the paper and leave to cool completely. *Continued*

5. While the sponges are cooling, make the syrup. Put 100ml cold water and the 100g caster sugar into a small pan. Finely grate the zest from one of the large unwaxed lemons and add it to the pan. Using a vegetable peeler, carefully peel the zest from the second lemon into strips, then cut the strips into fine needle-like shreds. Wrap tightly in clingfilm and set aside for decoration. Halve both lemons and squeeze the juice – add 3 tablespoons to the pan. Set the pan over a low heat and stir until the sugar has dissolved, then bring to the boil and simmer for 2 minutes to make a light syrup. Leave to cool.

6. To make the lemon curd, put the 125g butter, 225g caster sugar and the finely grated zest and juice of the 3 lemons into a large heatproof bowl. Set the bowl over a pan of just simmering water, not letting the base of the bowl touch the water, and stir gently with a wooden spoon until the mixture is completely melted and smooth.

7. Carefully remove the bowl from the pan and strain the 3 eggs into the mixture (this will make sure there are no fragments of shell or tough white membranes). Stir well, then set the bowl over the pan of simmering water again and stir constantly until the mixture becomes thick and opaque. Take your time – don't be tempted to turn up the heat as the eggs will scramble if the mixture gets anywhere near boiling. The lemon curd is ready when you can draw a finger through the mixture on the wooden spoon and leave a clear path.

8. Immediately lift the bowl from the pan and transfer the lemon curd to a clean bowl or a screw-topped jar. When cold, cover tightly and chill. The lemon curd can be kept in the fridge for up to 2 weeks.

9. To make the filling and covering, pour the 250ml chilled double cream into a mixing bowl and **whip** with an electric whisk or the whisk attachment (the cream whips better if the bowl and whisk have been chilled) until thick. Sprinkle the 2 tablespoons caster sugar into the bowl and whisk briefly just until soft peaks form when the whisk is lifted. Stir the lemon curd until smooth (reserving 3 tablespoons for the decoration), then mix 175g of it into the 400g ricotta, then gently fold this into the whipped cream. Cover and chill for about 30 minutes. Transfer slightly less than half the lemon cream to a separate bowl (this will be used to cover the cake), cover and return to the fridge.

10. Stir the 2–3 teaspoons limoncello (if using) into the rest of the lemon curd, cover and chill until needed.

11. When you're ready to assemble the cake, gently slice each sponge into two **layers** horizontally using a serrated bread knife.

12. Set one of the four sponge layers cut-side up on a serving plate. Brush with one-quarter of the syrup and leave for 2—3 minutes to soak in. Using a round-bladed knife or offset palette knife, spread one-third of the remaining lemon cream over the soaked sponge. Using another knife, carefully spread one-third of the limoncello lemon curd on top.

13. Set a second sponge layer, cut-side up, on top and repeat the process: brushing with syrup, spreading with lemon cream, then lemon curd. Set a third sponge layer on top, cut-side up, and repeat. Finally, top with the last sponge layer, this time with the crust-side uppermost, and brush with the last of the lemon syrup. Cover and chill for 30 minutes.

14. Spread the reserved lemon cream over the top and sides of the cake to cover.

15. Press the 50g flaked almonds around the sides of the cake using your hands.

16. Spoon the reserved lemon curd for the decoration into the **piping** bag, snip off the tip and pipe in a zigzag pattern over the top of the cake. Scatter the shreds of reserved lemon zest over the top of the cake.

Chess Cake

Appearances can be deceptive. An understated cake from the outside, but one that will impress when you cut the first slice to reveal a chequerboard of chocolate and vanilla squares inside.

For the sponge
350g unsalted butter, softened
350g caster sugar
6 medium eggs, at room temperature
1 teaspoon vanilla extract
350g self-raising flour
couple of pinches of salt
50g cocoa powder
4 tablespoons milk, at room temperature

For the white chocolate ganache filling
175g good-quality white chocolate (around 25 per cent cocoa solids), very finely chopped

125ml whipping cream
50g unsalted butter
pinch of salt

For the dark chocolate ganache covering
300g good-quality dark chocolate (around 70 per cent cocoa solids), very finely chopped
300ml whipping cream

For the decoration
Dark and white chocolate shavings and curls, or grated chocolate, or ready-made chocolate decorations

Up for a challenge

HANDS-ON TIME:
60 minutes

BAKING TIME:
22–25 minutes

MAKES:
1 large cake

SPECIAL EQUIPMENT:
3 × 20.5cm round deep sandwich cake tins (or springclip tins); 2 piping bags, each fitted with a 1.5cm plain piping nozzle

METHOD USED:
Creamed method, see page 24

STORAGE:
Bake the day before. Keep for up to 4 days in an airtight container

1. Preheat the oven to 180°C (160°C fan), 350°F, Gas 4. Grease and **line** the tins with butter and baking paper. Use springclip tins if you already have them, but sandwich tins are best as its easier to pipe the mixture into shallow tins.

To make the sponge
2. To make the whisked sponge, put the butter into a large mixing bowl or the bowl of a food-mixer and **beat** with a wooden spoon or the whisk attachment until very creamy and mayonnaise-like. Scrape down any mixture splattered on the sides of the bowl, then beat in the caster sugar a couple of tablespoons at a time, scraping down the sides of the bowl from every now and then. Beat well for a couple of minutes until the mixture is light and fluffy.

3. Break the eggs into a separate bowl, add the vanilla extract and beat with a fork until broken up. Gradually beat the eggs into the butter mixture, a tablespoon at a time, beating well after each addition and scraping down the sides of the bowl occasionally. Add 1 tablespoon of the flour with the last two additions of egg to stop the mixture curdling.

4. **Sift** the remaining flour and the salt into the bowl and carefully **fold** in using a large metal spoon. Divide the mixture in half – using scales or by eye. Put one half into a separate mixing bowl. Sift the cocoa powder into one portion with 2 tablespoons of the milk and fold in until combined and streak-free. Fill one of the **piping** bags fitted with the plain nozzle with the chocolate mixture.
Continued

5. Add the remaining 2 tablespoons milk to the other bowl of cake mixture and fold in with a clean spoon. Transfer this mixture to the other piping bag.

6. Set all three prepared tins in front of you. Take the bag containing the dark chocolate mixture and pipe a ring around the inside edge of one tin.

7. Now pick up the bag containing the vanilla mixture and pipe a ring inside the chocolate ring.

8. Repeat, piping alternate dark chocolate and white vanilla rings, until the tin is filled. Do not spread or even out the mixtures – leave them looking just like a bull's-eye. Do exactly the same thing with the second tin, starting with a dark chocolate ring around the edge.

9. For the third tin, do the reverse – use the vanilla mixture to pipe the outermost ring, then pipe a chocolate ring inside and repeat until it is filled.

10. Bake the sponges for 22–25 minutes. To **check** if the cakes are cooked, lightly press them in the centre – they should be well risen and springy. Run a round-bladed knife around the inside of the tins to loosen the sponges, leave to firm up for 1 minute, then **turn out** onto wire racks and leave to cool completely

To make the white chocolate ganache filling

11. Once the sponges are cold, make the white chocolate ganache filling. Put the 175g chocolate into a heatproof bowl. Put the 125ml cream, 50g butter and salt (this helps it set well) into a small pan and heat until steaming hot but not quite boiling. Pour onto the chocolate in a thin, steady stream. Leave to stand for a minute, then stir gently until melted and smooth. Leave for a few minutes until it is thick enough to spread easily.

12. Set one sponge with a dark chocolate outer ring crust- or top-side down on a cake board or serving platter. Spread with half the white chocolate ganache, then set the sponge with the white vanilla outer ring on top. Spread with the remaining white ganache and top with the last sponge, crust- or top-side uppermost. Leave to firm up while you make the other ganache.

To make the dark chocolate ganache filling

13. Make the dark chocolate ganache in the same way as the white: put the 300g chocolate into a heatproof bowl. Heat the 300ml cream until very hot but not boiling and pour over the chocolate. Leave to melt for a couple of minutes, then stir gently. Leave until thick enough to spread.

14. When it is nice and thick, using a knife, spread the ganache evenly over the top and sides of the cake. Leave in a cool spot – but not the fridge – until set and firm, then decorate with the grated chocolate, chocolate shavings and curls or decorations.

Porter
Fruitcake

A rich fruit cake hides beneath a light and pretty exterior. Perfect for celebrating the arrival of spring, the beautiful blooms look impressive but are surprisingly easy to make.

Up for a challenge

HANDS-ON TIME:
2½ hours

BAKING TIME:
2 hours

MAKES:
1 large cake

SPECIAL
EQUIPMENT:
20.5cm springclip tin
or deep round cake
tin; Newspaper;
Cake board; Tape
measure; Food
preparation gloves
(optional); Small
silicone flower
mould

METHOD USED:
Creamed method,
see page 24

STORAGE:
Ready after 5 days,
keep for up to
2 months in an
airtight container

For the cake mixture
500g mixed dried fruit
100ml Porter or stout
175g unsalted butter, softened
175g dark muscovado sugar
3 medium eggs, at room temperature
200g plain flour
good pinch of salt
50g ground almonds
1½ teaspoons ground mixed spice
85g walnut pieces or chopped toasted almonds

For covering the cake
2 tablespoons apricot jam, warmed
800g ready-made marzipan
icing sugar, for dusting
500g royal icing made with 500g royal icing sugar (or use ready-to-roll or rolled white or ivory icing or ready-coloured icing/sugarpaste)

For the rose decoration
250g ready-to-roll white icing/sugarpaste
yellow edible gel, liquid or paste food colour
cornflour, for dusting
edible lustre, for spraying (optional)

To make the cake mixture

1. Tip the dried fruit into a mixing bowl, pour over the Porter or stout and mix well. Cover tightly and leave to soak overnight on the worktop.

2. Next day, preheat the oven to 170°C (150°C fan), 325°F, Gas 3. Grease and **line** the tin with butter and baking paper.

3. Put the butter into a large mixing bowl or the bowl of a food-mixer and **beat** well with a wooden spoon or the whisk attachment for a couple of minutes until creamy and mayonnaise-like. Scrape down any mixture that has splattered on the sides of the bowl. Press out any lumps in the muscovado sugar (you may need to sieve it), then gradually beat it into the butter, scraping down the sides of the bowl from time to time. Once all the sugar has been added, beat well for 4 minutes or until the mixture turns much lighter in colour and texture. Scrape down the sides of the bowl again.

4. Break the eggs into a separate bowl and beat with a fork just until broken up, then gradually beat into the butter mixture, a tablespoon at a time, beating well after each addition. If it looks like it is about to curdle or separate, add a tablespoon of the plain flour with the last addition of egg.

5. **Sift** the remaining flour, salt, almonds and mixed spice into the bowl and gently but thoroughly **fold** in using a large metal spoon or plastic spatula. Add the soaked fruit (plus any liquid) and gently fold in.
Continued

6. When thoroughly combined, add the 85g walnut pieces or chopped toasted almonds and fold in. Spoon the mixture into the prepared tin and spread it out evenly. Bang the tin down on the worktop to knock out any pockets of air, then make a shallow hollow in the centre of the cake so that it will rise evenly.

7. Line the baking sheet with several sheets of newspaper and set the tin on top. Fold several more sheets into strips slightly wider than the depth of the tin and long enough to go all around it.

8. Wrap these strips around the tin and secure them with paper clips or string.

9. Bake the cake for about 2 hours. **Check** your cake is cooked by inserting a cocktail stick or skewer into the centre; if it comes out clean, it is ready. If necessary, turn the cake a couple of times during baking so that it cooks evenly and cover the top with a sheet of baking paper or foil if you think it is getting too brown. Remove the tin from the oven, set it on a wire rack and leave until cold, then turn out. Remove the lining paper, then wrap in baking paper then foil, and leave in a cool dry spot for at least a week – 4 weeks if possible – before finishing the cake.

To cover the cake

10. Unwrap the cake and set it upside down on the cake board or serving plate – the flat base of the cake is easier to cover. Brush all over with the 2 tablespoons warm apricot jam.

11. Knead the 800g ready-made marzipan until smooth and pliable. If there is a gap between the cake and the board, make a thin roll of marzipan and press it around the base of the cake so the sides are flat and straight. Lightly dust the worktop with icing sugar and roll out the remaining marzipan to a round large enough to cover the top and sides of the cake – for accuracy use a tape measure.

12. Carefully wrap the marzipan around the rolling pin and lift it over the cake. Gently unroll it so the edge just touches the board, then continue unrolling it over the cake so that it covers the cake evenly and touches the board all around.

13. Now remove all rings/bangles/watch – you don't want to make dents in the marzipan – then use the palms of your hands to smooth the marzipan on the top and down the sides of the cake, to make sure it is well fixed and there are no pockets of air. Find a sharp knife and roughly trim away the excess marzipan.

14. Lift the cake and board and trim the marzipan with a sharp knife until flush with the board. Leave the cake very loosely covered in a cool dry spot for a day or two to let the marzipan firm up.

15. Brush the marzipan very lightly with a little cooled boiled water (or brandy).

16. To make your own royal icing, mix the 500g royal icing with 80ml water, using an electric whisk or mixer, until smooth and thick. It should stand in soft peaks and leave a solid trail.

Continued

17. Spread the royal icing over the top and sides, smoothing it with a palette knife. (If you are using bought icing, knead and roll it out as for the marzipan then smooth and polish it with the palms of your hands.) Use the back of a small knife to tuck the icing under the edge of the cake (press the edge of the rolled icing under) so that it looks neat.

To make the decorations

18. When you are ready to decorate the cake, knead the 250g ready-to-roll white icing/sugarpaste until smooth, then tint it to the palest shade you want, kneading in just 1–2 drops of yellow edible gel, liquid or paste food colour for 4–5 minutes until even, with no streaks (it's a good idea to wear food preparation gloves to avoid staining your hands).

19. Divide the paste into four equal portions: wrap one portion tightly with clingfilm or put it in a snap-close plastic food bag, then add another 1–2 drops of food colour to the next portion, knead in and wrap tightly. Continue with all the remaining two portions of the sugarpaste.

20. When you are happy with the range of shades, you can make the shaped decorations. Make sure the silicone mould is clean and dry, then dust it lightly with cornflour. Mould a little of the lightest-coloured icing into a ball the size of a marble (or follow the instructions on the pack) and press it into the mould, making sure the icing is level with the edge of the mould.

21. Turn the mould over and gently release the blossom onto a sheet of baking paper. Repeat with the rest of the icing in this colour, then with the other three shades. Once dry and firm, the blossoms can be sprayed with edible lustre, if you like. You can paint the centres of the flowers darker yellow with edible cake decorating powder colour mixed with a couple of drops of vodka. For a little added sparkle, you could delicately brush dry powder lustre onto the petals – very fine brushes are available from specialist shops.

22. While the blossoms dry, if you like, cut a ribbon long enough to go around the cake and tie it around it tightly and neatly, securing it at the back.

23. When the blossoms are set and dry, start to attach them to the cake using small dabs of royal icing applied with a cotton bud.

24. Dot the flowers over the top of the cake, mixing up the colours for a pretty effect. Leave uncovered to firm up, then store carefully in a covered container in a cool and dry place.

Mile-high Chocolate Cake

An out-of-this-world chocolate cake; three very light layers of **creamed** sponge mixture filled and frosted with a whipped mousse-like chocolate ganache buttercream.

For the sponge

60g cocoa powder
250ml boiling water
30g good-quality dark chocolate (around 70 per cent cocoa solids), finely chopped
225g unsalted butter, softened
325g light muscovado sugar
2 medium eggs plus 2 yolks, at room temperature
½ teaspoon vanilla extract
4 tablespoons crème fraîche
225g self-raising flour
good pinch of salt

For the filling and frosting

200g good-quality dark chocolate (about 70 per cent cocoa solids), finely chopped
125ml double cream
2 medium egg whites, at room temperature
200g caster sugar
450g unsalted butter, softened and diced

To finish

75g chocolate-coated popping candy
100g good-quality dark chocolate (around 70 per cent cocoa solids), finely chopped

HANDS-ON TIME:
2¼ hours

BAKING TIME:
25–28 minutes

MAKES:
1 large cake

SPECIAL EQUIPMENT:
3 × 20.5cm deep round sandwich cake tins; 20.5cm cake board; Strip of acetate or chocolate transfer sheet

METHOD USED:
Creamed method, see page 24

STORAGE:
Bake the day before. Keep for up to 4 days in an airtight container in the fridge

1. Preheat the oven to 180°C (160°C fan), 350°F, Gas 4. Grease and **line** the tins with butter and baking paper.

To make the sponge

2. **Sift** the cocoa powder into a heatproof bowl and pour on the boiling water while whisking constantly with a hand wire whisk. When the mixture is smooth and lump-free, whisk the chocolate in until melted and perfectly smooth. Put to one side to cool.

3. Meanwhile, put the butter into a large mixing bowl or the bowl of a food-mixer and **beat** with a wooden spoon or the whisk attachment until creamy and mayonnaise-like. Scrape down any mixture splattered on the sides of the bowl. You need lump-free muscovado sugar for this, so push it through a sieve,

then gradually beat the fine sugar into the butter on a low speed. Once all the sugar has been added, scrape down the sides of the bowl, then beat on a high speed for about 4 minutes until the mixture looks fluffy and paler in colour. Stop and scrape down the sides of the bowl from time to time.

4. Put the 2 whole eggs and 2 yolks into a separate bowl (reserve the whites for the filling and frosting). Add the vanilla extract and beat with a fork just until combined. Gradually beat the egg mixture into the butter mixture a tablespoon at a time, beating well after each addition and scraping down the sides of the bowl as before.
Continued

5. Add the cooled chocolate mixture to the bowl and start to **fold** in, using just two movements, with a large metal spoon or plastic spatula. Spoon the 4 tablespoons crème fraîche into the bowl, sift over the 225g flour and a good pinch of salt, and gently fold everything together.

6. When thoroughly combined, divide the mixture equally among the three prepared tins – if you want to be more precise use your scales, or you can just judge it by eye – and spread evenly. Bake for 25–28 minutes. Check the cakes after 20 minutes and if they are not baking evenly, turn the tins round. **Check** if the cakes are cooked – they're ready when the sponges are well risen, starting to shrink away from the sides of the tins and the centre of each sponge springs back when gently pressed in the centre.

7. Run a round-bladed knife around the inside of each tin to loosen the sponges, then **turn out** onto a wire rack and leave to cool.

To make the filling and frosting
8. While the sponges are cooling, make the filling and frosting. Put the chocolate into a heatproof bowl. Heat the 125ml double cream until just boiling, then pour it over the chocolate and stir until melted and smooth. Leave to cool to room temperature, stirring occasionally.

9. Meanwhile, put the 2 egg whites into a large heatproof mixing bowl. Add the 200g caster sugar and **whisk** with a hand-held electric mixer for a minute until slightly frothy. Set the bowl over a pan of simmering water – don't let the base of the bowl touch the water – and whisk for 7 minutes to make a very thick, white, glossy stiff meringue. Lift the bowl off the pan and set it on a damp cloth (so it doesn't slip) and whisk for about 8 minutes until the mixture is completely cold.

10. Once the mixture is cold, gradually whisk in the 450g butter – if the meringue is even slightly warm the butter will melt and the mixture will turn oily. Once all the butter has been mixed in, whisk for 2 minutes to make a very light and fluffy buttercream.

11. Now whisk in the cooled but fluid ganache and whisk for 2 minutes to make a thick and light mousse-like mixture that stands in soft peaks when the whisk is lifted. It needs to be firm enough to spread easily and hold its shape so that it doesn't slide off the cake so, if necessary, cover the bowl and chill for a few minutes. Check the consistency every 5 minutes – you don't want it to become too firm to spread.

12. To assemble the cake, spoon half the buttercream into a separate bowl and reserve for covering the cake. Stir the 75g chocolate-coated popping candy into the remaining buttercream – this will be the filling. Set one sponge crust-side down on a cake board and spread with half the buttercream filling. Set a second sponge on top and cover with the rest of the buttercream filling. Place the third sponge on top, crust-side up.

13. Use half the reserved buttercream to cover the sides of the cake – use an off-set palette knife to spread the frosting evenly and neatly, making sure the sides are smooth and straight. Spoon the rest of the frosting on top of the cake and spread and swirl it to thickly cover. Leave in the fridge to firm up.

14. When the frosting feels just firm, gently **melt** the 100g chocolate in a heatproof bowl set over a pan of steaming hot but not boiling water – don't allow the base of the bowl to touch the water.

15. Cut the acetate or chocolate transfer sheet into a strip as wide as the cake is high and long enough to go around the cake – about 8 × 65cm. Set on a piece of baking paper, then spread with the melted chocolate so that the strip is completely and evenly covered.

16. Pick up the strip and press it around the sides of the cake so that the melted chocolate sticks to the frosting. If necessary trim the strip with small scissors so that it just meets. Leave in a cool spot until the chocolate has set. Carefully peel off the acetate, leaving the shiny chocolate band around the cake. Decorate with candles or more popping candy and leave in a cool spot until ready to serve.

Fraisier

An extravagant summery combination of orange biscuit sponge, Grand Marnier and strawberries. Crème diplomate is crème pâtissière lightened with the addition of whipped cream.

For the sponge
4 medium eggs, at room temperature
pinch of salt
125g caster sugar
1 large navel orange
125g plain flour
50g unsalted butter, melted and cooled

For the crème diplomate
500ml creamy milk
6 medium egg yolks, at room temperature
100g caster sugar
50g cornflour
1 tablespoon orange liqueur
50g unsalted butter, softened
150ml double cream, well chilled

For the syrup
75g caster sugar
4 tablespoons orange juice
1 tablespoon orange liqueur

To assemble
225g white marzipan
icing sugar, for dusting
pink or green gel/paste food colour (optional)
about 600g medium-sized strawberries (avoid 'giant' out-of-season ones)
50g dark chocolate, chopped

HANDS-ON TIME:
3 hours

BAKING TIME:
25 minutes

MAKES:
1 large cake

SPECIAL EQUIPMENT:
22cm springclip tin; Strip of acetate to fit inside the tin; Large piping bag fitted with a 1.5cm plain piping nozzle; Small disposable piping bag

METHOD USED:
Whisked method, see page 26

STORAGE:
Keep for up to 2 days in an airtight container

1. Preheat the oven to 180°C (160°C fan), 350°F, Gas 4. Grease the tin with butter, dust it with flour and **line** the base with baking paper.

To make the sponge
2. Separate the eggs, putting the whites into a large, spotlessly clean, grease-free mixing bowl or food-mixer bowl, and put the yolks into a separate bowl. Add the pinch of salt to the whites and **whisk** with an electric whisk or the whisk attachment until they stand in soft peaks. Gradually whisk in half the sugar, a couple of tablespoons at a time, to make a light meringue. Put the bowl aside for now. If you need to re-use the bowl, carefully spoon the whites into another bowl or dish. There's no need to wash the whisk.

3. Add the remaining caster sugar to the yolks. Finely grate the zest from the navel orange into a small bowl. Halve the orange and squeeze out the juice. Add half the zest to the yolks and 2 tablespoons of the juice – keep the rest of the juice and zest for later. Start on a low speed, then gradually increase the speed and whisk for 4–5 minutes until the mixture becomes very thick, light and mousse-like, and falls in thick ribbons from the whisk when it is lifted. *Continued*

4. Fold in the meringue in three batches, using a large metal spoon or plastic spatula. **Sift** the 125g plain flour on top and very gently but thoroughly fold it into the mixture. Drizzle the 50g cooled melted butter into the bowl and delicately fold it in. Take your time, it is essential that all the ingredients are really well combined and there are no blobs of meringue or streaks of flour.

5. Pour the mixture into the prepared tin and spread it evenly. Bake for about 25 minutes until pale golden brown. To **check** if the cake is cooked, gently press the centres – they should spring back and the sides should have shrunk away from the sides of the tin. Set the tin on a wire rack, run a round-bladed knife around the inside to loosen the sponge, then leave for 5 minutes to firm up (be patient here, the sponge is fragile). **Turn out** onto the wire rack and leave until cold. Wash and thoroughly dry the tin so that it is ready to assemble the cake.

To make the crème diplomate
6. This is a crème pâtissière with added butter, whipped cream and liqueur. Heat the 500ml creamy milk in a heavy-based pan until steaming hot but not boiling, then remove from the heat.

7. Put the 6 egg yolks, 100g caster sugar, 50g cornflour and the reserved orange zest into a heatproof bowl and **beat** well with a wooden spoon for a couple of minutes until it is lighter in colour and very smooth. Stir in the hot milk, then when it is well combined, pour the mixture back into the pan.

8. Set the pan over a medium heat and stir constantly until the mixture boils and thickens to make a very thick, smooth custard. Remove the pan from the heat and stir in the 1 tablespoon orange liqueur and the 50g butter. Wash and dry the heatproof bowl, then pour the hot crème pâtissière into it. Press a piece of clingfilm or dampened baking paper onto the surface of the custard (to prevent a skin forming), leave to cool, then chill thoroughly for at least 4 hours.

9. Whip the 150ml chilled double cream until it is thick and stands in soft peaks when the whisk is lifted. Whisk the cold crème pâtissière until smooth, then fold in the whipped cream using a large metal spoon or plastic spatula. Cover and chill for up to 1 hour.

To make the syrup
10. Put the 75g caster sugar and 4 tablespoons orange juice into a small pan, add 2 tablespoons cold water and heat gently, stirring until the sugar has dissolved, then bring to the boil. Simmer for 3 minutes to make a light syrup. Remove from the heat and stir in the 1 tablespoon orange liqueur. Put to one side for now.

11. Set the 225g white marzipan onto the worktop lightly dusted with icing sugar and knead for 1 minute until smooth and pliable. If you want, you can colour the marzipan with a couple of drops of pink or green food colour, add it very gradually using the tip of a cocktail stick dipped in the pot and gently knead in until evenly coloured.

12. Roll out the marzipan to a 3mm thickness and cut out a neat 22cm disc using the cake tin as a guide. Cover with clingfilm.

13. To assemble the cake, cut the cold sponge into two **layers** horizontally to make two thin and even discs of sponge. Place the acetate strip inside the clean tin so that it lines the edge. Instead of acetate sheets for the assembly, you can use clingfilm or parchment-lined foil.

14. Set one sponge disc cut-side up in the tin and brush liberally with the reheated syrup. With the back of a spoon, very gently press down the edges of the (slightly swollen) sponge cake so that it touches the acetate, with no gaps or holes.

15. Pick 12 strawberries of the same height and hull them to remove the green stalks. Cut them in half vertically, then arrange them, pointed-end up, on top of the sponge layer with the cut side pressed against the acetate – squidge them up so they fit together closely (depending on their size, you may need one more or one less). Set aside 5 good-looking strawberries as decoration, then hull and thinly slice the rest.
Continued

16. Set aside 1 tablespoon of the crème diplomate for the top of the cake and spoon the rest into a large **piping** bag fitted with a plain piping nozzle (depending on how big your bag is you may have to fill it in two batches). Pipe a spiral of the crème over the base.

17. Pipe vertically between the berries to fill in the gaps. Arrange the rest of the berries over the crème in an even layer to fill the space inside the strawberry ring, then pipe another spiral on top and spread it out so that it's level and the strawberries are completely covered.

18. Set the second sponge disc on top, cut-side down. Gently press the sponge with the palm of your hand so that there are no gaps between the crème and the sponge, and between the sponge edges and the acetate around the tin. Brush with the rest of the hot syrup, then leave to soak in for 10 minutes. Spread the reserved crème over the sponge using an offset palette knife to thinly cover. Press the marzipan disc on top, then cover and chill for at least 6 hours but preferably overnight.

19. Meanwhile, make the decorations. **Melt** the chocolate by putting the 50g chopped dark chocolate into a small heatproof bowl and set over a pan of steaming hot but not boiling water – don't let the base of the bowl touch the water. Dip the reserved strawberries in the chocolate so that they are half covered vertically – leaving half of each berry exposed. Leave to set on baking paper or acetate.

20. Spoon the rest of the chocolate into a small piping bag, snip off the tip and pipe small freehand flowers onto baking paper or acetate set on a baking tray. Leave to set.

21. To serve, unclip the tin and remove the acetate-wrapped cake. Set on a board or serving plate and gently peel off the acetate. Decorate the top with the dipped berries and the piped decorations. Once assembled, the cake needs plenty of time to firm up in the fridge – ideally overnight. Serve chilled and use a large sharp knife for cutting the slices.

Gâteau de
L'Opéra

Three layers of joconde – a **whisked** biscuit sponge flavoured with almonds – make up this glorious gâteau with layers of coffee buttercream, ganache and chocolate glaze.

Up for a challenge

HANDS-ON TIME:
3½ hours

BAKING TIME:
8–10 minutes

MAKES:
1 large cake

SPECIAL EQUIPMENT:
3 sheets of parchment-lined foil; 25cm square cake board; 1–3 baking sheets (see Step 2); Sugar thermometer; Small disposable piping bag; Tweezers

METHOD USED:
Whisked method, see page 26

STORAGE:
Keep for up to 3 days in an airtight container in the fridge. (Remove about 30 minutes before serving.)

For the sponge
6 medium egg whites, at room temperature
good pinch of cream of tartar
30g caster sugar
45g unsalted butter
6 medium eggs, at room temperature
225g icing sugar, sifted
225g ground almonds
75g plain flour

For the coffee syrup
60g caster sugar
1½ tablespoons instant coffee granules or powder
1 tablespoon brandy

For the coffee buttercream
85g caster sugar
2 medium egg yolks, at room temperature
150g unsalted butter, at room temperature, diced
1½ tablespoons instant coffee granules or powder
1 tablespoon boiling water

For the ganache
200g good-quality dark chocolate (about 70 per cent cocoa solids), finely chopped
175ml whipping cream
25g unsalted butter, at room temperature

For the under-glaze
50g good-quality dark chocolate (about 70 per cent cocoa solids), finely chopped

For the top glaze
100g unsalted butter
150g good-quality dark chocolate (about 70 percent cocoa solids), finely chopped

For the decoration
50g dark chocolate, finely chopped
edible gold leaf

1. Preheat the oven to 220°C (200°C fan), 425°F, Gas 7.

2. Cut each sheet of parchment-lined foil to a 26cm square, then set parchment-side up and fold in the sides by 1cm to make a shallow square cake case with 25cm sides – use the cake board to help form the shape. Set each case on a baking sheet – bake in batches if necessary.
Continued

Try Something Different

For a change of flavour, replace the ground almonds in the sponge layers with finely ground hazelnuts, and replace the brandy in the brushing liquid with rum, coffee liqueur or hazelnut liqueur.

To make the sponge

3. Put the 6 medium egg whites and a good pinch of cream of tartar into a large, spotlessly clean mixing bowl or the bowl of a food-mixer and **whisk** with an electric hand whisk or the whisk attachment until the whites stand in soft peaks when the whisk is lifted. Sprinkle the 30g caster sugar over the whites and whisk again for a few seconds until the whites form stiff peaks and the mixture is smooth and glossy. Put the bowl to one side until needed. If you need to re-use the bowl, gently spoon the meringue into a separate bowl or dish. There's no need to wash the beaters/whisk.

4. Melt the 45g butter and leave to cool while you whisk the eggs. Put the 6 whole eggs into a second large bowl or the bowl of the food-mixer, and add the 225g sifted icing sugar and the 225g ground almonds. Whisk on a high speed with the electric whisk or whisk attachment for about 4 minutes until the mixture is very thick and has massively increased in volume. **Sift** the 75g plain flour on top and very gently but thoroughly **fold** it in.

5. Once all the flour has been combined, fold in the meringue in three batches. Trickle the cool but still runny butter over the top and fold in until just combined. Divide the mixture equally – if you want to be precise use your scales – among the three cake cases set on baking sheets and spread it carefully to fill the corners. The surface should be flat and level and each sponge layer should be the same depth all over so that the cake is level when assembled.

6. Bake for 8–10 minutes. Check the cakes after 5 minutes to see if they are baking evenly, if not, turn the tins round. To **check** if the cakes are cooked, gently press the centres – the sponges should be lightly browned and spring back.

7. While the sponges are baking, cover two wire racks with baking paper. Remove the baked sponges from the oven and flip the baking sheets over onto the racks to **turn out** the sponges in their cake cases. Gently peel off the cake cases and leave the sponges to cool, loosely covered with a clean, dry tea towel or a sheet of baking paper. Once cold, the sponges can be wrapped individually in baking paper then clingfilm and left at room temperature overnight.

To make the coffee syrup

8. While the sponges cool, make the coffee syrup. Put the 60g caster sugar, 1½ tablespoons instant coffee granules or powder and 125ml cold water into a small pan and heat gently, stirring, until dissolved. Bring to the boil, then simmer for 1 minute to make a light syrup. Remove from the heat and stir in the 1 tablespoon brandy. Once cold, the syrup can be covered and left at room temperature for a couple of hours or stored in a jam jar in the fridge overnight (remove 1 hour before using).

To make the coffee buttercream

9. Next make the coffee buttercream filling. Put the 85g caster sugar and 4 tablespoons cold water into a small heavy-based pan and set over a low heat. Stir gently until the sugar has dissolved, then bring to the boil. Boil rapidly for 4–5 minutes until the syrup reaches 115°C (240°F) on a sugar thermometer. While the sugar is boiling, put the 2 medium egg yolks into a heatproof mixing bowl (put it on a damp cloth so it doesn't slip) or the bowl of a food-mixer and whisk for a few seconds until frothy with an electric whisk or the whisk attachment.

10. As soon as the syrup is up to temperature, pour it onto the yolks in a thin, steady stream while whisking at top speed – aim directly for the yolks or the syrup will harden before it is whisked in. Continue whisking for about 5 minutes until the mixture is very thick, pale and mousse-like. Then whisk for 1–2 minutes more until the mixture is completely cold. Whisk in the 150g soft (but not runny or oily) unsalted butter a few pieces at a time to make a smooth, thick buttercream. Dissolve the 1½ tablespoons instant coffee granules or powder in 1 tablespoon boiling water, leave to cool, then whisk in. Cover and chill until just spreadable (check the consistency every 5 minutes).

To make the ganache

11. To **melt** the chocolate, put the 200g dark chocolate into a heatproof bowl, heat the 175ml whipping cream until steaming hot but not quite boiling, and pour it over the chocolate. Leave it for a minute, then gently stir until melted and smooth. Gradually stir in the 25g butter to make a smooth and glossy ganache. Cover and chill until spreadable (check the consistency every 5 minutes).
Continued

To make the under-glaze

12. Now to assemble the cake: first **melt** the chocolate. Put the 50g finely chopped dark chocolate into a small heatproof bowl and set over a pan of steaming hot but not boiling water – don't let the base of the bowl touch the water – and leave to melt gently.

13. Set one sponge crust-side up on a sheet of baking paper and brush on a thin, even layer of melted chocolate. Leave until set hard (if you're impatient, chill it for 5 minutes), then gently flip the sponge over on the baking paper so that the chocolate-coated side is underneath. Carefully brush the upper surface with one-third of the coffee syrup so that the whole surface is evenly moistened. Leave for 10 minutes to soak in.

14. Spoon three-quarters of the coffee buttercream onto the sponge and spread evenly – take your time assembling the cake as it's vital it has a flat surface and doesn't tilt at the sides. Set a second sponge crust-side down on top, making sure all the sides are aligned. Brush this sponge with half the remaining coffee syrup as before and leave to soak in for 10 minutes.

15. Spoon all the ganache on top and spread evenly. Set the third sponge crust-side down on top and gently press it in place, checking again that the surface is level. Brush with the remaining coffee syrup and leave to soak in, as before. Spoon the remaining buttercream onto the sponge and spread to make a thin, even layer. Chill for 15 minutes until firm.

To make the top glaze

16. Meanwhile, make the top glaze. Melt the 100g unsalted butter in a small pan, then skim off the foam that rises to the top. Pour the clear butter into a small bowl, leaving behind and discarding the milky residue in the pan. Reheat the clarified butter until bubbling. Put 125g of the finely chopped dark chocolate into a heatproof bowl (reserve the remaining 25g for now) and pour in the very hot butter. Stir gently until the chocolate has melted, then stir in the reserved 25g chocolate to make a smooth, glossy glaze.

17. Take the cake out of the fridge and set it on the worktop still on its sheet of baking paper. Now, quickly pour the top glaze over the top of the cake to completely cover it – if necessary use a warmed offset palette knife to help spread the glaze evenly. Let the glaze drip down the sides of the cake (the sides will be trimmed off later). Return the cake to the fridge and chill until the glaze is firm and set.

18. Lastly, put the finishing touches to the cake. Dip a large, sharp knife in hot water, dry it quickly, then carefully trim the sides to make a perfectly square, neat cake. Transfer to the cake board.

19. Melt the chocolate for the decoration (as in Step 10) and spoon it into a small **piping** bag. Snip off the end to make a writing tip and pipe 'Opéra' diagonally across the cake, and decorate the edges with flourishes and musical notes. Finish with gold leaf – use tweezers or the tip of a small knife to very gently set the fragile flakes in place. Chill until firm, preferably overnight.

20. To cut neat slices, use a large sharp knife dipped in hot water, and keep kitchen paper at hand for cleaning the knife between slices.

What cake shall I bake?

Conversion table

WEIGHT

Metric	Imperial
25g	1oz
50g	2oz
75g	2½oz
85g	3oz
100g	4oz
125g	4½oz
140g	5oz
175g	6oz
200g	7oz
225g	8oz
250g	9oz
280g	10oz
300g	11oz
350g	12oz
375g	13oz
400g	14oz
425g	15oz
450g	1lb
500g	1lb 2oz
550g	1lb 4oz
600g	1lb 5oz
650g	1lb 7oz
700g	1lb 9oz
750g	1lb 10oz
800g	1lb 12oz
850g	1lb 14oz
900g	2lb
950g	2lb 2oz
1kg	2lb 4oz

VOLUME

Metric	Imperial
30ml	1fl oz
50ml	2fl oz
75ml	3fl oz
125ml	4fl oz
150ml	¼ pint
175ml	6fl oz
200ml	7fl oz
225ml	8fl oz
300ml	½ pint
350ml	12fl oz
400ml	14fl oz
450ml	¾ pint
500ml	18fl oz
600ml	1 pint
725ml	1¼ pints
1 litre	1¾ pints

SPOON MEASURES

Metric	Imperial
5ml	1 teaspoon
10ml	2 teaspoons
15ml	1 tablespoon
30ml	2 tablespoons
45ml	3 tablespoons
60ml	4 tablespoons
75ml	5 tablespoons

LINEAR

Metric	Imperial
2.5cm	1in
3cm	1¼in
4cm	1½in
5cm	2in
5.5cm	2¼in
6cm	2½in
7cm	2¾in
7.5cm	3in
8cm	3¼in
9cm	3½in
9.5cm	3¾in
10cm	4in
11cm	4¼in
12cm	4½in
13cm	5in
14cm	5½in
15cm	6in
16cm	6½in
17cm	6½in
18cm	7in
19cm	7½in
20cm	8in
22cm	8½in
23cm	9in
24cm	9½in
25cm	10in

Index

Acknowledgements

Hodder & Stoughton and Love Productions would like to thank the following people for their contribution to this book:

Linda Collister, Laura Herring, Caroline McArthur, Sam Binnie, Helena Caldon, Alasdair Oliver, Kate Brunt, Laura Del Vescovo, Joanna Seaton, Sarah Christie, Anna Heath, Damian Horner, Auriol Bishop, Anna Beattie, Rupert Frisby, Jane Treasure, Sharon Powers.

The author would also like to thank Alan Hertz, Barbara Levy and Simon Silverwood.

— BAKE IT BETTER —

Would you like to learn to be a better baker?

We know that so many people watch *The Great British Bake Off* for the tips and techniques you pick up – not only from the judges, but from watching the bakers too. We wanted to distil that knowledge into a library of cookbooks that are specifically designed to take you from novice to expert baker. Individually, each book covers the skills you will want to perfect so that you can master a particular area of baking – everything from cakes to bread, sweet pastries to pies.

We have chosen recipes that are classics of each type, and grouped them together so that they take you on a progression from 'Easy does it' through 'Needs a little skill' to 'Up for a challenge'. Put together, the full series of books will give you a comprehensive collection of the best recipes, along with all the advice you need to become a better baker.

The triumphs and lessons of the bakers in the tent show us that not everything works every time. But I hope that with these books as your guide, we have given you a head start towards baking it better every time!

—

Linda Collister
Series Editor

‑ BAKE it BETTER ‑

BISCUITS

Annie Rigg

HODDER &
STOUGHTON

Contents

BAKE IT BETTER
Baker's Guide

BAKE IT BETTER
Recipes

Easy does it   38

Need a little skill 88

Up for a challenge 134

Welcome bakers!

There are few greater pleasures than sitting down with a cup of tea and a home-made biscuit – and this book offers 40 classic biscuit recipes to get you going.

As well as being great bakes, the recipes have been carefully chosen to introduce you to all the key techniques, like rubbing-in, creaming, shaping and piping, that not only set you up to bake better biscuits, but which you can use in all sorts of other bakes.

Start with the 'Easy does it' section and master the basics with recipes like Icebox Cookies, then, as you grow in confidence, you can be ready to move to the recipes that 'Need a little skill' – Linzer Jammy Dodgers perhaps, some delectable Viennese Whirls. And the more you bake, the sooner you will find that you are 'Up for a challenge' with sophisticated Mochaccino Macarons, or testing your decorating skills with a stunning fairy tale Gingerbread House.

The colour strip on the right-hand side of the page tells you at a glance the level of difficulty of the recipe (from one spoon for easy to three spoons for more of a challenge), and gives you a helpful checklist of the special equipment you will use. Before you begin, have a look at the Baker's Guide at the beginning of the book. That will tell you what equipment you need to get started (just a bowl, a spoon and a baking tray will do!), introduce you to the most important ingredients, and explain some terms and techniques in more detail.

Biscuits can be a simple snack or a comforting mouthful of love, but even the most basic biscuit is a joy to make and eat. The *Bake It Better: Biscuits* book will show you just what you can do with butter, sugar, flour and eggs, so let's grab our wooden spoons and get baking!

HOW TO USE THIS BOOK

SECTION 1: BAKER'S GUIDE

Read this section before you start baking. The Baker's Guide contains key information on ingredients (page 10), equipment (page 16) and skills (page 22) relevant to the recipes in the book.

Refer back the Baker's Guide when you're baking if you want a refresher on a particular skill. In the recipes the first mention of each skill is highlighted in bold.

SECTION 2: RECIPES

Colour strips on the right-hand side and 1, 2 or 3 spoons show the level of difficulty of the recipe. Within the colour strips you'll find helpful information to help you decide what to bake: Hands-on time; Baking time; Quantity and Special equipment.

Refresh your knowledge of any Essential skills by referring to the Baker's Guide before you get started.

Refer back to the Baker's Guide when a skill is highlighted in bold in the recipe if you need a reminder.

Try Something Different options are given where the recipe lends itself to experimenting with ingredients or decorations.

BAKE IT BETTER

Baker's Guide

Ingredients

The simplest biscuits require just a few ingredients: butter, sugar, flour and maybe an egg, but usually you'll be adding flavourings to these key elements. Knowing a bit more about the ingredients before you use them will help to avoid problems and lead to more successful bakes. Here are a few simple guidelines to bear in mind when you're buying, storing and using your ingredients.

BAKING POWDER, BICARBONATE OF SODA AND CREAM OF TARTAR

Baking powder and bicarbonate of soda are chemical raising agents commonly used in baking, most often in small quantities, to lighten the texture of biscuits as well as to create volume and produce a tender crumb. Baking powder is a blend of bicarbonate of soda (an alkali) and cream of tartar (an acid) and sometimes also corn or rice flour to absorb any moisture that might be present. The two raising agents work by reacting with the moisture in your biscuit, and the heat from the oven, to produce carbon dioxide bubbles that lift, and lighten, the crumb.

Baking powder and bicarbonate of soda are not interchangeable and make sure you use exactly the amount stated. Check the best before date on the packets too, and discard any out-of-date or damp raising agents, as they lose their potency when they get past their best and they won't give you a good bake.

If you've run out of baking powder when you come to bake, you can make your own. For 1 teaspoon of baking powder, simply combine half a teaspoon cream of tartar with a quarter teaspoon of bicarbonate of soda.

BUTTER

In this book the recipes generally use **unsalted butter**, as it has a mild, delicate flavour, gives a lovely golden colour to your bakes and allows the baker to add salt to taste, if they wish. Unsalted butter usually contains slightly less whey than **salted butter** and it's this that bakers believe gives a more evenly coloured bake. Salted butter can also be used, but it may have a stronger taste. If you do use salted butter in a sweet recipe you won't need to add any extra salt.

Instructions are given in each recipe for whether your butter should be used at room temperature, softened or chilled. For recipes that require you to cream the mixture, use the butter at room temperature so that it's easier to smoothly incorporate dry ingredients, such as sugar; chilled and diced butter is needed for recipes that start by rubbing butter into dry ingredients, such as flour. To keep your butter at its best, store it tightly wrapped in its original wrapper in the fridge away from strong flavours, or you can freeze it, wrapped, for up to a month.

CHOCOLATE

Try to use the best-quality chocolate that you can find, as it can really affect the flavour of your final bake. Good chocolate is now widely available in supermarkets and you can buy chips in larger bags from specialist suppliers online.

Store bars of chocolate well wrapped in a cool, dry, dark cupboard, and away from other strong-tasting or flavoured ingredients. Always make sure that you've chopped your chocolate before melting it, to ensure that it melts quickly and evenly without scorching (see page 31 for more melting tips).

Dark chocolate with around 70 per cent cocoa solids is the type used in most of the recipes in this book as it gives the best flavour – chocolate with a higher percentage of cocoa (75 per cent and above) may be too bitter for general tastes, while a lower percentage may be too sweet.

Milk chocolate has a milder, sweeter flavour than dark, but the same rules apply and you should always use one that has the highest percentage of cocoa solids you can find, not only for better flavour but because the chocolate will set slightly firmer.

White chocolate doesn't contain any cocoa solids, just cocoa butter, and can vary a lot in quality, with some children's bars containing hardly any cocoa butter at all. Ideally, look for something with 30 per cent cocoa butter or more, but be aware that the higher fat content in white chocolate means that it will set less firmly than dark or milk chocolates.

COCOA POWDER
A dark, unsweetened powder made from pure cocoa with nearly all the cocoa butter removed – it is very bitter and strongly flavoured, and will give a powerful chocolate hit to your baking. Cocoa powder shouldn't be confused for, or substituted with, drinking chocolate, which has had sugar and dried milk powder added to it.

DRIED FRUIT
Keep stores of dried fruit such as raisins, sultanas and currants out of direct sunlight and in sealed containers for freshness, but bear in mind that dried fruit is best bought as and when you need it. Candied peel is widely available ready chopped, but can

also be found in boxes as whole pieces of orange, lemon or citrus peel, allowing you to cut the pieces into a size and mix that you prefer.

EGGS
Eggs bind your mixtures together, providing richness and lightening batters by incorporating air, particularly in recipes like Sponge Fingers (see page 70). All the recipes in this book use medium-sized eggs (about 62–65g each) – using a different-sized egg from the one specified can affect your recipe by altering the texture and moisture of the dough.

Storing eggs in the fridge, pointed-side down, protects the yolk from drying out and spoiling. Keep them in the box they came in and in the cooler body of the fridge, not the door, and use by the best before date on the box. If a recipe calls for only egg yolks, you can keep the spare egg whites, covered, in the fridge for 3–4 days, or they will freeze well for up to a month: defrost thoroughly before use. (A good tip is to mark the quantity on the container before you put it in the freezer.)

Eggs should be used at room temperature as they give a greater volume when beaten, so bring them out of the fridge 30–60 minutes before you need to use them.

EXTRACTS AND FLAVOURINGS
Avoid the synthetic versions of flavourings wherever possible, as these can give your bake a rather unpleasant 'fake' taste.

Vanilla extract is now widely available. Try to avoid the cheaper vanilla flavouring or essence on offer, which is a chemical, rather than natural flavouring. Check the label for 'natural' or 'pure' vanilla extract, which means it's been extracted from the vanilla pods and so you will only need to use a small amount. Whole **vanilla pods** are a good addition to your store cupboard, and once used you can dry them off and pop them into a jar of caster sugar. They will lightly infuse the sugar with their flavour and it can be used in biscuit recipes. Jars of highly concentrated **vanilla bean paste** are another good addition for the store cupboard, and are slightly less expensive than vanilla pods.

Coffee flavour can be added to recipes by using instant espresso powder or granules dissolved in a little boiling water. It adds a lovely strong coffee flavour to icings. You can also use coffee essence, although some find the flavour a little strange.

Ground spices should be measured carefully and kept in screw-topped jars rather than open packs. Try to use them when they are still fresh, preferably within a few months of opening.

Stem ginger in syrup is a wonderful store cupboard ingredient that adds an extra pop of gingery-ness to Gingersnaps (page 62). Drain the chunks of their syrup before using.

FLOUR
Poor-quality or past-its-best flour can really affect the final taste and texture of your bake, so only use flour when it's fresh and store it correctly between uses: keep opened packs of flour either in tightly sealed storage jars, plastic food boxes or plastic food bags to stop it getting damp. Don't add new flour to old in storage jars, and aim to use it within a month of opening or by its best before date.

Wheat flours are the most commonly used flours in baking. Most recipes call for **plain flour**, which needs sifting to give lightness to your biscuits. **Spelt flour** adds a slight nutty taste and a more crumby texture; it can be substituted in part for plain flour, but isn't really suitable for delicate biscuit work. **Wholemeal flour** is good for recipes that require a more oaty, wholesome flavour and texture and, along with oatmeal, is a key ingredient in Chocolate Digestives and Oatmeal Biscuits for Cheese (pages 96 and 58). **Rice flour**, used in small quantities, gives an almost gritty texture to your bake, while **cornflour** can be added to Shortbread and Viennese Whirls (pages 54 and 78) to give a delicate crumb.

Gluten-free flours are wheat-free mixtures made from several ingredients, including rice, potato, tapioca, maize, chickpea, broad bean, white sorghum or buckwheat, and are readily and inexpensively available. Ready-mixed gluten-free flours sometime suggest adding xanthum gum (which comes in powder form) to help improve the texture and crumb of your bake – check the packet and if your mix doesn't include it add 1 teaspoon xanthum gum per 150g flour. Some flours may also require a little more liquid to make the dough manageable. Gluten-free flours vary in taste and texture from brand to brand, so it's worth trying a few out to see which you prefer.

HONEY
Look out for honey that comes from the nectar of a single variety of flower or plant (such as orange blossom), as the flavour should be more distinct. As a general rule, the paler the honey, the milder the flavour. You can use almost any type in

baking, although soft-set honey (but not honeycomb) is the easiest to blend in. If you don't have any, solid honey can be softened first by gently warming it in the microwave, or in a dish set in a bowl of warm water.

ICING SUGAR

This fine, powdered white sugar dissolves easily in icings and buttercream, but also gives the light, melt-in-the-mouth texture to Viennese Whirls (page 78), and is used to dust finished biscuits. Sift it well to remove any lumps before use.

Royal icing sugar is a mixture of icing sugar and dried egg white that can be mixed with water to make a stiff white icing or a decorative 'glue' for recipes such as the Gingerbread House (page 154) – just add water, bit by bit, and beat well until the desired consistency is achieved.

Unrefined golden icing sugar has a slight butterscotch flavour and can be substituted for regular icing sugar in both biscuit doughs and icings, but you won't get the brilliant white colour you get from white icing sugar.

JAMS AND SPREADS

Perfect for sandwiching or filling biscuits, and for adding a splash of colour to your bakes. It's also useful to keep a jar of chocolate and hazelnut spread, or a caramel sauce like dulce de leche, in your cupboard, as both make utterly delicious quick cookie or macaron fillings.

MARGARINES AND SPREADS

These are based on vegetable oils, with added salt and flavourings. Some are made specifically for baking and can be used straight from the fridge; they give good results but they won't taste quite the same as bakes made with butter.

Spreads designed for use on breads and crackers are not meant for baking and won't give a good bake as they contain too much water and not enough fat.

Dairy-free spreads can be substituted for butter in recipes that require softened, or room-temperature, butter. These spreads are usually made from a blend of vegetable and sunflower oils and can be used straight from the fridge, although they may lack a little of the richness of pure butter.

NUTS AND SEEDS

It's best to buy nuts and seeds in small quantities as they can become oily and rancid when past their best, especially **walnuts** and **pine nuts**. Store them in a screwtop jar, or airtight container in a cool, dark spot and use them before their best before date.

Almonds are particularly versatile in baking and can be used whole, blanched and flaked or ground.

Blanched hazelnuts have had their thin, papery brown skin removed, but this is easy enough to do if you only have unblanched – just tip the nuts onto a baking sheet and toast them in a medium oven for 4–5 minutes. Gather the toasted nuts into a clean tea towel and rub them vigorously to remove the skins.

Look out for packs of **mixed seeds** (usually a combination of sunflower, pumpkin, sesame and linseed) to add to flapjacks and oatmeal cookies. Toasting nuts increases their flavour, but they do burn easily, so watch them carefully.

OILS

Some recipes for softer, chewier biscuits require **sunflower oil** or **groundnut oil**, both of which have a mild, neutral flavour and should not be confused with **vegetable oil**, a frying oil which will give a distinctive, unpleasant 'savoury' flavour to your baking.

Coconut oil is now widely available from health food shops and larger supermarkets and can be substituted for butter or to make recipes dairy-free. It often comes in jars and you'll need to gently melt it, either in the microwave, or in a pan, over a low heat, before using.

SUGAR

There are various ways to sweeten biscuits, but it is very important to use the type of sugar specified in the recipe. They all combine with other ingredients in slightly different ways and this affects the end result.

Caster sugar is the refined white version. It has a mild, neutral sweetness and is easily combined with other ingredients.

Golden caster sugar is unrefined and gives a warmer, richer flavour, but it is not so easily combined, so techniques such as creaming will take slightly longer.

Soft light brown sugar, **demerara sugar** or **light muscovado sugar** are all good when a warmer butterscotch or caramel flavour is needed and add a good, rich colour to biscuits. All these sugars should be stored in airtight bags or jars to stop them drying out, but if lumps do form, just press them out through a sieve.

SYRUPS AND TREACLE

Syrups and treacles are perfect for adding sweetness and flavour to fillings and icings. **Golden syrup** and sticky **black treacle** will give your bakes a rich, rounded and warm toffee-ish flavour.

Treacle can be awkward and messy to measure and weigh, but if you sit the whole tin in a bowl of just-boiled water, or warm the measuring spoon in a mug of boiled water beforehand, you will find it much easier and less messy by far.

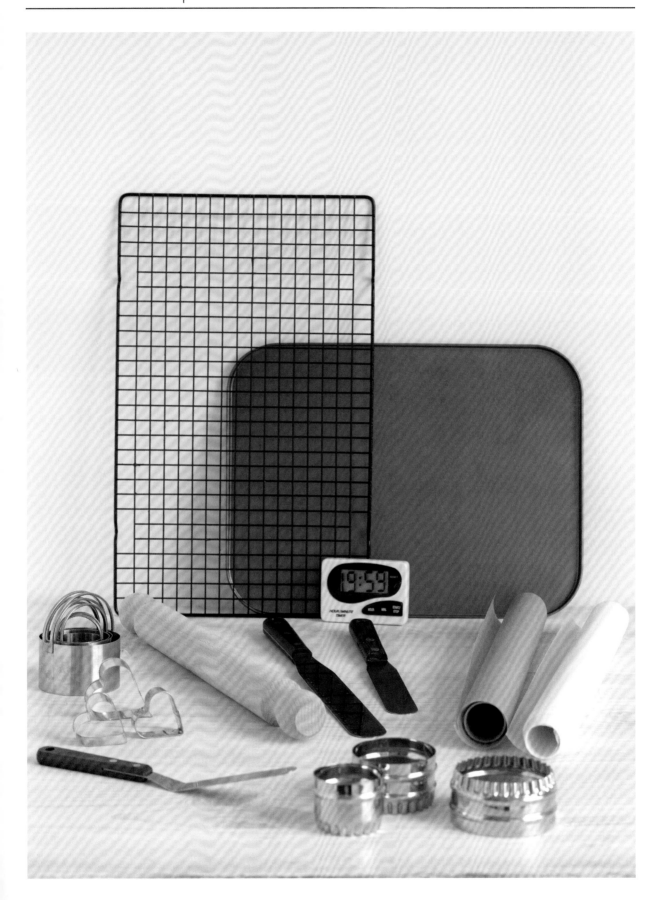

Equipment

One of the best things about baking biscuits is that you can get started without a cupboard full of expensive equipment. In fact, you can probably produce your first tray of delicious biscuits with what you already have in your kitchen. But having a few key pieces of kit will make your life easier and more importantly will ensure your bakes are more consistently successful.

BAKING PAPER AND SILICONE BAKING MATS

Non-stick baking paper, parchment paper and **silicone baking mats** are all non-stick liners and are invaluable for stopping biscuits sticking to trays and sheets. Silicone baking mats are expensive but they are reusable and if looked after properly they will last a long time. **Greaseproof paper** is best kept for wrapping cooked biscuits as it is water resistant, but its waxy coating doesn't stand up well to the heat of the oven. It is also not non-stick, so you will end up wrestling your biscuits off the paper after baking.

BAKING SHEETS AND TRAYS

Sturdy sheets and trays that won't buckle and twist in the oven ensure your biscuits bake evenly. **Baking sheets** with only one raised edge make it easy to slide a palette knife under very thin biscuits. For other types of biscuits, a **baking tray** with sides is perfectly fine, just so long as you can easily get 10–12 biscuits per tray. It's worth having two or three baking sheets so that you can portion out and prepare a whole recipe's worth of dough at once, without having to wait for your sheets to cool down between batches.

BISCUIT CUTTERS

A nest of cutters in various sizes is ideal – double-sided ones (plain and fluted) mean you won't need to buy two separate sets. Metal cutters will give you the cleanest edge when cutting out your biscuits. There's a cutter shape for just about any occasion or theme, as well as cutters for specific biscuits, such as bourbons or custard creams, and kits for embossing lettering into dough.

BOWLS

If you're buying new, a nest of small, medium and large bowls is ideal. **Heatproof glass** bowls are perfect for sitting over a pan of simmering water and for putting in the microwave. **Stainless steel** are also good, but not microwave-proof. **Ceramic** bowls are pretty, can go in the dishwasher and are good for mixing by hand as they are less likely to slide all over the work surface, but they're quite heavy and break easily. **Plastic** bowls are cheap and good for weighing ingredients – some even have rubber bases, helping to make them non-slip. (You can solve the slip issue by placing a damp cloth underneath any bowl.) **Anodised aluminium** bowls are very durable and will last a lifetime, but, gaian, are no good in the microwave.

COOLING RACKS

Wire cooling racks allow the air to circulate underneath your bakes, helping prevent the dreaded soggy bottom. For biscuits, look out for large rectangular cooling racks that will hold at least 24 biscuits in rows. If you need to, you can always improvise by using clean wire grill-pan racks for bigger biscuits, but smaller bakes are better on the finer wires of a cooling rack.

FOOD-PROCESSOR OR MINI WHIZZER

Like a free-standing electric mixer, a food-processor is not essential, but it certainly makes light work of tasks like rubbing butter into flour (see page 23), or finely chopping nuts. If space is at a premium, a mini whizzer or chopper (a mini food-processor that chops about 100g of ingredients) is useful – they're good for small quantities and can be stored away quite easily when not in use.

ICE CREAM SCOOP

Not essential, but a really useful piece of equipment for scooping out balls of biscuit dough in recipes that don't require rolling and stamping out.

KNIVES

You'll probably find that a **medium-sized sharp knife** is useful for most purposes. When choosing a knife, hold it first to check that it feels well balanced, and that the weight and shape suits the size of your hand – a 20cm knife is probably the most versatile, but choose the one that you feel most comfortable with. If you can, spend a bit more on a good-quality knife; it will be worth every penny as it will be sturdier and last longer, and will be easier to keep sharp (a **knife sharpener** is vital too) for those really clean lines when trimming rolled-out dough and slicing up logs of biscuit dough.

Knives are made from different materials. The main ones to consider are stainless steel, which is cheaper but needs to be sharpened regularly; carbon steel, which is more expensive, harder and easier to keep sharp; and ceramic, which is far harder than carbon steel, much lighter and doesn't require sharpening – but can chip easily.

LARGE METAL SPOON

A large, long-handled metal spoon for folding wet ingredients into dry is invaluable.

MEASURING JUGS

Pick a heat-resistant and microwave-safe jug that's easy to read in both metric and imperial measures, starting from 50ml, if you can find one, otherwise 100ml and going up to about 2 litres. A small jug or cup that measures from 1 teaspoon (5ml) up to 4 tablespoons (60ml) is a useful extra, but remember you can also weigh liquids, as well as measuring the volume: 1ml = 1 gram. This is the most precise method.

MEASURING SPOONS

Most measuring spoons come in sets of 4–6 different sizes, from ⅛ teaspoon to 1½ tablespoon, and are essential for ensuring absolute accuracy, especially when adding spices or raising agents. Day-to-day teaspoons, dessertspoons and tablespoons can vary enormously in size and will give inconsistent results to your bakes, so do invest in some proper measuring spoons. Look out, too, for measuring spoons with narrow pointed ends that will easily fit into small spice jars. Unless otherwise indicated, all spoon measures in these recipes are level – knock off the excess using a finger or the back of a knife.

OVEN THERMOMETER

We all know how varied ovens can be, with some getting hotter than they should and some not getting hot enough; to be really accurate it's a good idea to get an oven thermometer. You can then check that your oven is reaching the correct temperature – and you can discover where the hot and cooler spots are – so your bakes cook evenly and perfectly.

PALETTE KNIVES

An essential piece of kit for biscuit baking, **palette knives** are useful for spreading mixtures in tins, smoothing icing and for lifting biscuits from baking sheets. A small **offset palette knife**, with a kink in the frame, is perfect for spreading buttercream onto your biscuits or fillings when sandwiching them together.

PASTRY BRUSH

This is an indispensable tool, particularly useful when sandwiching together strips of dough, as in the Chocolate and Vanilla Checkerboard Biscuits (see page 148). Brushes with smooth, fine-hair bristles and a wooden handle are ideal. Choose one that is heat-resistant and can go in the dishwasher.

PIPING BAGS

If you can, go for large, seamless, plastic-coated **nylon** piping bags for piping biscuit dough. They have a little more weight and strength to them and don't have seams for the mixtures to leak through. They can be rinsed and then washed inside out in very hot water. Always make sure they are completely dry before putting them away. **Disposable plastic** piping bags are indispensible for piping royal icing and for finer, more detailed work and are now available in most supermarkets in the baking aisle. If you are in desperate need or for smaller jobs in which you don't need to pipe with precision, you can snip the corner off a plastic food bag to use as a piping bag. You can use the bag without a nozzle or snip a larger hole and include a nozzle.

PIPING NOZZLES

These conical tubes fit into the end of piping bags and come in scores of different shapes and sizes, from the finest writing tip to large, sharp-toothed star nozzles, for different aesthetic and practical purposes. Although they're usually used for icing and decorating cakes, some biscuit recipes will also call for a plain nozzle, as the uncooked biscuit dough is piped into lines before baking. Boxed sets usually provide the best value, but you can start with a small selection that includes a plain 1cm nozzle and a star. Stainless-steel nozzles are the most durable, but plastic ones are also good.

ROLLING PIN

A good rolling pin should be heavy and big enough to roll out a full batch of dough at once; solid wooden pins are easier to use than old-fashioned ones with handles. Look after your rolling pin and it should last a lifetime, so never leave a wooden rolling pin soaking in washing-up water, don't put it in the dishwasher and don't use it for anything other than rolling out dough or pastry – which means no crushing ice or tenderising meat with it!

SCALES

Baking is really a science, so it pays to be accurate if you want perfect results every time. As you'll be dealing with some quite small quantities, **digital** scales are preferable to spring, or balance, scales as they are much more precise and can weigh ingredients that are as little as 1 gram. You can see the weight easily at a glance and you can add multiple items to one bowl simply by resetting the balance to zero after adding each ingredient. A helpful tip: always keep a spare battery on standby.

SIEVE

Fine-mesh sieves for sifting dry ingredients will not only rid your mixture of lumps, but are the first step to combining, and aerating, dry ingredients. A sieve with a large bowl will be the most useful, but it's also handy to have a tea-strainer size for dusting icing sugar or cocoa over your finished bakes. Stainless steel is the best option.

SPATULA

A good-quality, heat-resistant rubber or plastic spatula is really useful for thoroughly combining your ingredients, cleaning out bowls and spreading mixtures. A smaller one is a useful extra, too.

STORAGE CONTAINERS

You don't need to buy expensive ones, but dishwasher-proof containers with secure locking clips are a good purchase. Otherwise, use a stainless-steel tin with a tight-fitting lid, or a heavy-duty plastic container with a secure lid. Store your biscuits in them well away from any heat sources (radiators, sunlight, kitchen light fittings, your fridge or cooker) and mark the container with a dated sticker so that you know when your biscuits are still good to eat.

TIMER

A digital timer is essential for biscuit-baking. It's easy to get distracted and suddenly 10 minutes has become 15 and you have several trays of burnt biscuits. Go for a timer with seconds as well as minutes, as well as a loud ring, and set it for 1 minute less than the suggested time in the recipe, especially if you are unsure of your oven temperature – you can always increase the cooking time if needed.

WHISKS AND MIXERS

These range from the most basic, which means the baker has to do the energetic whisking, to free-standing food mixers that do it all for you.

Wire whisks can be balloon-shaped or flat. A sturdy, classic hand-held whisk with an easy-grip handle makes light work of whisking eggs and whipping cream. You might find a mini/magic hand whisk is useful for stirring small quantities, for lightly beating eggs or for smoothing out lumpy mixtures.

Rotary whisks with two beaters in a metal frame that are turned by hand are next up in terms of power. They're perfect for whisking egg whites, for whisking mixtures over heat (no trailing leads) and for whisking out lumps.

Hand-held electric whisks are more expensive, but much more powerful and can be used for more general mixing. Look for models with a set of attachments and a retractable cord for easy storage.

Free-standing electric mixers, although non-essential and expensive, are the workhorse in any keen baker's kitchen. Not only do they make light work of creaming mixtures, they also rub butter into flour and knead dough in half the time (and with a fraction of the effort) that it takes by hand. Most free-standing mixers come with three different attachments: a whisk for eggs, meringues and light sponge mixtures; a creamer, or paddle attachment, which is ideal for creaming butter and sugar, and for rubbing cold butter into flour (see page 23); and a dough hook, which makes short work of kneading heavy dough. They do take up worktop space but they will cut your preparation time in half.

....

WOODEN SPOONS

You can never have enough wooden spoons – they're heat-resistant, won't scratch non-stick pans and are ideal for beating mixtures. The handles are also invaluable for making and shaping Tuiles (see page 72). It's a good idea to keep ones for baking separate from those that are used for savoury cooking, as wooden spoons are porous and will absorb strong flavours.

Skills

Now that you have all your ingredients and equipment ready, it's time to get baking!

The recipes in this book are designed to take you stage-by-stage through all the skills you need, from absolute beginner to baking your very own spectacular showstoppers. All the recipes tell you exactly what you need to do, step-by-step, but you'll notice that some of the baking terms are highlighted in bold, which means you can refer back to this section if you want a bit more detail, or to refresh your memory.

From basic biscuit mixes to shaping, piping and decorating skills, the following pages contain invaluable hints and tips from the experts to help you bake perfect biscuits.

THE THREE KEY BISCUIT-MAKING TECHNIQUES

The starting point for all biscuit recipes is a dough or soft batter mixture. All the recipes in this book are made with the same simple ingredients – butter, sugar, flour and sometimes eggs, used in different ratios and with various added extras to make them unique – but all of them are made using one of three methods, each of which produces a very different biscuit.

The three methods are explained in detail here, and below each method are some examples of recipes in the book that use them. Try these and you'll soon be an expert in each technique.

RUBBED-IN METHOD

This is the most basic method and the skill used most frequently in baking – and specifically in pastry making. The key to this method is chilled, diced butter being combined with flour without melting, creaming or adding any liquids. It can be done in a food-processor, by hand, or using a free-standing mixer fitted with the creamer/paddle attachment. Tiny little crumbs of cold butter are left in the dough once they have been rubbed in and these create little pockets of steam as it bakes, giving a crumbly and crisp, rather than chewy and dry, texture. Using warm butter to rub in would make the dough greasy, tough and hard to bind together, and you'd probably need to add more liquid to bind it. Any liquid added to rubbed-in dough later on also needs to be cold, to prevent melting the butter.

Learn with: Garibaldi Biscuits (page 76), Custard Creams (page 106) and Gingerbread House (page 154)

How to rub in by hand

1. Sift the flour, plus any raising agents and/or spices, into a large mixing bowl. Add the cold, diced butter.

2. Using either a palette knife or round-bladed knife, cut the butter through the flour into smaller pieces so that the butter is covered with flour. (Or toss the butter with your fingertips to cover it in the flour.)

3. Use your fingers to lift up some flour and butter in both hands, allowing it to fall back into the bowl while gently pressing and rolling the butter pieces between your fingertips and thumbs. Repeat until there are no visible flecks of butter remaining, and the mixture is the texture of light sand (*see photo, right*).

4. Mix in your sugar, then make a well in the middle of the mixture and add any liquid and/or egg. Use the palette knife again to flick the dry ingredients into the middle of the wet ingredients and then continue mixing with your knife by gently cutting and mixing the dough to combine. (Or just use your fingers.)

5. When the dough starts to lump together, use your hands to gently gather it into a smooth ball, but take care not to overwork the dough as this will stretch the gluten, resulting in a tough finish to your bake.

How to rub in using a food-processor

1. Tip the flour into your food-processor bowl, add the chilled, diced butter and pulse in short bursts until there are no visible butter pieces remaining.

2. Add the sugar and pulse again until combined, then slowly pour the liquid through the feeder tube, pulsing until the dough starts to clump together.

3. Tip into a bowl and use your hands to very gently knead and gather the dough into a ball.

How to rub in using a free-standing mixer

1. Fit the machine with the creamer/paddle attachment and slowly mix your dry ingredients with the chilled, diced butter until the butter is no longer visible.

2. Add the sugar and mix again. You can then add the liquid and gently mix until starting to clump together.

3. Gather the dough into a smooth ball, flatten into a disc, wrap up in clingfilm and chill.

MELT AND MIX METHOD

This is a wonderfully simple one-pan technique where diced butter is gently melted in a saucepan along with sugar, and often another sweetener like honey or golden syrup. Most of the recipes using this method have a high sugar to flour (and also sometimes fat to flour) ratio, which would make rubbing-in or creaming tricky. This method is used when you want a chewy, sticky biscuit.

1. Put the diced butter and sugar (plus any other sweetener) in a pan over a low heat and stir almost constantly until the butter has melted, the sugar has completely dissolved, and the mixture is smooth (*see photo, left*).

2. Remove the pan from the heat and leave it to cool for a minute or two before adding the dry ingredients directly to the pan.

3. Mix well with a wooden spoon or rubber spatula until everything is evenly combined and coated in the butter and sugar mixture.

Learn with: Florentines (page 88) and Brandy Snaps (page 126)

CREAMED METHOD

This method produces a smoother, more even texture, without the crumbly shortness of a rubbed-in dough. You can use a wooden spoon or electric whisk in a mixing bowl, or a free-standing mixer fitted with a creamer/paddle attachment. The butter and eggs (if using) should always be at room temperature so that they combine easily with the sugar – caster and icing sugars are most often used for creaming as they combine quickly and give even, consistent bakes. The result is a dense biscuit with a crisp exterior and a more robust, chewier centre.

1. Put the butter in a large bowl (or the bowl of a free-standing mixer), add the sugar and beat until light, pale and silky smooth (*see photo, right*) – this can take 2–3 minutes using a mixer or electric whisk, twice as long using muscle power. Whichever method you are using, you'll need to scrape down the sides of the mixing bowl with a rubber spatula from time to time, to ensure the ingredients are combined evenly.

2. Lightly beat the eggs (if using) in a small jug or cup before gradually adding them to the bowl, about a tablespoon at a time – mix well after each addition and scrape down the sides of the mixing bowl to make sure your ingredients are incorporated.

3. Sift the dry ingredients into the bowl and gently mix or **fold** in with a large metal spoon or rubber spatula, until smooth.

Learn with: Classic Chocolate Chip Cookies (page 46), Almond, Pistachio and Rosewater Biscuits (page 100) and Chocolate and Vanilla Checkerboard Biscuits (page 148).

EXPERT ADVICE FROM START TO FINISH

This section takes you through every stage of the biscuit-making process, explaining the how, what and why behind the key techniques.

HOW TO LINE A BAKING TIN OR BAKING SHEET

All the recipes in this book require a baking paper-lined baking sheet or tin. Baking paper has a non-stick coating that prevents your bakes sticking to it (or the tin) during cooking. It can be white or brown in colour and shouldn't be confused with greaseproof paper, which is an entirely different beast and is used for wrapping food.

Tear off a sheet of baking paper the same size as your baking sheet and lay it flat on the surface of the sheet. For items that need spreading or piping, or that are light and delicate, it is a useful trick to stick each corner of the paper down onto the baking sheet with a dab of mixture (*see photo, left*), but this is not necessary for more substantial bakes. It's always best to use a clean sheet of paper for each batch you bake.

HOW TO WHISK

When making macarons and other biscuits that have a base of eggs and sugar you'll need good whisking skills. Whisking incorporates air into a mixture to create a light batter that holds its structure once cooked. It can be done in three different ways: by hand, using a balloon or rotary whisk, mixing bowl and muscle power; using an electric hand-held whisk; or in a free-standing mixer fitted with a whisk attachment. If you're whisking by hand, a large whisk will make light work of creating large pockets of air.

If you like, you can rest a medium-large mixing bowl on a damp tea towel to prevent the bowl slipping and sliding across the work surface, otherwise you can simply hold the whisk firmly in one hand and the bowl with the other. With a movement that starts at the elbow rather than the shoulder, work your whisk in rapid, large circular movements through the mixture, trying to incorporate as much air as possible as you do so. You may find it easier to tilt the bowl at an angle towards the whisk (*see photo, right*). Scrape down the sides of your bowl with a rubber spatula from time to time to ensure everything is evenly incorporated.

HOW TO FOLD IN

When adding dried fruit, nuts or chocolate chips to biscuit or cookie dough, they'll need to be thoroughly and evenly incorporated by folding in with a large metal spoon or a sturdy rubber spatula. Using a large, deep, almost cutting action, lift the dough up from the bottom of the bowl, and over the dry ingredients. Turn the bowl clockwise slightly, and repeat this cutting, lifting and folding until the additions are evenly distributed.

It's always best to rinse glacé cherries of any sticky syrup and pat them dry on kitchen paper before using. Nuts should be toasted early on so that they can cool to room temperature before being added to the dough.

Most added extras such as nuts, dried fruit and chocolate chips are added to the dough just before the flour is completely incorporated, to reduce the chances of over-mixing the dough, which would result in tough and chewy biscuits. You should stop mixing as soon as the ingredients are evenly distributed.

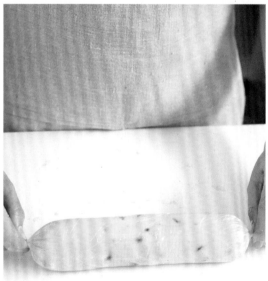

HOW TO SHAPE YOUR BISCUITS

Biscuits come in all shapes and sizes and there are various techniques used to create each one.

How to hand-roll biscuits into balls

This is a great technique for simple, neat, but freeform cookie doughs, where chunks or spoonfuls of (often chilled) dough are rolled into neat, smooth balls between the palms of your hand (*see photo, left*). To make sure your biscuits are evenly sized (and will therefore bake to a consistent colour) you can roll one ball, weigh it and then make sure that all subsequent balls are the same weight. Always use cool, clean hands for rolling biscuit dough into balls, but if your dough is on the sticky side you can lightly dust your hands with a little flour.

How to shape dough into a log

This technique enables you to make 'cut and come again' dough – unbaked logs can be stored in the fridge for a few days (or weeks in the freezer) and sliced and baked as needed, meaning you can bake a few or a whole batch of biscuits at any one time. Before slicing frozen dough, defrost it slowly in the fridge and slice it while it is still cold.

How to shape a log

1. Once the dough is mixed, divide it into two even portions (you can freeze the second log after step 4 if you don't want to bake it now).

2. Using your hands, squeeze the dough into a rough, fat sausage shape so that there are no air pockets in the middle, then roll the dough on the work surface into a smooth, even log – if the dough is very sticky, it helps to lightly dust your hands with a little plain flour.

3. When the dough log has reached the right width, lay it on a piece of clingfilm, fold the clingfilm over to completely encase the log and twist the ends to seal it up like a Christmas cracker (*see photo, below left*).

4. You can then gently roll the log, holding the twisted ends of clingfilm, back and forwards a couple of times along the work surface to further smooth it.

5. Pop the wrapped dough logs in the freezer on a flat surface for at least 20–30 minutes to firm up the dough and ensure that the logs keep their shape when cutting. Store them in the fridge or freezer until needed.

6. When you want to bake your biscuits, all you need to do is unwrap the dough and, using a sharp kitchen knife, slice the log into discs of the thickness required for the recipe (usually 3–5mm). If you find that your dough is still sticky, you can simply dust the knife blade with a little plain flour between each cut.

How to stamp out shapes using a cutter
This technique results in perfectly uniform biscuits. Evenly roll out the dough on a lightly floured work surface to the thickness required by your recipe. Place the cutter as close as possible to one edge and stamp out a shape. If the dough is slightly sticky you can dip the bottom of the cutter into plain flour before stamping out shapes. Press the cutter into the dough using your hands, applying even pressure across the cutter to create neat biscuits with straight sides. Cut as close as possible to previous stamps to get the maximum number of biscuits from the dough at one time (*see photo, right*). Gather the off-cuts into a neat smooth ball and re-roll it so that you can stamp out more biscuits.

How to pipe even-sized biscuits

To pipe your delicate piped finger biscuits to a uniform size you will need to be either very precise with your piping – practice makes perfect, which is a great excuse for making lots of batches – or you can make life easier by drawing markers on your baking paper. Using a ruler and pencil, measure out two sets of parallel lines on each sheet of baking paper, each 9cm apart. Flip the paper over so that you can still see the lines through the paper from the other side (so that you don't get any pencil or ink on your biscuits). Pipe the biscuits into fingers between your parallel lines (*see photo, left*).

How to portion dough for chocolate chip cookies

Chocolate chip dough needs to be divided accurately to give even-sized bakes as this dough is much softer than other shaped or cut biscuits. For absolute perfection you can weigh each mound of dough, but for ease simply scoop the dough with a tablespoon or ice-cream scoop as if you were serving ice cream and arrange the mounds on prepared baking sheets, allowing plenty of space between each cookie for them to spread during baking (*see photo, left*).

HOW TO TELL WHEN YOUR BISCUITS ARE READY

Most recipes will tell you how your bakes should look and feel when they're ready to come out of the oven. Keep an eye on them, as they near the end of the baking time, and bear in mind that some cookies may appear to be still soft after the baking time is up but will firm up quite considerably on cooling. This particularly applies to flapjacks, and cookies or biscuits with a high sugar or butter content.

MELTING CHOCOLATE

Melting chocolate isn't tricky, but it needs a little preparation and patience. Finely chop your chocolate to ensure it melts quickly and evenly, or use good-quality chocolate chips (not to be confused with the chocolate chips that are used for cookies – these are often chocolate of a lower quality, with a higher sugar and lower cocoa content).

When melting white chocolate, try not to overheat it – white chocolate pieces may keep their shape even when the chocolate is melted because of the high fat and sugar content. If you do happen to scorch the chocolate as you melt it, it will become greasy, grainy (known as 'seizing') and unusable. Dark chocolates with a very high cocoa solid content (more than 70 per cent) and sugary white chocolate are more delicate and prone to overheating and seizing. It's not generally recommended to melt chocolate in the microwave as you will have less control over the temperature.

How to melt chocolate

1. Tip the chocolate into a heatproof bowl that fits snugly over a saucepan of gently simmering water – the bottom of the bowl should not come into contact with the water below.

2. Leave the chocolate to melt in the heat from the water for a couple of minutes (*see photo, right*) and then gently stir with a spoon or spatula until it is completely glossy and smooth. It's ready to use as melted chocolate as soon as it is smooth and liquid – at around 30°C (86°F).

3. Some recipes might need the chocolate to cool slightly to prevent it melting any butter in your dough.

HOW TO DIP BISCUITS IN CHOCOLATE

To chocolate-coat the top of biscuits, melt the chocolate following the instructions on page 31. Remove the bowl from the heat, stir until smooth and leave to cool slightly. Take one biscuit at a time, hold it at the edges with the tips of your fingers and dip the flat top evenly into the chocolate. Hold the biscuit above the bowl to let any excess chocolate drip back into the bowl – the chocolate should evenly and smoothly coat the surface of the biscuit (*see photo, left*). Lay the biscuits, chocolate-side-up, on a wire cooling rack or baking paper-lined baking sheet until the chocolate has set.

FILLING PIPING BAGS

The recipes in this book use two types of piping bag: disposable and large nylon plastic-coated bags. Disposable piping bags are more often used when you are working with small quantities of batter or icing and/ or you need to pipe fine lines or shapes. The larger nylon bags are better for piping larger quantities, or batters such as macarons or sponge fingers (see pages 138 or 70).

How to fill a piping bag

1. For a large plastic-coated piping bag, drop the nozzle, if you are using one, into the piping bag, then snip off enough of the tip so the nozzle fits snugly and just peeps out.
2. Twist the bag right above the nozzle (so the filling doesn't ooze out while you're filling it), then put the bag in a tall container and fold the top of the bag over the rim so the bag is supported and easier to fill).
3. Spoon the filling into the bag to about two-thirds full (*see photo, left*).
4. Unfold the bag from the rim and twist the top to push the filling down to the (still

twisted) nozzle end, pushing out any air pockets, then twist it again to compact the filling and prevent it from escaping.

5. Untwist the nozzle end and squeeze the bag so the filling fills the nozzle. Practise the flow and shape of the filling before you begin, by squeezing a little out onto a plate.

How to fill a disposable piping bag
Disposable piping bags are filled in the same way but for much smaller quantities. Spoon the mixture into the bag, twist the top to seal and push the mixture towards the point end. Using sharp scissors, snip a very tiny point off the end to make a nozzle – you can always snip a bigger point if it's too small, but you'll have to throw the bag away and use another if you snip too big.

HOW TO SANDWICH BISCUITS
Pair up your biscuits so they're evenly matched. Flip one biscuit in each pair over so the flat base is uppermost, then either pipe the filling onto the flat surface or spread it on top with a small off-set palette knife, or a spoon (*see photo, right*). Then, just top the filling-topped biscuit with its partner.

HOW TO STORE YOUR BAKES
If you're not eating or serving a full batch of cookies and biscuits immediately, you can store them until needed. Line a plastic food storage box with a sheet of baking paper and stack the biscuits in layers with baking paper in between each one. Cover with a tight-fitting, secure lid.

Most biscuits will keep for up to a week in an airtight box or tin, but thinner, delicate wafer biscuits like brandy snaps or iced biscuits will start to soften after a couple of days – they'll still be delicious, but perhaps not quite as perfect.

Help!

No matter how many biscuits you've baked in your lifetime, sometimes things will just go wrong. But don't worry, here are the most frequently encountered baking pitfalls, and how to avoid them.

MY BISCUITS AREN'T BAKING EVENLY!

Many ovens have hot spots. You can make sure that each tray of biscuits or cookies bakes to an even colour and crispness by rotating the baking tray halfway through baking – if you're baking two trays at a time, swap them from one shelf to the other.

It can also help to double-check the temperature of your oven. Oven thermometers either sit on, or hook onto, the oven shelf, and give an accurate reading of the temperature in a particular spot so you can check for hot spots and your overall oven temperature.

MY BISCUITS ARE UNEVENLY SIZED!

To ensure that each and every biscuit is equally sized, weigh the first scoop of dough, then match each subsequent scoop to it. If your uneven sizing happens with sandwich biscuits, you'll need to match the biscuits together as best you can, and hope you have an even number of oddly sized ones to pair up. This could be a result of not measuring your biscuits evenly if you used a ruler rather than cutter to make the shapes; chilling your rolled and cut biscuits before baking can help, too.

CREAMING BUTTER SEEMS TO TAKE FOREVER AND IT WON'T CREAM SMOOTHLY!

It could be that your butter is too cold – this can happen even if you've left the butter out overnight to soften if your kitchen is on the cool side. Simply pop the butter in the microwave for a few seconds (in a microwave-safe bowl) on a medium heat to soften slightly.

If you've already started creaming you can still do this, as long as you haven't added the eggs. Failing that, take your time over creaming the mixture – the butter will eventually soften and cream smoothly and evenly.

MY BISCUITS ARE STICKING TO THE BAKING PAPER!

Check that you are using baking parchment/non-stick baking paper to line your trays and not greaseproof paper. They look similar but behave very differently: bakes will stick like crazy to greaseproof paper during cooking but will easily lift off baking parchment. If you do happen to mix them up and your biscuits have got stuck, cut them off carefully with a knife and disguise the ragged bases by spreading with a buttercream filling or dipping them in melted chocolate (see page 32).

MY DOUGH IS TOO SOFT TO ROLL OUT AND STAMP OUT SHAPES!

Give yourself a little extra time and set the dough in the fridge for 30–60 minutes, or in the freezer for 20 minutes to chill.

MY CUTTERS ARE STICKING TO THE DOUGH AS I CUT OUT SHAPES!

If your dough is on the sticky or soft side, you might find the cutter sticks as you stamp out shapes. This is easily solved by dipping the cutter in plain flour in between each stamping.

MY BISCUITS HAVE SPREAD DURING COOKING AND MERGED INTO ONE!

Try to leave plenty of space between each of your biscuits or cookies to allow room for them to spread. If, however, your bake has spread so that you have one large biscuit instead of 12, simply cut the still-warm bake into pieces – if you wait until they cool, the biscuit will crumble. Which is another solution: crumble the biscuit into chunks and you have a fancy cheesecake base, or fold it into melted dark chocolate along with a handful of mini marshmallows, glacé cherries and some chopped nuts. Press the whole lot into a lined tin, leave in the fridge until set and – voila! – tasty tiffin.

ICING DISASTER!

If you're unsure of your icing skills, have a practice run on some parchment paper before committing your design to the baked biscuits. Feathered icing (see Lemon Butter Cookies on page 80) is a brilliant way of covering a multitude of icing mistakes, but if your feathering is not as delicate as you'd hoped, simply turn it into marbling: rather than dragging the point of a wooden skewer or cocktail stick neatly back and forth through the icing lines, be more freestyle by swirling two coloured icings.

If you do make a glaring mistake on intricately iced biscuits that absolutely cannot be rectified, just scrape the icing off with a palette knife and start again – or cover the mistake with a generous flourish of sprinkles.

BAKE IT BETTER
Recipes

Thumbprint Cookies

These crumbly cookies couldn't be easier, with no fancy cutters or rolling out. They're fun to make with kids and can be filled with different jams for a colourful party spread.

200g unsalted butter, at room temperature
100g caster sugar
1 large egg yolk
1 teaspoon vanilla extract
275g plain flour
pinch of salt
150g raspberry jam

HANDS-ON TIME:
10 minutes, plus 1 hour chilling

BAKING TIME:
15 minutes

MAKES:
24 biscuits

SPECIAL EQUIPMENT:
2 baking sheets

METHOD USED:
Creamed method, page 25

1. Cream together the butter and caster sugar until really pale and light – you'll find this easiest using a free-standing mixer fitted with the creamer/paddle attachment but a hand-held mixer or bowl and wooden spoon will do just as well. Scrape down the sides of the bowl with a rubber spatula from time to time as you are working.

2. Add the egg yolk and vanilla extract and mix again until thoroughly combined. Sift the flour into the bowl with the salt and mix until the dough comes together into a smooth ball. Don't overwork the dough or the cookies could end up tough rather than crisp and crumbly. Cover the bowl with clingfilm and chill for 1 hour, until firm.

3. Preheat the oven to 180°C (160°C fan), Gas 4 and **line** two baking sheets with baking paper. Using your hands, roll the dough into walnut-sized balls and arrange on the lined baking sheets, leaving a little space between each biscuit, as they will spread slightly during cooking.

4. Using your thumb or finger, press into the middle of each cookie. Bake on the middle shelf of the oven for about 15 minutes, or until pale golden. Remove from the oven and gently press your thumb into the indent again. Fill each indent with ½–1 teaspoon of jam, depending on its depth, and return the cookies to the oven for another minute.

5. Leave to cool on the baking sheet for a few minutes, then transfer to a wire rack to cool completely.

Try Something Different

Add the finely grated zest of 1 unwaxed lemon to the dough and fill the indent with lemon curd, or swap 15g of the plain flour for the same amount of cocoa powder and fill the indent with chocolate and hazelnut spread. Reduce the flour by 75g and add 50g ground almonds or hazelnuts and 25g of cocoa powder. Fill the indents with raspberry jam, chocolate and hazelnut spread or peanut butter.

Flapjacks

These flapjacks are delicious and moreish and have a crunchier texture with the addition of mixed seeds. For your perfect flapjack – crunchy or chewy – follow the timings below.

100g golden syrup
100g demerara sugar
125g unsalted butter, diced
250g rolled porridge oats
75g mixed seeds (sunflower, pumpkin, golden linseed and sesame)
¼ teaspoon ground ginger
pinch of salt

HANDS-ON TIME:
10 minutes

BAKING TIME:
20–25 minutes

MAKES:
16 squares

SPECIAL EQUIPMENT:
20cm square baking tin

METHOD USED:
Melt and mix method, page 24

1. Preheat the oven to 180°C (160°C fan), Gas 4 and **line** the base and sides of the baking tin with baking paper.

2. To make it easy to measure golden syrup from a tin, first heat a tablespoon in a mug of boiling water for a minute before using. If you have digital scales, place a small pan on the scales, making sure they are registering zero, and use the hot spoon to scoop the syrup from the tin and into the pan. Re-set the scales to zero and add the demerara sugar and unsalted butter. Set the pan over a low heat to melt the butter and dissolve the sugar. Stir until smooth and remove from the heat.

3. Mix the porridge oats, mixed seeds, ginger and salt in a mixing bowl. Add the melted butter mixture and stir well to thoroughly combine. Spoon into the prepared tin and press level with the back of a spoon.

4. Bake on the middle shelf of the oven for 20–25 minutes, until starting to firm, remembering to use the shorter cooking time for more chewy flapjacks and the longer time if you prefer them crisper. The flapjacks will firm up and crisp as they cool.

5. Remove from the oven and mark the flapjack into squares. Cool in the tin on a wire rack.

Try Something Different

Increase the amount of ground ginger to 1 tsp and add a nugget of stem ginger, finely chopped, or add 50g raisins, sultanas, chopped dates or apricots to the dry ingredients. for a thinner, crisper flapjack, bake it in a 23cm square tin for 20 minutes.

Icebox Cookies

These are infinitely adaptable cookies – the options for added extras are endless. The dough is shaped into a neat log and sliced after chilling, so it can be prepared in advance.

100g dried or glacé cherries, roughly chopped
225g unsalted butter, at room temperature
125g icing sugar

2 medium egg yolks
1 teaspoon vanilla extract
300g plain flour
pinch of salt

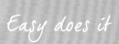
HANDS-ON TIME:
15 minutes,
plus 1 hour chilling

BAKING TIME:
12 minutes

MAKES:
about 40 biscuits

SPECIAL EQUIPMENT:
2 baking sheets

METHOD USED:
Creamed method,
page 25

1. If you are using glacé cherries tip them into a sieve, rinse in warm water to remove any excess syrup and pat dry on kitchen paper. Roughly chop the cherries, whichever type you are using, and set aside.

2. Cream the butter and icing sugar together until pale and light, scraping down the mixing bowl from time to time with a rubber spatula. Add the egg yolks, one at a time, mixing well between each one and then add the vanilla extract.

3. Sift the flour and salt into the bowl and mix until almost combined. Add the chopped cherries and mix again until thoroughly combined. Divide the dough into two equal-sized portions. Lightly flour your work surface and hands and then **shape** each piece into a neat, smooth log, 4–5cm in diameter. Wrap tightly in clingfilm and chill for at least 1 hour, until firm.

4. Preheat the oven to 180°C (160°C fan), Gas 4 and **line** two baking sheets with baking paper.

5. Cut the logs into slices, roughly 5mm thick, and arrange on the prepared baking sheets. Bake on the middle shelf of the oven for about 12 minutes, or until firm and pale golden brown. Leave the cookies to cool on the baking sheets for a few minutes before transferring to a wire rack to cool completely.

Try Something Different

Brush the chilled log with milk or lightly beaten egg white and roll in crushed flaked almonds or cinnamon sugar for a crisp edge to each cookie. Add finely grated orange or lemon zest and finely chopped candied peel to the dough instead of the cherries, or try adding 50g grated chocolate to the dough and roll the logs in finely chopped pistachios.

Anzac Biscuits

These delicious biscuits are named after the Australian and New Zealand soldiers they were sent to in World War 1; with no eggs in the recipe they could withstand the voyage to Europe.

150g plain flour
125g porridge oats
75g desiccated coconut
50g soft light brown sugar
25g caster sugar

pinch of salt
125g unsalted butter
100g golden syrup
½ teaspoon bicarbonate of soda
2 tablespoons boiling water

HANDS-ON TIME:
10 minutes

BAKING TIME:
12 minutes

MAKES:
20 biscuits

SPECIAL EQUIPMENT:
2 baking sheets

METHOD USED:
Melt and mix method, page 24

1. Preheat the oven to 180°C (160°C fan), Gas 4 and **line** two baking sheets with baking paper.

2. In a large mixing bowl stir together the flour, oats, coconut, soft light brown sugar, caster sugar and salt.

3. Melt the butter and golden syrup together in a small pan set over a low heat (or in the microwave on a low-medium setting). Remove the pan from the heat, add the bicarbonate of soda and boiling water and quickly mix with a whisk to combine.

4. Pour the melted butter mixture into the dry ingredients and mix with a wooden spoon or rubber spatula until thoroughly combined. Using your hands, roll level tablespoons of the mixture into walnut-sized balls and arrange on the prepared baking sheets, leaving plenty of space between each one as they will spread during cooking. Using the back of a spoon, slightly flatten each biscuit and bake in batches on the middle shelf of the oven for about 12 minutes, until almost firm and starting to crisp. The biscuits will crisp and firm up more as they cool.

5. Leave the biscuits on the trays for a few minutes, then transfer to a wire rack to cool completely.

Try Something Different

Add a handful of pumpkin, sunflower or sesame seeds to the mixture, or use coconut sugar instead of the soft light brown sugar.

Classic Chocolate Chip Cookies

In a twist on the classic recipe, here hazelnuts are baked with a generous helping of chocolate chips. Preparing the dough 24 hours before baking gives a better texture and shape.

100g blanched hazelnuts
200g unsalted butter, at room temperature
125g soft light brown sugar
100g caster sugar
2 medium eggs, lightly beaten
1 teaspoon vanilla extract

275g plain flour
½ teaspoon bicarbonate of soda
¼ teaspoon baking powder
pinch of salt
200g chocolate chips (dark or milk or a combination of both)

HANDS-ON TIME:
15 minutes, plus overnight chilling

BAKING TIME:
12 minutes

MAKES:
24 biscuits

SPECIAL EQUIPMENT:
2 baking sheets

METHOD USED:
Creamed method, page 25

1. Preheat the oven to 180°C (160°C fan), Gas 4 and **line** two baking sheets with baking paper. Roughly chop the hazelnuts and set aside.

2. Cream the butter with the soft light brown sugar and caster sugar until pale and light – using a free-standing mixer makes light work of this but a hand-held mixer works too. Gradually add the beaten eggs, mixing well between each addition and scraping down the sides of the bowl with a rubber spatula from time to time. Add the vanilla extract and mix again.

3. Sift the plain flour, bicarbonate of soda, baking powder and salt into the bowl and mix until almost combined. Add the chocolate chips and chopped hazelnuts and mix again until they are evenly distributed throughout the dough. If you like, you can now chill the dough for up to 24 hours until ready to bake.

4. Portion the dough to create biscuits of an even size – a good tip is to use an ice-cream scoop or tablespoon to drop even-sized mounds of dough onto the baking sheets. Leave plenty of space between each to allow the cookies to spread during cooking. Flatten the cookies slightly using your fingers and bake on the middle shelf of the oven for 12 minutes, until the cookies are lightly browned but the middle is still slightly soft. They will crisp up more as they cool.

5. Leave to cool on the baking sheets for 5 minutes, then use a palette knife or fish slice to transfer to a wire rack to cool completely.

Try Something Different

Replace the hazelnuts with macadamia nuts and use white chocolate chips. For a chunkier cookie, roughly chop a 200g bar of chocolate instead of using chocolate chips.

Oatmeal Raisin Cookies

These cookies may be loaded with good stuff but are still deliciously sweet and chewy. Use whole rolled oats for a better flavour and texture rather than quick-cook porridge oats.

225g unsalted butter, at room temperature
200g soft light brown sugar
50g soft dark brown sugar
1 teaspoon vanilla extract
2 large eggs, lightly beaten
175g plain flour
1 teaspoon bicarbonate of soda

½ teaspoon ground cinnamon
good pinch of salt
200g rolled porridge oats
150g raisins
100g pecans, roughly chopped
50g desiccated coconut
50g mixed seeds (sunflower, pumpkin, sesame and golden linseed)

HANDS-ON TIME:
15 minutes,
plus 1 hour chilling

MAKES:
about 30 biscuits

BAKING TIME:
12–14 minutes

SPECIAL EQUIPMENT:
2 baking sheets

METHOD USED:
Creamed method,
page 25

1. Cream the butter with the light and dark brown sugars in a free-standing mixer until pale and light – this will take about 3 minutes. Scrape down the insides of the bowl from time to time so that all of the ingredients are thoroughly incorporated. Add the vanilla extract and mix again.

2. Gradually add the beaten eggs, mixing well between each addition. Sift the flour, bicarbonate of soda, ground cinnamon and a good pinch of salt into the bowl and mix until barely combined. Add the oats, raisins, chopped pecans, coconut and seeds and mix again until all of the ingredients are thoroughly incorporated. Cover the bowl with clingfilm and chill for 1 hour.

3. Preheat the oven to 180°C (160°C fan), Gas 4 and **line** two baking sheets with baking paper.

4. Scoop level tablespoons of dough into balls and place on the prepared baking sheets, leaving plenty of space between each one to allow for spreading during cooking. Flatten each cookie with your hands and bake in

batches on the middle shelf of the oven for 12–14 minutes, until crisp and golden brown. The cookies are better when slightly soft and chewy, and as they crisp up as they cool, don't overcook them.

5. Remove from the oven and leave on the baking sheets for 2–3 minutes to firm up, then transfer the cookies to a wire cooling rack using a palette knife or fish slice. These cookies can be rolled into balls and frozen in bags, then baked from frozen or defrosted first.

Try Something Different

Swap the raisins with other dried fruit, depending on your tastes and what you have in your store cupboard – sultanas make a delicious alternative, or use walnuts instead of pecans. Try using coconut sugar in place of the soft light brown sugar for a hint of coconut as well as a more caramelly flavour.

Gingerbread Men

These nostalgic biscuits are ideal for making with children. You can easily get classic gingerbread men cutters, but look out for gingerbread ladies and children for the whole family.

HANDS-ON TIME:
10 minutes

BAKING TIME:
12 minutes

MAKES:
10–12 biscuits

SPECIAL
EQUIPMENT:
2 baking sheets,
gingerbread man
cookie cutter

METHOD USED:
Rubbed-in method,
page 22

2 tablespoons golden syrup
I large egg yolk
200g plain flour, plus extra for rolling
½ teaspoon bicarbonate of soda
2 teaspoons ground ginger
I teaspoon ground cinnamon

½ teaspoon mixed spice
pinch of salt
100g unsalted butter, chilled and diced
75g light muscovado sugar
currants, to decorate

1. Preheat the oven to 180°C (160°C fan), Gas 4 and **line** two baking sheets with baking paper.

2. Mix together the golden syrup and egg yolk in a small bowl.

3. Tip the flour, bicarbonate of soda, ginger, ground cinnamon, mixed spice and salt into a large bowl and add the diced butter. **Rub** the butter into the flour using your fingers but trying not to overwork the mixture. You can also do this step in a food-processor or in a free-standing mixer fitted with the creamer/paddle attachment.

4. When the mixture resembles fine sand and there are no visible lumps of butter remaining, add the light muscovado sugar and mix again to incorporate. Add the golden syrup and egg yolk mixture and mix again until the dough starts to clump together. Use your hands to gently knead the dough into a smooth ball.

5. Lightly dust the work surface with flour and roll the dough out to a thickness of 2–3mm. Using the gingerbread man cutter, stamp out **shapes** from the dough and carefully arrange on the prepared baking sheets, leaving a little space between each cookie. Gather any dough scraps together and knead gently into a ball, re-roll and stamp out more cookies. Press 3–4 currants onto each gingerbread man for buttons and bake on the middle shelf of the oven for about 12 minutes, until starting to brown slightly at the edges.

6. Leave to cool and firm up on the baking sheets for 5 minutes before transferring to a wire rack to cool completely.

Spiced Apple Cookies

The secret ingredient in these soft, moreish cookies makes them an ideal bake for those following a vegan diet – thick apple purée replaces eggs and sunflower oil replaces butter.

HANDS-ON TIME:
15 minutes

BAKING TIME:
10 minutes

MAKES:
24 biscuits

SPECIAL EQUIPMENT:
2 baking sheets

METHOD USED:
Melt and mix method, page 24

175g thick apple purée or good-quality ready-made apple sauce
100ml sunflower oil
50g dark treacle
125g light muscovado sugar
75g raisins or sultanas
300g plain flour

½ teaspoon baking powder
1 teaspoon bicarbonate of soda
1 teaspoon ground ginger
2 teaspoons ground cinnamon
good grating of nutmeg
pinch of salt
100g granulated sugar, for rolling

---

1. Heat the apple purée in a small pan over a low heat for a minute to cook off any excess liquid. Tip into a medium bowl, add the sunflower oil, treacle, light muscovado sugar and raisins or sultanas. Mix to combine and leave to cool to room temperature.

2. Preheat the oven to 180°C (160°C fan), Gas 4 and **line** two baking sheets with baking paper.

3. Sift the flour, baking powder, bicarbonate of soda, ginger, cinnamon, nutmeg and salt into the bowl with the apple and treacle mixture and stir well until thoroughly combined.

4. Tip the granulated sugar and remaining cinnamon onto a large plate or tray. Using a dessertspoon and your hands, scoop walnut-sized balls of dough into balls and roll in the cinnamon sugar to completely coat. Arrange on the prepared baking sheets, leaving plenty of space between each cookie to spread during baking, and flatten slightly with your fingers.

5. Bake on the middle shelf of the oven for 10 minutes, until the top of the cookies are crisp. Leave to cool on the baking sheets for 5 minutes and then transfer to a wire rack to cool completely.

Try Something Different

The dark treacle can easily be swapped for blackstrap molasses if that is what you happen to have to hand – molasses will give a slightly warmer, toffee-ish flavour. Add a finely chopped nugget of stem ginger or a handful of chopped pecans with the dry ingredients. Mix 1–2 tbsp of maple syrup with about 150g icing sugar to make a drizzly icing to zigzag over the cookies.

Shortbread

Crumbly, light and buttery shortbread is a good introduction to using different flours – cornflour gives a more delicate crumb, while rice flour adds a slight grittiness.

125g unsalted butter, at room temperature
50g caster sugar, plus 1 tablespoon
150g plain flour, plus extra for dusting
50g cornflour or rice flour
pinch of salt

1. Cream the butter with the caster sugar until pale and light – this is easiest in a free-standing mixer fitted with the creamer/paddle attachment. Scrape down the sides of the bowl with a rubber spatula from time to time.

2. Add the plain flour, cornflour (or rice flour) and salt and mix to combine, but don't overwork the dough.

3. Very lightly dust a sheet of baking paper with plain flour and press or roll the dough into a 20cm disc – you can use a cake tin as a guide to get it really neat. Carefully lift the shortbread dough, still on its paper, onto the middle of a baking sheet. Use your fingers to crimp the shortbread circle, making a decorative pattern around the edges. Use a knife to mark the shortbread into eight equal sections, but do not cut all the way through the dough. Prick with a fork and chill for 30 minutes to 1 hour while you preheat the oven to 150°C (130°C fan), Gas 2.

4. Bake the shortbread on the middle shelf of the oven for about 45 minutes to 1 hour, until light golden. Remove from the oven, sprinkle with the extra caster sugar and leave to cool on the baking sheet for 10 minutes, then carefully slide onto a wire rack to cool completely. Cut into sections to serve.

Try Something Different

Use vanilla sugar instead of regular caster or add the seeds from 1 vanilla pod when creaming the butter and sugar, or swap regular caster for golden caster sugar for slightly more crumbly shortbread with a faint hint of caramel. Add 1 tbsp of finely chopped candied peel and the finely grated zest of ½ unwaxed lemon.

Easy does it

HANDS-ON TIME:
10 minutes,
plus 1 hour chilling

BAKING TIME:
45 minutes

SERVES:
8

SPECIAL EQUIPMENT:
baking tray

METHOD USED:
Creamed method,
page 25

Cheese and Sun-Dried Tomato Sables

Crisp and cheesey, these bite-sized biscuits are perfect served with drinks or as canapés – perhaps topped with a little pesto, cherry tomato and goat's cheese.

HANDS-ON TIME:
15 minutes,
plus 2 hours chilling

BAKING TIME:
12–15 minutes

MAKES:
30 biscuits

SPECIAL EQUIPMENT:
2 baking sheets

75g sun-dried tomatoes in oil (drained weight)
100g plain flour
75g white spelt flour
½ teaspoon sea salt
good pinch of cayenne pepper
good pinch of English mustard powder
1 teaspoon caraway seeds, lightly crushed

125g unsalted butter, chilled and diced
50g mature Cheddar, finely grated
75g Parmesan, finely grated
2 tablespoons sesame seeds
1 tablespoon black sesame or black onion (nigella) seeds
1 tablespoon milk
freshly ground black pepper

1. Pat the drained sun-dried tomatoes with kitchen paper to remove as much oil as possible. Chop into small pieces and set aside.

2. Tip the plain flour, spelt flour, salt, cayenne pepper, mustard powder and caraway seeds into the bowl of a food-processor and season with a good grind of black pepper. Add the diced butter and, using the pulse button, mix the butter into the dry ingredients until there are no visible flecks of butter remaining.

3. Add the grated Cheddar and Parmesan and pulse again until the dough just starts to come together in clumps. Add the sun-dried tomatoes and pulse again to combine.

4. Tip the dough into a bowl and use your hands to bring it together into a smooth ball. Lightly flour your hands and **shape** the dough into a log, roughly 5cm in diameter, by rolling it on a clean work surface. Wrap tightly in clingfilm and chill for 2 hours, or until firm.

5. Preheat the oven to 180°C (160°C fan), Gas 4 and **line** two baking sheets with baking paper.

6. Mix the sesame seeds and black sesame or onion seeds together on a tray. Unwrap the sablé logs, brush with the milk and roll in the seeds, pressing them into the dough so that they stick evenly. Slice the logs into discs, around 5mm thick, and arrange on the baking sheets, spacing them well apart.

7. Bake on the middle shelf of the oven for 12–15 minutes, or until crisp and golden. Leave to rest on the baking sheets for 2 minutes, then transfer to a wire rack to cool. **Store** in an airtight container for up to 4 days and reheat in a moderate oven to crisp up.

Try Something Different

Swap the sun-dried tomatoes for the same amount of chopped black olives or replace the caraway seeds in the dough with cumin or fennel seeds. Roll the logs in poppy seeds instead of sesame and black onion seeds.

Oatmeal Biscuits
for Cheese

These lightly spiced, crumbly biscuits are ideal to serve alongside cheeses. For a perfect crumbly texture, don't overwork the dough as it will stretch the gluten in the flour.

HANDS-ON TIME:
10 minutes

BAKING TIME:
12 minutes

MAKES:
30–40 biscuits

SPECIAL EQUIPMENT:
2 baking sheets

METHOD USED
Rubbed-in method, page 22

100g medium oatmeal
175g wholegrain spelt flour
2 teaspoons baking powder
2 teaspoons mustard powder
1 teaspoon coarsely ground black pepper
¼ teaspoon cayenne pepper
1 teaspoon sea salt flakes, plus extra for sprinkling

125g unsalted butter, chilled and diced
2 tablespoons soft light brown sugar
2 teaspoons poppy seeds, plus extra for sprinkling
3 tablespoons whole milk
plain flour for dusting

1. Preheat the oven to 170°C (150°C fan), Gas 3 and **line** two baking sheets with baking paper.

2. Sift the oatmeal, spelt flour, baking powder, mustard powder, pepper and cayenne into a large bowl. Tip any bran left in the sieve back into the bowl. Add the salt and diced butter and, using your hands, **rub** the butter into the flour.

3. When there are no visible flecks of butter remaining and the mixture resembles damp sand, add the sugar and poppy seeds and mix again to combine. Add the milk and mix into the dry ingredients using a palette knife, until the dough starts to clump together and then use your hands to gently bring the dough into a neat ball. Do not over-work the dough otherwise your biscuits will be tough rather than crisp.

4. Lightly dust the work surface with plain flour and **roll** out the dough out to a thickness of no more than 2mm. Cut into neat 6–7cm squares and arrange on the lined baking sheets. Gather the dough scraps together, re-roll and cut out more biscuits. Prick each biscuit with a fork, sprinkle with a little salt flakes and/or poppy seeds and bake on the middle shelf of the oven for about 12 minutes, until lightly golden and crisp.

5. Transfer to a wire rack to cool.

Try Something Different

Use smoked sea salt flakes instead of regular flakes. Add a teaspoon of finely chopped fresh rosemary or thyme. You can also make the dough using a food-processor if you prefer and stamp out the biscuits using a round or square cookie cutter.

Coconut, Almond and Date Cookies

These wholesome biscuits are not only very tasty but are packed with goodness, too. Coconut oil is a new favourite and is available in health food stores, supermarkets and online.

150g blanched almonds
100g coconut chips or unsweetened desiccated coconut
100g pitted medjool dates
50g coconut oil

50g coconut nectar/syrup or agave syrup
1 teaspoon vanilla extract
½ teaspoon mixed spice
pinch of salt

1. Preheat the oven to 160°C (140°C fan), Gas 3 and **line** two baking sheets with baking paper.

2. Tip the blanched almonds into a food-processor or mini blender and pulse until finely ground. Tip into a mixing bowl. Add the coconut chips to the food-processor and pulse these until very finely chopped and then add to the almonds. Repeat with the pitted dates and finely chop, almost to a paste. Add to the almonds and coconut.

3. Melt the coconut oil, either in a small pan over a low heat or in the microwave on a low setting. Add the coconut nectar (or agave syrup) and vanilla extract and pour into the mixing bowl, along with the mixed spice and salt. Mix together, at first with a spoon to combine, and then with your hands to bring all the ingredients together until thoroughly combined.

4. Using your hands, roll the mixture into neat walnut-sized balls and arrange on the lined baking sheets. Flatten into neat 1cm-thick rounds and bake on the middle shelf of the oven for about 10 minutes, until starting to turn golden at the edges. The biscuits will seem quite soft but will harden further on cooling – leave them on the baking sheet for 2–3 minutes and then transfer to a wire rack to cool completely.

Try Something Different

Use honey instead of the coconut nectar or agave syrup, but remember that will mean these biscuits are no longer suitable for vegans.

Easy does it

HANDS-ON TIME:
15 minutes

BAKING TIME:
10 minutes

MAKES:
about 20 biscuits

SPECIAL EQUIPMENT:
2 baking sheets

METHOD USED:
Melt and mix method, page 24

Gingersnaps

These crisp biscuits pack a powerful punch, with ground ginger and chewy ginger chunks. The pinch of cayenne pepper adds extra heat, but feel free to leave it out if you prefer.

HANDS-ON TIME:
15

BAKING TIME:
12 minutes

MAKES:
30 biscuits

SPECIAL EQUIPMENT:
2 baking sheets

METHOD USED:
Creamed method, page 25

200g unsalted butter, at room temperature
125g caster sugar
175g golden syrup
50g treacle
1 large egg, lightly beaten
50g stem ginger in syrup, drained

425g plain flour
2 teaspoons bicarbonate of soda
4–5 teaspoons ground ginger
1 teaspoon ground cinnamon
large pinch of cayenne pepper
pinch of salt
100g granulated sugar

---

1. Preheat the oven to 180°C (160°C fan), Gas 4 and **line** two baking sheets with baking paper.

2. Cream together the butter and caster sugar until light and fluffy – this is easiest using a free-standing mixer fitted with a creamer/paddle attachment. Add the golden syrup, treacle and beaten egg and mix until smooth, scraping down the bowl with a rubber spatula from time to time. Finely chop the stem ginger, add to the bowl and mix again.

3. Sift the flour, bicarbonate of soda, ground ginger, ground cinnamon, cayenne pepper and salt into the bowl and mix again until thoroughly combined. Tip the granulated sugar onto a tray.

4. Using your hands, roll the gingersnap mixture into walnut-sized balls and roll in the granulated sugar to coat completely. Arrange on the prepared baking sheets, allowing plenty of space for the biscuits to spread during baking and flatten the top of each using a fork.

5. Bake in batches on the middle shelf of the oven for about 12 minutes, or until golden brown and the edges of the cookies are crisp and the middle is still slightly soft. (The gingersnaps will crisp further as they cool.) Leave the biscuits on the trays for 5 minutes and then transfer to a wire rack to cool completely.

Try Something Different

Add 2 tsp finely grated fresh ginger to give a really powerful ginger hit to these biscuits, or for less ginger, replace the stem ginger with 1 tbsp finely chopped mixed peel. Dip the underside of each gingersnap in **melted** dark chocolate (see the recipe for Florentines, page 88, for tips on how to do this).

Double Chocolate Peanut Butter Cookies

These delicious cookies are packed with dark and white chocolate chunks and a double dose of peanuts. The trick is not to over-bake them so they are slightly soft in the middle.

HANDS-ON TIME:
20 minutes

BAKING TIME:
12 minutes

MAKES:
24 biscuits

SPECIAL EQUIPMENT:
2 baking sheets

METHOD USED:
Creamed method,
page 25

125g dark chocolate, preferably a minimum of 65 per cent cocoa solids, chopped
125g white chocolate
100g salted roasted peanuts
100g unsalted butter, at room temperature
125g crunchy peanut butter
225g soft light brown sugar

2 large eggs, lightly beaten
1 teaspoon vanilla extract
200g plain flour
40g cocoa powder
1 teaspoon bicarbonate of soda
½ teaspoon baking powder
pinch of salt
2 tablespoons milk

1. Preheat the oven to 170°C (150°C fan), Gas 3 and **line** two baking sheets with baking paper.

2. **Melt** the dark chocolate in a heatproof glass or ceramic bowl, either over a pan of barely simmering water, making sure the bottom of the bowl doesn't touch the water. Stir until smooth, remove from the heat and leave to cool slightly. Chop the white chocolate into chunks and very roughly chop the peanuts and put to one side.

3. Cream the butter with the peanut butter and soft light brown sugar until pale and light – this will be easiest using a free-standing mixer fitted with the creamer/paddle attachment. Gradually add the eggs, mixing well between each addition and scraping down the sides of the bowl with a rubber spatula from time to time. Add the vanilla extract and mix again.

4. Add the cooled melted chocolate and mix until smooth. Sift the flour, cocoa powder, bicarbonate of soda, baking powder and a pinch of salt into the bowl and mix until barely combined before adding the milk, white chocolate chunks and chopped peanuts. Mix again to thoroughly combine.

5. Using a tablespoon, scoop even-sized mounds onto the lined baking sheets, leaving plenty of space between each cookie to allow them to spread during baking. Bake in batches, for 10 minutes on the middle shelf of the oven. Remove from the oven and flatten each cookie slightly with a fish slice or palette knife and return to the oven for a further minute. The cookies will still be slightly soft at this point but will harden as they cool – if you can wait that long. Cool the cookies on the baking sheets for a few minutes and then transfer to a wire rack to cool completely.

Honey and Pine Nut Cookies

Aromatic orange blossom honey adds a sweetness to these slightly soft pine nuts and candied peel cookies. Flattening them slightly before baking makes them crisp rather than cakey.

225g plain flour
½ teaspoon bicarbonate of soda
I teaspoon ground cinnamon
pinch of ground allspice
pinch of ground cloves
pinch of salt
150g unsalted butter, at room temperature
150g golden caster sugar, plus 50g extra for coating

75g clear orange blossom honey, plus I tablespoon for brushing
finely grated zest of ½ orange
I tablespoon orange juice
I medium egg, lightly beaten
100g pine nuts
50g candied peel, finely chopped

HANDS-ON TIME:
15 minutes

BAKING TIME:
12 minutes

MAKES:
24 biscuits

SPECIAL EQUIPMENT:
2 baking sheets

METHOD USED:
Creamed method, page 25

1. Sift the plain flour, bicarbonate of soda, spices and salt into a bowl.

2. Cream the butter with 100g of the golden caster sugar until pale and light – this is quickest in a free-standing mixer fitted with a creamer/paddle attachment. Scrape down the sides of the mixing bowl with a rubber spatula from time to time. Gradually add the clear honey, orange zest and juice and beaten egg and mix again until smooth.

3. Tip the sifted dry ingredients into the bowl and mix again until almost combined. Add 50g of the pine nuts and 25g of the candied peel and mix until combined. Cover the bowl with clingfilm and chill for 30 minutes to help make shaping the dough easier.

4. Preheat the oven to 180°C (140°C fan), Gas 4 and **line** two baking sheets with baking paper.

5. Tip the remaining 50g caster sugar onto a tray. Scoop level tablespoons of the cookie mixture and roll into

balls. Drop into the sugar, roll to coat and then arrange on the lined baking sheets, leaving space between each cookie. Flatten each one slightly with your fingers. Divide the remaining pine nuts and candied peel between the cookies, pressing slightly into the top of each, and bake on the middle shelf of the oven for 12 minutes, until golden brown, slightly risen and starting to firm at the edges.

6. Remove from the oven and brush the top of each hot cookie with a little honey. Leave to rest on the baking sheets for 3 minutes and then, using a fish slice or palette knife, transfer to a wire rack to cool completely.

Try Something Different

Use chopped walnuts instead of the pine nuts, or add a teaspoon of finely chopped fresh rosemary to the mix.

Sesame Crisps

Delicious with fresh mint tea or coffee these sesame cookies are flavoured with tahini and the merest hint of cocoa, giving them an exotic flavour that is similar to halva.

100g sesame seeds
125g unsalted butter, at room temperature
75g caster sugar
2 tablespoons clear honey or agave syrup
2 tablespoons tahini

1 teaspoon vanilla extract
150g plain flour
25g ground almonds
15g cocoa powder
½ teaspoon baking powder
pinch of salt

HANDS-ON TIME:
20 minutes, plus
1 hour chilling

BAKING TIME:
10 minutes

MAKES:
about 20 biscuits

SPECIAL
EQUIPMENT:
2 baking sheets

METHOD USED:
Creamed method,
page 25

1. Preheat the oven to 170°C (150°C fan), Gas 3 and **line** a baking sheet with baking paper. Tip the sesame seeds onto the lined baking sheet and toast in the oven for about 4 minutes, until golden – keep an eye on them as they can easily burn due to their high oil content. Remove from the oven and cool. You can turn the oven off for now.

2. Cream the butter with the caster sugar until pale and light, scraping down the sides of the mixing bowl from time to time. Add the honey (or agave syrup), tahini and vanilla extract and mix again.

3. Sift the flour, ground almonds, cocoa powder, baking powder and salt into the bowl. Add 40g of the toasted sesame seeds and mix until thoroughly combined, scraping down the bowl with a rubber spatula to ensure that the ingredients are thoroughly incorporated. Scoop the mixture into a clean bowl, cover with clingfilm and chill for 1 hour.

4. Preheat the oven to 170°C (150°C fan), Gas 3 and **line** two baking sheets with baking paper.

5. Using a dessertspoon and your hands, **roll** large cherry-sized nuggets of the dough into balls. Roll the balls in the reserved toasted sesame seeds to coat, arrange on the prepared baking sheets and flatten slightly with your hands. Allow a little space between each ball to allow them to spread during cooking. Bake the biscuits on the middle shelf of the oven for 10 minutes, until firm (they will crisp further on cooling).

6. Leave the biscuits to cool on the baking sheets for 10 minutes and then transfer to a wire rack to cool completely.

Try Something Different

For a savoury version, replace the cocoa powder with spelt or rye flour, omit the vanilla extract and roll the balls in za'atar instead of sesame seeds. Za'atar is a Middle Eastern spice blend usually consisting of sumac, sesame seeds and thyme.

Sponge Fingers

Also known as Lady Fingers or Savoiardi Biscuits, these light-as-air biscuits are piped, so are a good introduction to using a piping bag. Slow and steady makes perfect piping.

3 large eggs, separated
125g caster sugar, plus extra
for sprinkling
½ vanilla pod, slit lengthways and
seeds scraped out or ½ teaspoon
vanilla bean paste
pinch of salt
60g plain flour

HANDS-ON TIME:
15 minutes,
plus 20 minutes
resting

BAKING TIME:
10 minutes

MAKES:
36 biscuits

SPECIAL
EQUIPMENT:
2 baking sheets,
large piping bag,
1cm plain nozzle

1. **Line** two baking sheets with baking paper.

2. Tip the egg yolks into a bowl and add half of the caster sugar and all of the vanilla (seeds or paste). Using a hand-held or free-standing mixer, **whisk** on high speed until thick, pale and the mixture will hold a ribbon trail when the whisk is lifted from the bowl.

3. In another, spotlessly clean bowl whisk the egg whites with the salt until stiff but not dry. Add the remaining caster sugar in three batches, whisking well between each addition, until the egg whites are silky smooth and glossy. Using a large metal spoon, **fold** the egg whites into the yolk mixture. Sift the flour into the bowl over the mixture and fold in until thoroughly combined.

4. Fit the 1cm plain nozzle into the piping bag and then fill the piping bag with the mixture. **Pipe** even-sized lengths, roughly the size of your finger, in neat lines onto the baking paper. Keep the biscuits 2cm apart to allow enough space for them to spread during baking. Sprinkle each one with caster sugar and leave to one side for 15 minutes while you preheat the oven to 170°C (150°C fan), Gas 3.

5. Bake the biscuits in batches on the middle shelf of the oven for about 10 minutes, until crisp and pale golden brown. Remove from the oven and leave to cool on the baking sheets.

Tuiles

Delicate tuile biscuits are ideal for serving with ice cream, sorbet or creamy desserts. You need to work fast to shape them as they harden quickly as they cool.

75g unsalted butter
2 large egg whites
pinch of salt
125g icing sugar
1 teaspoon vanilla extract
75g plain flour

1. Melt the butter, either in a small pan or carefully in the microwave on a low setting; cool slightly. Place the egg whites in a large bowl, add the salt and **whisk** until they will almost hold a soft, floppy peak. Add the icing sugar and whisk for a further minute until the egg whites are glossy and the sugar has been thoroughly incorporated.

2. Add the vanilla extract, Sift over the flour and gently **fold** in using a large metal spoon. Pour the cooled melted butter around the edges of the bowl and fold in until thoroughly combined. Cover and chill for 30 minutes to 1 hour.

3. Preheat the oven to 170°C (150°C fan), Gas 3 and **line** two baking sheets with baking paper.

4. Drop 4 dessertspoons of the mixture onto each tray and spread each spoonful into a thin, neat disc roughly 10–12cm in diameter with plenty of space between each tuile.

5. Bake one tray at a time on the middle shelf of the oven for about 10–12 minutes, until starting to turn golden brown at the edges. Working quickly, slide a palette knife under each tuile, lift off the tray and drape over a lightly oiled rolling pin. The tuiles harden very quickly which is why you bake only a few at a time. Repeat this baking and shaping until all of the batter has been used up. Leave to cool and finish hardening. these are best eaten on the day you bake them, but they can be **stored** in an airtight container for 2–3 days, then crisped up in a medium oven.

Try Something Different

To make baskets for serving ice cream, use a tablespoon of mixture for each basket, spread into a slightly larger disc (15cm in diameter) and bake for 8 minutes. Working quickly, drape the hot tuiles over upturned glasses and use your hands to press each tuile into delicate folds. Leave to cool over the glass for at least 4 minutes then carefully remove and cool completely before serving. To vary the tuiles, add a teaspoon of finely grated orange or lemon zest to the batter, or scatter the tuiles with flaked almonds, pistachios or cocoa nibs halfway through baking.

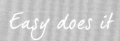

Easy does it

HANDS-ON TIME:
10 minutes,
plus 30 minutes
chilling

BAKING TIME:
7–8 minutes

MAKES:
24 biscuits

SPECIAL
EQUIPMENT:
2 baking sheets,
palette knife,
rolling pin

METHOD USED:
Melt and mix
method, page 24

Langues de Chat

Langues de Chat, so-called because they look like a bit like a cat's tongue, are crisp wafers that are perfect for serving with ice cream, sorbets, creamy desserts or an espresso.

125g unsalted butter, at room temperature
125g icing sugar, sifted
1 teaspoon vanilla extract
finely grated zest of ½ orange
3 medium egg whites
140g plain flour
pinch of salt

1. Preheat the oven to 180°F (160°C fan), Gas 4 and **line** two baking sheets with baking paper.

2. Cream the butter with the icing sugar until pale and light, this is easiest in a free-standing mixer fitted with the creamer/paddle attachment but can be done by hand in a large bowl with a wooden spoon. Scrape down the sides of the bowl from time to time using a rubber spatula. Add the vanilla extract and orange zest and mix to combine.

3. Add the egg whites one at a time and mix again – at this point the mixture may look curdled but don't worry. Add the flour and salt and mix until thoroughly combined and the batter is smooth.

4. Fit a large piping bag with a 1cm plain nozzle. Spoon the biscuit mixture into the piping bag and **pipe** neat lines on the prepared baking sheets, 8–10cm long, leaving plenty of space between each biscuit to allow them to spread during baking. Bake in batches on the middle shelf of the oven for about 10 minutes, until the biscuits are golden brown at the edges and set in the middle. (They will crisp up further as they cool.)

5. Leave to cool on the baking sheets for 2–3 minutes and then, using a palette knife, carefully transfer to a wire rack to cool completely.

Try Something Different

Scatter the top of the biscuits with flaked almonds halfway through baking. **Sandwich** the biscuits with chocolate ganache (see page 145), **dip** one end of each biscuit in **melted** dark chocolate or **pipe** the tops with chocolate in zigzag lines.

Easy does it

HANDS-ON TIME:
10 minutes

BAKING TIME:
10–12 minutes

MAKES:
36 small biscuits

SPECIAL EQUIPMENT:
2 baking sheets, large piping bag, 1cm plain nozzle, palette knife

METHOD USED:
Creamed method, page 25

Garibaldi Biscuits

This is a slightly more indulgent version of the classic, shop-bought 'squashed fly biscuit' with a hint of nutmeg and lemon zest and plumped, juicy raisins and currants.

200g mixed raisins and currants
finely grated zest of ½ unwaxed lemon
2 tablespoons orange juice
grating of nutmeg
225g plain flour, plus extra for dusting
½ teaspoon baking powder
good pinch of salt

100g unsalted butter, chilled and diced
75g caster sugar, plus extra for sprinkling
2 medium egg yolks (save 1 white for use later)
3 tablespoons milk
1 teaspoon lemon juice
1 egg white

HANDS-ON TIME:
15 minutes,
plus 1–2 hours
chilling

BAKING TIME:
12 minutes

MAKES:
30 biscuits

SPECIAL
EQUIPMENT:
2 baking sheets

METHOD USED:
Rubbed-in method,
page 22

1. Start by preparing the filling. Tip the raisins and currants into a bowl, add the lemon zest, orange juice and nutmeg. Mix well, cover and set aside for about 2 hours, until the dried fruit has absorbed all of the liquid and become plump. You can speed up this process by popping the bowl (making sure that it is heatproof ceramic or glass) into the microwave for a minute and then stirring well. Leave until cold.

2. To make the dough, tip the flour, baking powder and salt into a large mixing bowl and mix to combine. Add the diced butter and use your fingertips to **rub** the butter into the flour. When you can no longer see or feel any butter pieces add the caster sugar and mix again until the mixture has a sandy texture.

3. Make a well in the centre, add the egg yolks, milk and lemon juice and mix using a palette knife to combine. Gather the dough into a neat ball, flatten into a disc, cover with clingfilm and chill for 1 hour until firm. **Line** two baking sheets with baking paper.

4. Lightly dust the work surface with flour and roll the dough out to a neat rectangle, 2–3mm thick. Scatter the soaked fruit in an even layer neatly over one half of the dough. **Fold** the other half of the dough over the top to completely encase the fruit. Lightly dust the rolling pin with flour and give the dough a couple of turns of the rolling pin to press the dried fruit into the dough.

5. Use a long knife to trim the edges to neaten and cut the dough into neat even rectangles, each measuring 7 × 4cm and arrange on the lined baking sheets. Chill the biscuits for 20 minutes while you preheat the oven to 180°C (160°C fan), Gas 4.

6. Prick each biscuit three times with a fork. Lightly beat the egg white and use to glaze the biscuits. Sprinkle with caster sugar. Bake in batches on the middle shelf of the oven for about 12 minutes, until crisp and golden brown, cool for a couple of minutes on the baking sheets and then transfer to a wire rack to cool completely.

Viennese Whirls

These delicate, melt-in-the-mouth sandwich biscuits show off your skills in piping swirls or fingers.

For the biscuits

250g unsalted butter, softened
100g icing sugar, Sifted
1 teaspoon vanilla extract
250g plain flour
30g cornflour
½ teaspoon baking powder
pinch of salt
1 tablespoon milk

For the buttercream filling

75g unsalted butter, at room temperature
1 teaspoon vanilla extract or
½ teaspoon vanilla bean paste
175g icing sugar, plus extra for dusting
3 tablespoons raspberry jam

HANDS-ON TIME:
15 minutes,
plus 20 minutes
chilling

BAKING TIME:
12 minutes

MAKES:
18-20 biscuits

SPECIAL EQUIPMENT:
2 baking sheets,
large piping bag,
large star nozzle

METHOD USED:
Creamed method,
page 25

1. **Line** two baking sheets with baking paper.

2. The butter needs to be really soft, so tip it into the bowl of a free-standing mixer fitted with the creamer/paddle attachment. Cream for 2–3 minutes until pale, light and soft. Add the icing sugar and vanilla and beat again for 2–3 minutes, until smooth and soft.

3. Sift the flour, cornflour, baking powder and salt into the bowl and mix until smooth and thoroughly combined. Add the milk and mix for another 30 seconds to combine.

4. Spoon the dough into a **piping** bag fitted with a large star nozzle and pipe 10–12 tight rosette spirals, each 5cm in diameter, onto each prepared baking sheet, leaving a little space between them to allow for spreading during cooking. Chill the biscuits for 20 minutes while you preheat the oven to 170°C (150°C fan), Gas 3.

5. Bake on the middle shelf of the oven for 10–12 minutes, until pale golden at the edges. Cool on the baking sheet for 5 minutes, then use a palette knife or fish slice to carefully transfer them to a wire rack to cool completely.

6. To make the buttercream filling, beat the butter until pale and really soft, add the vanilla and mix again. Gradually add the icing sugar until the buttercream is pale, light and soft.

7. Spoon the buttercream into the clean piping bag fitted with the star nozzle. Turn half the biscuits upside down and pipe a rosette of buttercream on each. Spread the underside of the remaining biscuits with a scant teaspoon of jam and **sandwich** the halves together. Lightly dust with icing sugar to serve.

Lemon Butter Cookies

These lemon biscuits are fresh looking and tasting. They look especially pretty when iced in contrasting colours, which makes them ideal for children's birthday parties.

For the cookie dough

125g unsalted butter, at room temperature
125g caster sugar
finely grated zest of ½ unwaxed lemon
½ teaspoon lemon extract
1 medium egg, lightly beaten
200g plain flour, plus extra for dusting
30g cornflour
¼ teaspoon baking powder
pinch of salt

For the icing

500g royal icing sugar
1–2 teaspoons lemon juice
food colouring pastes in assorted colours

HANDS-ON TIME:
10 minutes,
plus 2–3 hours chilling

BAKING TIME:
10 minutes

MAKES:
about 30 biscuits

SPECIAL EQUIPMENT:
2 baking sheets,
7cm and 2cm round fluted cookie cutters,
3 disposable piping bags

METHOD USED:
Creamed method,
page 25

Easy does it

1. Cream together the butter and caster sugar until pale and light – this is easiest and quickest using a free-standing mixer fitted with a creamer/paddle attachment or with a hand-held mixer but can also be done using the old-fashioned wooded spoon and bowl method.

2. Add the lemon zest and extract and mix well. Scrape down the sides of the bowl with a rubber spatula, add the egg and mix again until thoroughly combined.

3. In a separate bowl Sift together the flour, cornflour, baking powder and salt and gradually add to the creamed mixture. Mix until smooth and bring the dough together into a neat ball using your hands. Flatten into a disc, wrap in clingfilm and chill for 2 hours, or until firm.

4. **Line** two baking sheets with baking paper and lightly dust the work surface with flour. Roll the dough out to a thickness of about 2mm and, using the 7cm cutter, stamp out as many rounds from the dough as you can. Arrange on the prepared baking sheets and then use the smaller cutter to stamp out circles from the middle of each biscuit. Gather the dough off-cuts into a ball and re-roll to make more **shape**s. Chill the biscuits for 30 minutes and then preheat the oven to 180°C (160°C fan), Gas 4.

5. Bake on the middle shelf for about 12 minutes, until the edges of each biscuit are lightly golden and firm to the touch. Leave to cool on the baking tray for about 5 minutes before transferring to a wire rack to cool completely.
Continued

6. Tip the 500g royal icing sugar into a bowl and gradually add the 1–2 teaspoons of lemon juice and enough cold water to make an icing that is thick enough to coat the back of a spoon, **whisking** continuously until the icing is glossy and the right consistency. Divide the icing between three bowls and tint each a different colour using food colouring pastes. (Add the paste gradually on the point of a cocktail stick or wooden skewer until the desired shade is reached.)

7. **Dip** the top of each biscuit into icing to coat, allowing any excess to drip back into the bowl, and return the biscuits to the cooling racks. Spoon 1–2 tablespoons of each coloured icing into disposable piping bags and snip the end of each bag into a fine point.

8. **Pipe** fine lines across each biscuit in contrasting colours and then drag a clean cocktail stick or wooden skewer through the icing in opposite directions to feather. Leave until the icing has set before eating.

Try Something Different

Replace 30g of the flour with 30g cocoa powder and use orange zest and juice instead of lemon, or add the seeds of 1 vanilla pod instead of the lemon zest and lemon extract. Replace 30g of the plain flour with 30g finely ground pistachios and replace the lemon extract with the same amount of rosewater.

Palmiers

Crumbly, crunchy, crisp, sugary puff pastry palmiers are a staple in most French patisseries. With only two ingredients in this recipe, the technique here is all in the shaping.

200g caster sugar
1 × 500g block all-butter puff pastry

1. Liberally dust the work surface with some of the caster sugar and place the block of puff pastry on top. Dust the pastry with a coating of sugar and **roll** out to a neat 40–42cm square with a thickness of about 2mm. Turn the pastry over and around as you roll so that it is of even thickness, dusting the top and underneath with more sugar as needed to prevent the pastry from sticking to either the work surface or rolling pin.

2. Using a large knife, trim the edges to neaten and cut the pastry in half to make two neat 40 × 20cm rectangles. You will find it easier to work with two smaller pastry sections rather than one large one.

3. Scatter the work surface and the top of one pastry rectangle with more caster sugar and with one of the longer sides nearest to you, measure the long side and make a nick in the pastry to mark the middle.

Continued

HANDS-ON TIME:
15 minutes,
plus 1 hour chilling

BAKING TIME:
20 minutes

MAKES:
about 24

SPECIAL EQUIPMENT:
2 baking sheets

Try Something Different

Mix the caster sugar with either the finely grated zest of ½ unwaxed lemon or 1 tsp of ground cinnamon, then **sandwich** the cooked palmiers with a thin layer of lemon curd or chocolate and hazelnut spread. For a savoury version, replace the caster sugar with 2–3 tbsp of finely grated Parmesan mixed with a good ½ tsp of smoked paprika or 1 tsp of toasted and finely ground cumin seeds

4. Fold the outside edges in to meet in the middle and scatter the top with more caster sugar. Fold the outside edges in again to meet in the middle so that you have two neat rolls of four layers of pastry on either side of the middle. Fold the pastry rolls on top of each other as if you were closing a book. Set aside and repeat with the second pastry rectangle.

5. Wrap the rolls in clingfilm and chill in the fridge for 1 hour or the freezer for 30 minutes until firm.

6. Preheat the oven to 190°C (170°C fan), Gas 5 and **line** two baking sheets with baking paper. Lay the two rolls on top of the paper.

7. Using a sharp knife, cut the pastry rolls into slices no thicker than 1 cm and arrange, cut side uppermost, on the prepared baking sheets, leaving plenty of space between each one to allow the palmiers to spread during cooking.

8. Dust the tops of the palmiers with more caster sugar and bake on the middle shelf of the oven for 20 minutes, until golden brown and crisp.

9. Leave to cool on the baking sheets for 5 minutes and then transfer to a wire rack to cool completely.

Florentines

The fruit and nut combination in these elegant biscuits can be varied, but for a jewelled, festive look for Christmas gifts, choose a brightly coloured combination.

75g glace cherries, preferably natural coloured
75g chopped mixed candied peel
50g blanched almonds
25g shelled and unsalted slivered pistachios
25g flaked almonds
25g unsalted butter
50g demerara sugar
1 tablespoon clear honey
2 tablespoons double cream
25g plain flour
pinch of ground ginger
pinch of salt

For the chocolate coating
175g dark chocolate, 70 per cent cocoa solids
75g white chocolate

Need a little skill

HANDS-ON TIME:
15 minutes,

BAKING TIME:
12 minutes

MAKES:
16 biscuits

SPECIAL EQUIPMENT:
2 baking sheets, disposable piping bag

METHOD USED:
Melt and mix method, page 24

1. Preheat the oven to 170°C (150°C fan), Gas 3 and **line** two baking sheets with baking paper.

2. Prepare the dried fruit and nuts first. Rinse the glacé cherries to remove any sticky syrup and pat dry on kitchen paper. Quarter the cherries and tip into a bowl with the candied peel. Chop the blanched almonds and add to the cherries along with the slivered pistachios and flaked almonds. Mix to combine and set aside.

Continued

Try Something Different

Add a nugget of finely chopped stem ginger to the mix or a handful of dried cranberries. Look out for packets of whole candied peel that you can cut into small pieces, then you can choose your favourite citrus peels and decide how large to chop the pieces.

3 Melt the 25g butter, 50g demerara sugar and 1 tablespoon of honey in a small pan over a low heat, stirring continuously to prevent the sugar catching on the bottom of the pan. Add the 2 tablespoons of double cream, mix to combine and pour into the bowl of fruit and nuts; mix well to combine.

4 Add the 25g plain flour, pinch of ground ginger and salt and mix again until smooth.

5 Spoon level dessertspoons of the mixture onto the prepared baking sheets, leaving plenty of space between each mound, and flatten slightly with the back of a spoon.

6 Bake on the middle shelf of the oven for about 12 minutes, or until the edges of the Florentines are tinged golden brown. Remove from the oven and leave to cool on the baking sheets until crisp.

7. **Melt** the 175g dark and 75g white chocolate separately in heatproof glass or ceramic bowls, either set over pans of barely simmering water. Stir until smooth, remove from the heat and leave to cool slightly. **Dip** the underside of each Florentine into the melted dark chocolate so that they have an even layer.

8. Spoon the melted white chocolate into a disposable **piping** bag, snip the end into a fine nozzle and drizzle over the dark chocolate. Leave until the chocolate has set and hardened before serving..

Linzer Jammy Dodgers

These crumbly, nutty sandwich biscuits can be stamped into whatever shape takes your fancy – just make sure you can see the jam and they are dusted with icing sugar.

100g blanched hazelnuts
250g plain flour, plus extra for rolling out
225g unsalted butter, at room temperature
100g caster sugar
50g icing sugar
3 medium egg yolks
1 teaspoon vanilla extract
½ teaspoon baking powder
pinch of salt
4–5 tablespoons good-quality raspberry jam
icing sugar, for dusting

1. Tip the hazelnuts into a food-processor, add 1 tablespoon of the flour and whizz until finely ground. Adding the flour will prevent the nuts becoming oily as they are ground.

2. Cream together the butter, caster sugar and icing sugar until pale, light and fluffy – this will be quickest and easiest using a free-standing mixer fitted with the creamer/paddle attachment. Scrape down the sides of the mixing bowl using a rubber spatula. Add the egg yolks one at a time, mixing between each one, and then add the vanilla extract and mix again until combined. *Continued*

Try Something Different

Use ground almonds or pistachios instead of the hazelnuts. Replace the raspberry jam with apricot jam, or use three different types of jam for a colourful assortment of biscuits. For a chocolatey hit, **sandwich** the biscuits with chocolate and hazelnut spread or dulce de leche, or with a thin layer of chocolate bourbon buttercream – you will need about the same amount as that given on page 114.

HANDS-ON TIME:
15 minutes,
plus 1 hour chilling

BAKING TIME:
10 minutes

MAKES:
about 24
sandwiched biscuits

SPECIAL EQUIPMENT:
2 baking sheets,
6–7cm round
cookie cutter,
2cm round cookie
cutter (or use smaller
shaped cutters)

METHOD USED:
Creamed method,
page 25

3. Sift the remaining plain flour, baking powder and salt into the bowl. Add the ground hazelnuts and slowly mix into the creamed mixture until smooth. Flatten the dough into a disc, wrap in clingfilm and chill for 1 hour until firm. **Line** two baking sheets with baking paper.

4. On a lightly floured work surface roll half of the dough out to a thickness of 2mm. Stamp out biscuits using a 6–7cm round cookie cutter. Re-shape any leftover dough into a ball, re-roll and cut out more biscuits. Repeat with the other half of the dough.

5. Arrange the uncooked biscuits on the lined baking sheets and using smaller cutters, stamp out **shapes** from the middle of half the cookies. Chill again for 15 minutes while you preheat the oven to 170°C (150°C fan), Gas 3.

6. Bake the biscuits in batches on the middle shelf of the oven for about 12–14 minutes, or until pale golden brown. Cool on the baking sheets for 2 minutes and then carefully transfer to a cooling rack.

7. Once the biscuits are completely cold, spread a scant teaspoon of jam onto the solid biscuits leaving a 1cm border around the edge. Dust the biscuits for the top of the **sandwich** with icing sugar and press onto each jam-covered biscuit.

Chocolate Digestives

Chocolate digestives are especially good when home-made. You can use dark or milk chocolate here or an equal mix of both – but always use 70 per cent cocoa solids dark chocolate.

175g plain wholemeal flour
100g medium oatmeal
75g plain flour, plus extra for rolling out
½ teaspoon bicarbonate of soda
pinch of salt
200g chilled unsalted butter, diced
80g soft light brown sugar
3 tablespoons milk
225g milk or dark chocolate (or a combination of both)
1 teaspoon sunflower or groundnut oil

1. Sift the wholemeal flour, oatmeal, plain flour, bicarbonate of soda and salt into a large mixing bowl. Any bran left in the sieve can be tipped back into the bowl. Add the diced butter and **rub** into the dry ingredients using your hands. You can also do this in a free-standing mixer fitted with the creamer attachment. When there are no visible flecks of butter remaining and the mixture is the texture of coarse sand, add the soft light brown sugar and mix to combine.

2. Make a well in the middle of the mixture, add the milk and use a palette knife to bring the dough together into clumps.
Continued

Need a little skill

HANDS-ON TIME:
10 minutes,
plus 1 hour chilling

BAKING TIME:
12 minutes

MAKES:
30 biscuits

SPECIAL EQUIPMENT:
2 baking sheets,
7cm plain round cutter

METHOD USED:
Rubbed-in method,
page 22

Try Something Different

Use wholemeal spelt flour in place of regular wholemeal flour. For a savoury version to serve with crumbly blue cheese such as Stilton, reduce the amount of sugar to 40g and omit the chocolate coating.

3. Very gently knead the dough in your hands, just to bring the dough into a neat, smooth ball. Try not to overwork the dough otherwise the resulting biscuits will be tough rather than crisp and crumbly. Flatten the dough into a disc, wrap in clingfilm and chill for 1 hour until firm.

4. **Line** two baking sheets with baking paper.

5. Lightly dust the work surface with plain flour and roll the chilled dough out to a thickness of 2–3mm. Using the cutter, stamp out as many rounds from the dough as you can and arrange on the prepared baking sheets, leaving a little space between each one. Gather any scraps and off-cuts together into a ball, re-roll and stamp out more biscuits. Prick each biscuit a couple of times with a fork and chill for 20 minutes while you preheat the oven to 170°C (150°C), Gas 3.

6. Bake the digestives on the middle shelf of the oven for about 11 minutes, until firm and light gold in colour. Cool on the trays for about 3 minutes then transfer to a wire cooling rack until cold and crisp.

7. Chop the 225g chocolate into chunks and tip into a heatproof glass or ceramic bowl. Add the 1 teaspoon of oil and place the bowl over a pan of barely simmering water to **melt**, making sure the bottom of the bowl doesn't touch the water. Stir occasionally until smooth and then remove from the heat and leave to cool slightly.

8. **Dip** the underside of each digestive biscuit into the melted chocolate, allow any excess chocolate to drip back into the bowl.

9. Place the digestive, chocolate side uppermost, either back on the wire rack or on a sheet of baking paper. Before the chocolate sets dip the flat side of the tines of a fork across each biscuit to leave ripples in the chocolate. Leave until the chocolate has set before serving or storing in an airtight container.

Almond, Pistachio and Rosewater Biscuits

These crumbly, nutty mounds are known as Mexican Wedding Cakes or polvorones, but this recipe nods to the Middle East with rosewater, cardamom and cinnamon.

100g blanched almonds
50g pistachios (shelled and unsalted)
250g plain flour
5 green cardamom pods
125g unsalted butter, at room temperature

100g caster sugar
1–2 teaspoons rosewater
½ teaspoon ground cinnamon
pinch of salt
150g icing sugar

HANDS-ON TIME:
20 minutes,
plus 1hour chilling

BAKING TIME:
14 minutes

MAKES:
about 30 biscuits

SPECIAL EQUIPMENT:
2 baking sheets

METHOD USED:
Creamed method,
page 25

1. Preheat the oven to 170°C (150°C fan), Gas 3.

2. Tip the blanched almonds onto a baking sheet and toast in the oven for 4–5 minutes, until very pale golden. Watch them carefully so they don't brown too much. Leave until cold and turn the oven off for the time being.

3. Once the almonds are completely cold, tip them into a food-processor, add the pistachios and flour and whizz until finely ground. Put to one side.

4. Pound the cardamom pods using a pestle and mortar to release the small black seeds from the husks. Discard the husks and continue to pound the seeds until finely ground.

5. Cream the butter with the caster sugar until soft, pale and light – this is easiest and quickest using a free-standing mixer fitted with a creamer/paddle attachment. Scrape down the sides of the bowl with a rubber spatula from time to time. Add the rosewater and mix again.

6. Sift the remaining flour, cinnamon salt into the bowl, add the ground nuts and crushed cardamom seeds and mix again until thoroughly combined. Scoop the dough into a clean bowl, cover with clingfilm and chill for 1–2 hours.

7. Preheat the oven to 170°C (150°C fan), Gas 3 and **line** two baking sheets with baking paper. Tip the 150g icing sugar into a large, shallow bowl.

8. Using a dessertspoon and your hands, scoop up walnut-sized nuggets of dough and roll into balls. Arrange on the lined baking sheets, leaving a little space between each one to allow for spreading, and bake on the middle shelf of the oven for about 12–14 minutes, until firm and pale golden brown.

9. Leave the biscuits to cool on the baking sheets for 10 minutes and then toss them in the icing sugar to coat. Transfer to a wire rack and leave until cold before dusting with more icing sugar to serve.

Stained Glass Biscuits

These cookies look beautiful hanging at a window, the light shining through the 'stained glass'. Try to fill the holes neatly so you don't scatter sweets over the dough or overfill the holes.

225g unsalted butter, softened
150g icing sugar
1 medium egg, beaten
1 egg yolk
1 teaspoon vanilla extract
350g plain flour, plus extra for rolling out

1 teaspoon ground ginger
1 teaspoon ground cinnamon
pinch of salt
1 tablespoon milk, if needed
200g boiled sweets in assorted flavours and colours

1 Using a free-standing mixer fitted with the creamer/paddle attachment, cream together the softened butter and icing sugar until pale and light, scraping down the sides of the bowl from time to time with a rubber spatula. You can also use an electric hand-held whisk or a wooden spoon and plenty of muscle power. Add the whole egg and egg yolk and vanilla extract and mix again until thoroughly combined.

Continued

HANDS-ON TIME:
12 minutes,
plus 1–2 hours
chilling

BAKING TIME:
12 minutes

MAKES:
24 biscuits

SPECIAL EQUIPMENT:
snowflake or star-shaped cutters in assorted sizes, 2 baking sheets

METHOD USED:
Creamed method,
page 25

Sift the 350g plain flour with the
1 teaspoon of ground ginger and
1 teaspoon of ground cinnamon and
a pinch of salt into the bowl and mix
again adding a drop of milk if needed
to make the dough come together
smoothly.

Gather the dough into a ball, flatten
into a disc and wrap in clingfilm. Chill for
a couple of hours, or until firm.

Meanwhile, divide the 200g boiled
sweets into separate colours, and
crush each colour separately into small
pieces in a pestle and mortar. Wash the
pestle and mortar between each colour.
Alternatively, you could just place each
colour in a double thickness of freezer
bags, and crush them using a rolling pin.

Preheat the oven to 180°C (160°C
fan), 350°F, Gas 4 and **line** two baking
sheets with baking paper.

6 Lightly dust the work surface with plain flour and roll out the dough until it is 3mm thick. Using the snowflake or star-shaped cookie cutters, stamp out **shapes** in assorted sizes and arrange on the prepared baking sheets. Stamp out and remove smaller shapes from the middle of each biscuit, leaving a neat hole in the middle. Carefully and neatly fill the holes in the snowflakes with one colour of the crushed boiled sweets, filling them just shallower than the

depth of the biscuits. Bake in batches on the middle shelf of the preheated oven for about 12 minutes, until the cookies are pale golden and the boiled sweets have melted and filled the holes.

7 Gather any dough scraps into a neat ball, re-roll and shape more biscuits and fill and bake as before. Leave the biscuits to cool on the baking sheets until they are firm and the 'stained glass' centres have hardened.

Custard
Creams

These old school favourites have a few added extras that you won't find in shop-bought packs – a double hit of custard powder in the biscuit dough and also in the buttercream.

225g plain flour, plus extra for rolling out
½ teaspoon baking powder
50g custard powder
50g icing sugar
pinch of salt
175g unsalted butter, chilled and diced
1 tablespoon milk
1 teaspoon vanilla extract

For the filling
50g white chocolate, chopped
100g unsalted butter, softened
50g icing sugar
1 tablespoon custard powder
1 teaspoon vanilla extract

1. Sift the flour, baking powder, custard powder, icing sugar and salt into the bowl of a food-processor and whizz for 30 seconds to combine. Add the diced butter and process until it has been completely rubbed into the dry ingredients. You can also do this step using a free-standing mixer fitted with a creamer/paddle attachment or **rub** the butter into the dry ingredients using your hands.

2. Add the milk and vanilla extract and mix again just until the dough starts to clump together. Tip the dough into a large mixing bowl and use your hands to squeeze and very lightly knead the dough into a smooth ball but don't overwork the mixture or your resulting cookies will shrink and toughen as they bake. Flatten into a disc, cover with cling film and chill for 1 hour.

3. Preheat the oven to 180°C (160°C fan), Gas 4 and **line** two baking sheets with baking paper.
Continued

Try Something Different

These biscuits can be made with various flavours. Add desiccated coconut to the custard, or a few drops of lemon juice, or cocoa powder.

HANDS-ON TIME:
15 minutes,
plus 1 hour chilling

BAKING TIME:
10 minutes

MAKES:
20 biscuits

SPECIAL EQUIPMENT:
2 baking sheets,
5cm square cookie cutters

METHOD USED:
Rubbed-in method,
page 24

4 Lightly dust the work surface with plain flour and roll out the dough to a thickness of 2mm. Using cookie cutters, stamp out **shapes** and arrange on the lined baking sheets. Gather any scraps of dough together and shape into a smooth-ish ball, then re-roll and stamp out more cookies. Press decorative indent patterns into the top of each cookie (one trick is to use the lemon zesting side of a box grater) and bake on the middle shelf of the oven for about 10–11 minutes, or until firm and starting to turn very pale golden at the edges.

5 Remove from the oven and leave the biscuits to rest on the baking sheet for few minutes and then transfer to a wire rack to cool completely.

6. Meanwhile prepare the custard filling. **Melt** the 50g white chocolate in a small heatproof bowl, over a pan of barely simmering water. (Make sure the bottom of the bowl doesn't touch the water.) Remove from the heat, stir until smooth and leave to cool. Beat the 100g butter, 50g icing sugar, 1 tablespoon of custard powder and 1 teaspoon of vanilla extract together until smooth, pale and light. Add the cooled, melted white chocolate and stir until smooth.

7. Use a palette knife to spread the underside of half of the cookies with buttercream and **sandwich** with the remaining cookies, making sure that they are pretty-side outermost.

Malted Milk Sandwich Biscuits

Malty, sweet, light and crisp, these biscuits can either be filled with a rich chocolate buttercream or eaten singly and simply, just coated in a melted chocolate glaze.

HANDS-ON TIME:
10 minutes,
plus 1 hour chilling

BAKING TIME:
11 minutes

MAKES:
about 24
sandwiched
biscuits

SPECIAL
EQUIPMENT:
2 baking sheets,
5–6cm round cutter

METHOD USED:
Creamed method,
page 25

For the biscuits

150g unsalted butter, at room temperature
100g caster sugar
1 teaspoon vanilla extract or vanilla bean paste
1 medium egg
1 medium egg yolk
250g plain flour
75g malted milk powder
½ teaspoon baking powder
pinch of salt

For the malted chocolate buttercream

75g dark chocolate, preferably a minimum of 70 per cent cocoa solids
75g unsalted butter, at room temperature
50g icing sugar, sifted
2 tablespoons malted milk powder
1 tablespoon milk

1. Cream the softened butter and caster sugar until pale and light – this is easiest using a free-standing mixer fitted with the creamer/paddle attachment. Scrape down the sides of the bowl from time to time using a rubber spatula. Add the vanilla and mix again to combine.

2. In a small bowl lightly beat the egg and egg yolk together and gradually add to the creamed butter mixture, mixing well between each addition and scraping down the sides of the mixing bowl. Sift the plain flour, malted milk powder, baking powder and salt directly into the bowl and mix again until smooth and thoroughly combined. Do not over-mix the dough as this

will result in tough rather than crisp cookies. Gather the dough into a ball, flatten into a disc and wrap in clingfilm. Chill for 1 hour until firm.

3. Preheat the oven to 170°C (150°C fan), Gas 3 and **line** two baking sheets with baking paper.

4. Lightly dust the work surface with plain flour and roll the dough out to a thickness of 2mm. Stamp out biscuits using the plain round cutter.
Continued

Try Something Different

Omit the buttercream filling and instead **dip** one side of each biscuit in **melted** milk or dark chocolate.

5. Arrange the biscuits on the prepared baking sheets leaving a little space between each one. If you like, gently press the top (thicker) side of a smaller cutter into the discs to make a rim, and use the end of the skewer to indent little button holes in the centre.

6. Bake in batches on the middle shelf of the oven for about 11 minutes, until firm and golden at the edges. (Swap the baking sheets around halfway through baking to ensure that they bake evenly.)

Leave to cool on the trays for a few minutes before transferring to wire racks to cool completely.

7. Meanwhile prepare the malted chocolate buttercream. Break the 75g chocolate into chunks and place in a heatproof ceramic or glass bowl. Set the bowl over a pan of barely simmering water (make sure the bottom of the bowl does not touch the water) to **melt** the chocolate. Stir until smooth, remove from the heat and leave to

cool slightly. Tip the 75g butter into a bowl and beat until soft and light, either using a free-standing mixer, hand-held electric whisk or with a wooden spoon. Gradually add the 50g sifted icing sugar, one tablespoon at a time, and mix until really pale and light.

8. In another small bowl mix the 2 tablespoons of malted milk powder with the 1 tablespoon of milk to a smooth paste. Add to the creamed butter and icing sugar along with the melted, cooled chocolate. Beat until smooth and thoroughly combined.

9. Turn half of the malted milk biscuits upside down and top with a teaspoon of the malted chocolate buttercream. **Sandwich** with a naked biscuit and press gently together. Leave until set firm before serving.

Chocolate Bourbon Creams

Two rich, crisp chocolate biscuits sandwiched together with a layer of decadent chocolate buttercream – these are the biscuits of fond teatime childhood memories.

HANDS-ON TIME:
10 minutes,
plus 1 hour chilling

BAKING TIME:
12 minutes

MAKES:
about 24
sandwiched
biscuits

SPECIAL
EQUIPMENT:
2 baking sheets
Bourbon biscuit
cutter (optional)

METHOD USED:
Creamed method,
page 25

For the biscuits

125g unsalted butter, at room temperature
100g caster sugar, plus extra for sprinkling
1 tablespoon golden syrup
½ teaspoon vanilla extract
1 large egg yolk
225g plain flour, plus extra for dusting
30g cocoa powder
½ teaspoon bicarbonate of soda
pinch of salt
1 tablespoon milk

For the chocolate buttercream

150g unsalted butter, at room temperature
225g icing sugar
75g cocoa powder
1–2 tablespoons milk

1. Cream the softened butter and caster sugar until pale and light – this is easiest and quickest using a free-standing mixer fitted with a creamer/paddle attachment. Scrape down the sides of the bowl from time to time using a rubber spatula. Add the golden syrup, vanilla extract and egg yolk and mix again until smooth and thoroughly combined.

2. Sift the flour, cocoa powder, bicarbonate of soda and salt into the bowl. Add the milk and mix again until the dough is smooth. Shape into a ball, flatten into a disc and wrap in clingfilm. Chill for 1 hour to firm up.

Continued

Try Something Different

For a white chocolate filling simply replace the cocoa powder with **melted** and cooled white chocolate and replace the milk with 1 teaspoon of vanilla extract.

3. Cover two baking sheets with baking paper. Lightly dust the work surface with plain flour and roll out the chilled dough to a neat rectangle with a thickness of 2mm. Using a ruler as a guide, cut the dough into neat 4 x 8cm rectangles, or use a rectangular cutter. Arrange on the prepared baking sheets, leaving a little space between each biscuit. Gather the dough off-cuts into a ball and re-roll to make more shapes.

4. Prick with a fork or stamp bourbon lettering across each biscuit and chill again for 15 minutes while you preheat the oven to 180°C (160°C fan), Gas 4.

5. Sprinkle the biscuits with caster sugar and bake in batches on the middle shelf of the oven for 10–12 minutes, until firm and crisp. Cool the bourbons on the baking sheet for a few minutes and then carefully transfer to a wire rack to cool completely.

6 Meanwhile prepare the chocolate buttercream filling. Beat the 150g butter in a bowl with a wooden spoon until soft and light. Sift the 225g icing sugar and 75g cocoa powder into a bowl and gradually add to the creamed butter, mixing well between each addition until smooth. Add the 1–2 tablespoons of milk, a little at a time, until the buttercream is a good spreading consistency.

7 Turn half of the bourbon biscuits upside down and spread with a teaspoon of the buttercream. Top with another biscuit gently pressing the two together.

Biscotti

Serve these crisp Italian cookies alongside a creamy dessert for a crunchy contrast, or eat after dinner alongside an espresso or dunked into a glass of vin santo.

100g whole almonds
275g plain flour
150g caster sugar
½ teaspoon baking powder
1 teaspoon anise seeds
pinch of salt
finely grated zest of ½ orange
finely grated zest of ½ lemon
2 large eggs
1 tablespoon Marsala or orange juice
1 teaspoon vanilla extract

1. Preheat the oven to 170°C (150°C fan), Gas 3 and **line** a large baking sheet with baking paper.

2. Roughly chop the almonds and tip into a large mixing bowl with the plain flour, caster sugar, baking powder, anise seeds and salt. Add the orange and lemon zests and mix well to thoroughly combine. Make a well in the centre.

3. **Beat** together the eggs, Marsala or orange juice and vanilla extract in a separate bowl. Pour into the well in the centre of the dry ingredients and mix until thoroughly combined and the dough comes together into a smooth ball. You will find this easiest initially using a wooden spoon or rubber spatula but then switch to your hands to bring the dough into a smooth ball.
Continued

Try Something Different

Make a chocolate and pistachio version. Follow the recipe above, using the following ingredients: 75g shelled and unsalted pistachios, 230g plain flour, 175g caster sugar, 40g cocoa powder, ½ tsp baking powder, pinch of salt, 75g dark chocolate chips, 1 tsp finely grated orange zest, 2 large eggs, 1 large egg yolk, 1 tbsp Marsala or orange juice and 1 tsp vanilla extract. **Dip** half of each biscotti in either white or dark **melted** chocolate. Add a handful of either dried sour cherries or cranberries to the dough along with the nuts.

Need a little skill

HANDS-ON TIME:
10 minutes,

BAKING TIME:
1 hour

MAKES:
about 30 biscuits

SPECIAL EQUIPMENT:
2 baking sheets

Lightly dust your hands with plain flour and divide the dough into two even pieces. Roll out each piece into a log roughly 20cm long and 4–5cm in diameter. Arrange on the prepared baking sheet, placing the logs well apart to allow for spreading during baking.

Cook on the middle shelf of the oven for 20–25 minutes, or until light golden in colour, turning the tray around after 10–15 minutes to ensure that the logs brown evenly. Remove from the oven and leave to cool for 30–45 minutes, turn the oven down to 150°C (130°C fan), Gas 2 and line another baking sheet with a clean piece of baking paper.

6. Using a long serrated or bread knife, cut the cooled biscotti logs on the diagonal into slices, each about 5mm thick. Lay the slices in a single layer on the prepared baking sheets and return to the oven for a further 10 minutes, until pale golden brown and crisp.

Turn the biscotti over and swap the baking sheets around halfway through the baking time to ensure that they crisp evenly. Transfer to a wire rack to cool and keep in an airtight container until required.

Millionaire's Shortbread

These indulgent squares have something for everyone: a crisp, buttery shortbread base, topped with luscious, slightly salted caramel and a thin layer of dark chocolate.

For the shortbread
125g plain flour
pinch of salt
125g unsalted butter, chilled and diced
50g icing sugar

For the caramel
125g caster sugar
75g golden syrup
50g light muscovado sugar
250ml double cream
½ teaspoon vanilla bean paste
75g unsalted butter
a pinch of sea salt flakes
25g dark chocolate, finely chopped

For the topping
125g dark chocolate, preferably a minimum of 70 per cent cocoa solids
50g white chocolate

Need a little skill

HANDS-ON TIME:
20 minutes,
plus 2 hours chilling

BAKING TIME:
15 minutes

MAKES:
16 squares

SPECIAL
EQUIPMENT:
20cm square
baking tin

METHOD USED:
Rubbed-in method,
page 22

1. Preheat the oven to 180°C (160°C fan), Gas 4 and **line** the base and sides of the baking tin with baking paper.

2. Start by making the shortbread base. Tip the flour and salt into either a large mixing bowl or the bowl of a food-processor. Add the diced butter and **rub** into the flour, either using your fingertips or the pulse button on the food-processor. When there are no visible specks of butter remaining add the icing sugar and mix again to combine. Continue pulsing or rubbing in until the dough just starts to clump together.

3. Tip the shortbread mix into the prepared tin and press level using your fingertips or the back of a spoon.

Continued

4 Bake on the middle shelf of the oven for 12–14 minutes, or until golden brown. Remove from the oven and leave to cool.

5 To make the caramel, tip the 125g caster sugar, 75g golden syrup and 50g light muscovado sugar into a medium sized saucepan. Add the 250ml double cream, ½ teaspoon vanilla bean paste and 75g unsalted butter. Set the pan over a low heat and, stirring frequently, melt the butter and dissolve the sugar.

6 When the mixture is smooth, pop a sugar thermometer into the pan and raise the heat slightly to bring the caramel to the boil. Continue cooking at a steady but not furious pace, stirring from time to time to prevent the caramel scorching on the bottom of the pan. When the caramel reaches 120°C or just over the soft ball stage, slide the pan off the heat. If you don't have a sugar thermometer you can test the caramel by dropping a ½ teaspoonful of the caramel into a cup of very cold water – it should set into a firm but not hardball.

7 Remove the thermometer from the pan and when the bubbling subsides add the chopped chocolate and a good pinch of sea salt flakes. Stir to

combine and pour the caramel into the tin over the baked shortbread. The caramel should cover the shortbread in a smooth layer. Leave until completely cold and set firm.

8. Finely chop the 125g dark chocolate for the topping and tip into a heatproof glass or ceramic bowl. Set over a pan of barely simmering water – do not allow the bottom of the bowl to touch the water or you could scorch the chocolate. Stir until smooth and completely **melted**, then remove from the heat and leave to cool for about 10 minutes.

9. Pour over the top of the caramel and spread the chocolate in an even layer using an offset palette knife; leave until set firm. Melt the 50g white chocolate in the same way, stirring until smooth. Remove from the heat and leave to cool slightly before spooning it into a disposable piping bag. Snip the end into a fine point and **pipe** lines of white chocolate over the dark chocolate and drag the point of a cocktail stick or wooden skewer through the lines to make a delicate feathered pattern in the chocolate. Leave until set before cutting into squares to serve.

Brandy Snaps

Success in making these delicate brandy snaps is down to timing; you need to work quickly to shape them while pliable, but when cool enough to handle. Practice makes perfect.

Need a little skill

HANDS-ON TIME:
10 minutes

BAKING TIME:
9 minutes

MAKES:
about 20 biscuits

SPECIAL
EQUIPMENT:
2–3 baking sheets,
4 wooden spoons

METHOD USED:
Melt and mix
method, page 24

sunflower oil, for greasing
125g unsalted butter
125g caster sugar
125g (4 level tablespoons) golden syrup
pinch of salt
125g plain flour
1 teaspoon ground ginger
1 tablespoon lemon juice

1. Preheat the oven to 190°C (170°C fan), Gas 5 and **line** two or three baking sheets with baking paper. Using kitchen paper, lightly grease the handles of four wooden spoons with a little sunflower oil.

2. Place the butter, caster sugar, golden syrup and salt into a small, heavy-based pan. You'll find it easier to measure the golden syrup if you heat the measuring spoon in a mug of boiling hot water for a minute or so beforehand. Heat the mixture gently, stirring from time to time until it is smooth and the butter has melted and the sugar completely dissolved. Remove from the heat and leave to cool for 1 minute.

3. Sift the flour and ground ginger together into the pan with the lemon juice. Beat with a wooden spoon until smooth and then leave to rest for a further 2 minutes.

Continued

Try Something Different

For a more indulgent treat fill the cooled brandy snaps. Whip 300ml double cream to soft peaks with either ½ tsp vanilla bean paste or the finely grated zest of ½ orange, one tablespoon of brandy and a pinch of ground cinnamon. Spoon into a **piping** bag fitted with a large star nozzle and pipe the cream into each end of the brandy snaps. Serve immediately.

Spoon level dessertspoons of the mixture onto the prepared baking sheets, spacing each mound well apart and with no more than four brandy snaps on each sheet as they will spread during baking. You will also find it hard to juggle shaping more than four brandy snaps at a time.

Bake in batches on the middle shelf of the oven for 8–9 minutes, until the brandy snaps are thin, lacy in texture and a light amber colour. Remove from the oven and leave to cool for about 20–30 seconds to firm up slightly.

Working quickly, slide a palette knife under one brandy snap and carefully drape one end of the biscuit over the handle of a wooden spoon with the top of the biscuit uppermost. Turn the handle of the spoon around so that the

brandy snap forms a neat tube with the spoon handle inside – use your other hand to gently press the biscuit into shape. Rest the spoon over an empty bowl to allow the brandy snap to cool and harden.

7 Repeat with the remaining baked biscuits. Cool for about 3 minutes and then carefully slide the brandy snaps off the wooden spoons and onto a wire rack. If you leave the biscuits on the spoons for too long you may find that they are too crisp and will be tricky to remove from the spoons without breaking.

8 Repeat the baking and shaping until all the mixture is used up. **Store** in layers between sheets of baking paper in an airtight container for up to 3 days

Jaffa Cakes

These biscuits (or are they cakes?) are elevated to lofty heights when home-made with the best ingredients.

For the orange jelly

3 leaves platinum-grade leaf gelatine
225ml freshly squeezed orange juice
150g shredless orange marmalade

For the chocolate layer

200g dark chocolate, preferably a minimum of 70 per cent cocoa solids, chopped
1 teaspoon sunflower or groundnut oil, plus extra for greasing

For the cake bases

100g unsalted butter, at room temperature, plus extra for greasing
75g caster sugar
1 medium egg
1 medium egg yolk
½ teaspoon vanilla extract
60g plain flour
¼ teaspoon baking powder
40g ground almonds
pinch of salt
2 teaspoons milk

Need a little skill

HANDS-ON TIME:
2 hours,
plus overnight
setting

BAKING TIME:
12 minutes

MAKES:
20–24 biscuits

SPECIAL
EQUIPMENT:
20 × 30cm
baking tin,
2 × 12-hole
muffin tins,
4–5cm plain
round cutter,
palette knife

METHOD USED:
Creamed method,
page 25

1. Prepare the orange jelly first. Lightly grease the 20 × 30cm baking tin with oil and **line** the base and sides with a piece of clingfilm. Soak the 3 gelatine leaves in a bowl of cold water for 10 minutes, until soft and floppy.

2. Pour the orange juice and marmalade into a small pan and heat gently to melt the marmalade. Bring to the boil and then remove from the heat. Lift the softened gelatine leaves from the cold water, blot briefly on kitchen paper or a clean tea towel to remove any excess water and add to the hot orange juice. **Whisk** to melt and then pour into the clingfilm-lined baking tin. Leave until cool and then chill for at least 4 hours or preferably overnight until set firm.

3. Preheat the oven to 170°C (150°C fan), Gas 3 and grease the holes of the muffin tins with a little butter. Line the base of each muffin cup with a small disc of buttered baking paper.

Continued

Cream the 100g butter with the 75g caster sugar until light and fluffy. Gradually add the 1 egg and 1 egg yolk, a little at a time, scraping down the sides of the bowl with a rubber spatula between additions. Add the ½ teaspoon of vanilla extract and mix again. Sift the 60g flour, ¼ teaspoon of baking powder, 40g ground almonds and a pinch of salt into the bowl. Add the 2 teaspoons of milk and mix again until smooth.

Divide the mixture between the prepared muffin tins – each muffin cup should have just over 1 teaspoon of mixture; you should have enough batter to make 20 cakes. Spread level with either an offset palette knife or the back of a teaspoon and bake on the middle shelf of the oven for about 12 minutes, until pale golden at the edges.

Run a palette knife around the edge of each cake to release it and turn out onto a wire rack. Peel off the baking

8

paper circles, turn the cakes the right side up and leave to cool completely.

7. Using the clingfilm to help you, carefully lift the orange jelly from the tray and onto a board. Using the 4–5cm cutter, stamp out circles from the jelly. Carefully lift the jelly circles off the clingfilm using a palette knife and place on top of each sponge base.

8. Chop the 200g chocolate, tip into a heatproof bowl and add the 1 teaspoon of sunflower oil. **Melt** the chocolate by placing the bowl over a pan of barely simmer water, making sure the bottom of the bowl doesn't touch the water. Stir until smooth, remove from the heat and leave to cool for a few minutes. Carefully spoon melted chocolate over each jelly-topped cake, allowing it to completely cover the jelly and any exposed sponge. Press the tines of a fork into the chocolate to make decorative ridges and leave in a cool place until the chocolate has set firm.

Lemony
Spiced
and Iced
Biscuits

Let your imagination run wild, and shape these as numbers and letters or fancy dancing shoes and Fabergé eggs.

225g unsalted butter, softened
150g icing sugar
1 medium egg, lightly beaten
grated zest of ½ unwaxed lemon
1 teaspoon vanilla bean paste
350g plain flour, plus extra for rolling out
pinch of salt

For the icing
500g royal icing sugar
75–100ml water
pink and blue food colouring pastes

Up for a challenge

HANDS-ON TIME:
30 minutes, plus chilling and decorating

BAKING TIME:
12 minutes

MAKES:
about 20 biscuits, depending on cutters used

SPECIAL EQUIPMENT:
baking sheets, large number cutters, disposable piping bags

METHOD USED:
Creamed method, page 25

1 In a large bowl cream the softened butter and icing sugar until pale, light and fluffy. This will be easiest and quickest using a free-standing mixer fitted with a creamer/paddle attachment but can also be done by hand with a wooden spoon. Scrape down the sides of the bowl with a rubber spatula and gradually add the beaten egg, mixing well until smooth. Add the lemon zest and vanilla bean paste and mix again.

2 Sift the plain flour and salt into the bowl and mix until smooth. Shape the mixture into a disc, wrap in clingfilm and chill for a couple of hours or until firm. **Line** two baking sheets with baking paper.

3 Lightly dust the work surface with plain flour and roll the cookie dough out to a thickness of 2–3mm. Using the number cookie cutters, stamp out biscuits and arrange on the prepared baking sheets. Gather any off-cuts, re-roll and stamp out more biscuits. Chill for 20 minutes while you preheat the oven to 180°C (160°C fan), 350°F, Gas 4.

4 Bake the biscuits in batches on the middle shelf of the oven for 10–12 minutes, or until pale golden. Remove from the oven and cool on the baking sheets until firm before carefully transferring to a wire rack to cool completely.

Continued

5 Sift the 500g royal icing sugar into a bowl and gradually add the 75–100ml water – you want just enough to make a smooth, spreadable icing. Beat or **whisk** until smooth and lump-free. The icing should be thick enough to hold a firm ribbon trail when the spoon or whisk is lifted from the bowl.

6 Divide the icing between 3 separate bowls. Leave one bowl of icing white and cover with clingfilm until ready to use. Using a wooden skewer or cocktail stick add pink food colouring paste in small increments to one bowl and mix well until the desired shade is reached. Always add the colour a little at a time, mixing well between each addition, it's easier to add more colouring to build up the depth of colour and impossible to take it away if you've been a little too enthusiastic! Cover and set aside. In the same way add blue food colouring to the third bowl of icing, cover and set aside.

7 Now you can fill your **piping** bag. Spoon 2–3 tablespoons of the white icing into a piping bag and squeeze or press the icing towards the nozzle end. Twist the open top to seal and prevent any icing escaping all over your hands then use sharp scissors to snip the nozzle end into a fine point. Taking

one biscuit at a time, and with a steady hand, pipe a fine, continuous line of white icing around the top outside edge of the biscuit and another round the inside edge of each shape – this inside line only applies to numbers that have a hole in the middle such as 4, 6, 8 and 9. This will create a section in the middle of the biscuit that will later be flooded with coloured icing. Repeat with all of the biscuits and then leave the icing to dry for 30 minutes.

8 Divide the biscuits in half – half will be iced pink and the other half with the blue icing. Add a drop more water to the reserved pink icing to make it just slightly runnier than the piping icing – about the consistency of double cream – and use a teaspoon to spoon the icing into the middle of the outline that you have previously piped. Using a small palette knife, carefully spread the icing in a smooth layer to fill the outline. Leave to dry for about 2 minutes and then pipe white polka dots all over the pink icing. Repeat this icing and dotting until all of the biscuits are fully decorated in either pink or blue icing.

9 Leave for at least 1 hour for the icing to dry and set firm before serving.

Mochaccino Macarons

Mastering macarons is not as tricky as you'd think – the skill is in piping the mixture into neat and even circles. Eat them the day after they are made for the best flavour and chewy texture.

Up for a challenge

HANDS-ON TIME:
20 minutes,
plus 30 minutes
reasting

BAKING TIME:
12–13 minutes

MAKES:
about 30 biscuits

SPECIAL
EQUIPMENT:
4cm plain round
cookie cutter,
2 baking sheets,
large piping bag,
1cm plain round
piping nozzle

For the macaron shells

175g ground almonds
175g icing sugar
150g egg whites (about 4 medium egg whites – keep 2 yolks for use later)
pinch of salt
200g caster sugar
2 teaspoons instant espresso powder/granules
½ teaspoon brown food colouring paste

For the mocha cream filling

100g dark chocolate, preferably a minimum of 70 percent cocoa solids, chopped
2 large egg yolks
50g caster sugar
½ teaspoon instant espresso powder/granules
150g unsalted butter, at room temperature

1. Take two sheets of baking paper and, using the cookie cutter as a guide, draw around the cutter to make 30 evenly spaced, 4cm circles on each piece of baking paper. Try to keep the circles in neat lines, leaving a little space between each. Turn the paper over so that the pencil lines are now on the underside – you should be able to see them through the paper – and place one piece on each baking sheet. Fit the large piping bag with the 1cm round nozzle, twist the bag just above the nozzle and sit the bag in a jug so that the top is folded back and open wide.

2. Tip the ground almonds and icing sugar into a food-processor and blitz for 30 seconds to 1 minute to thoroughly mix. Add 70g of the egg whites and pulse again until combined into a smooth, thick paste.

3. Tip the remaining egg whites and a pinch of salt into a medium-large heatproof glass or ceramic mixing bowl and add the caster sugar. Dissolve the coffee in 1 tablespoon of boiling water, add to the egg whites and set the bowl over a pan of simmering water. Be sure that the bottom of the bowl does not come into contact with the water or you will scramble the egg whites. Beat constantly with a balloon whisk or electric hand whisk for 3–4 minutes until the sugar has completely dissolved and the egg whites are glossy white, silky smooth, thickened enough to hold a ribbon trail and are hot to the touch.

4. Quickly scoop the meringue mixture into the bowl of a free-standing mixer, add the brown food colouring and **whisk** over a medium-high heat for a further 3 minutes, until the meringue is glossy and has cooled and thickened enough to hold a firm ribbon trail when the whisk is lifted from the bowl.
Continued

5. Using a rubber spatula, scoop the almond mixture from the food-processor into a bowl (use the one that you used for the bain-marie to save on washing up) and add one quarter of the meringue. **Fold** in using a rubber spatula or large metal spoon to loosen the almond paste. Add this back to the meringue and fold in using large strokes, continuing to mix until thoroughly combined and the mixture resembles thick molten lava that will hold a ribbon trail for about 5 seconds.

6. Working quickly, scoop the mixture into the prepared piping bag and **pipe** 30 even sized macarons onto each baking paper-lined sheet, using the circles as a guide. Sharply bang the baking sheets on the work surface to pop any air bubbles and set aside for about 30 minutes, until a light skin has formed on the surface of each macaron shell. Preheat the oven to 170°C (150°C fan), Gas 3.

7. Bake the macarons, one tray at a time, on the middle shelf of the oven for 12–13 minutes until well risen and crisp with well-defined 'feet'.

8. Remove from the oven and leave to cool completely on the trays while you prepare the mocha cream filling. **Melt** the 100g chocolate in a heatproof bowl over a pan of barely simmering water. Stir until smooth and leave to cool slightly.

9. Place the 2 egg yolks in a medium heatproof glass or ceramic bowl and set aside. Tip the 50g caster sugar into a small pan, add 3 tablespoons of water and set over a low heat to dissolve the sugar. Bring to the boil and simmer for 30 seconds to thicken slightly. Dissolve the ½ teaspoon of instant espresso in 1 teaspoon of boiling water, add to the syrup and pour over the egg yolks, whisking continuously until smooth. Set the bowl over a pan of simmering water and continue to whisk for a further 2–3 minutes until pale and thickened. Remove from the heat and whisk for a further 2–3 minutes until cool.

10. Gradually add the 150g butter, a little at a time and whisking between each addition until smooth. Add the melted chocolate, fold in and leave for 30 minutes to firm up slightly.

11. To assemble the macarons: turn half of the shells over so that they are flat side uppermost and top with a teaspoon of mocha cream. Top with another shell, pressing them gently together so that the cream is visible from the sides. Stack the macarons in a tray, cover with clingfilm and chill overnight before serving.

Cigarettes
Russes

Practice make perfect for these delicate biscuits. The technique needed for rolling these wafers is similar to that used in brandy snaps – just on a finer scale, using a straw.

For the biscuits

75g unsalted butter
4 large egg whites
pinch of salt
150g icing sugar, sifted
1 teaspoon vanilla extract
100g plain flour
1 teaspoon cocoa powder

For the ganache filling

100g dark chocolate, preferably a minimum of 70 per cent cocoa solids, finely chopped
100ml double cream
1 tablespoon light muscovado sugar
drop of vanilla extract
pinch of salt

For the decoration

75g white chocolate
75g dark chocolate, preferably a minimum of 70 per cent cocoa solids
2 tablespoons very finely chopped toasted hazelnuts
2 tablespoons finely chopped blanched pistachios

HANDS-ON TIME:
10 minutes, plus overnight resting

BAKING TIME:
3–4 minutes per baking sheet but 1 hour in total

MAKES:
20–24 biscuits

SPECIAL EQUIPMENT:
plastic ice cream tub lid, several baking sheets, silicone baking mats (optional), disposable piping bags, offset palette knife, 6 drinking straws

1. For best results you will need to make the mixture for these biscuits at least 2 hours (but preferably the day before) you plan to start baking.

2. Melt the butter, either in a small pan over a low heat or in a heatproof bowl in short bursts in the microwave. Set aside to cool slightly.

3. Tip the 4 egg whites and a pinch of salt into a large mixing bowl and beat with a balloon whisk until just foamy. Add the 150g sifted icing sugar and 1 teaspoon of vanilla extract and **whisk** again until smooth. Sift the 100g plain flour into the bowl and beat until combined. Pour the melted butter around the inside edge of the bowl and whisk until the batter is smooth.

4. Spoon 100g of the batter into a small bowl, add the 1 teaspoon of cocoa powder and mix to combine. Cover both bowls with clingfilm and chill for at least 2 hours but preferably overnight.
Continued

143

5. While the batter is resting prepare the plastic template. Take your ice cream tub lid and with the help of a ruler draw an 8 × 12cm rectangle in the middle. Using a craft knife or sharp scissors, cut out the rectangle, leaving a neat hole in the middle of the plastic. This will be your template.

6. Preheat the oven to 180°C (160°C fan), Gas 4 and **line** two baking sheets with baking paper or use silicone baking sheets.

7. You will need to bake these biscuits in batches of no more than two on each sheet, as once they are cooked you will need to work quickly to **shape** them. When you get the hang of shaping them and into a rhythm you'll be able to have two trays in the oven while you are shaping a batch of biscuits.

8. Scoop the chocolate batter into a disposable piping bag and snip the end into a very fine point. Lay your template over one half of the baking paper or silicone baking mat, spoon 1 scant level tablespoon of plain batter

into the middle of the template and use an offset palette knife to quickly spread into a thin, even layer. Lift off the template and repeat on the other side of the baking paper or silicone mat.

9. Now take your disposable piping bag and **pipe** fine diagonal lines of the chocolate batter across each rectangle, keeping the chocolate lines neat and within the edges of the rectangle. Bake on the middle shelf of the oven for about 3–4 minutes, until just starting to brown at the edges.

10. Working quickly, remove the tray from the oven and slide a palette knife underneath each biscuit to loosen them from the paper. Flip the biscuits over and lay a drinking straw along one of the longer edges. Roll the biscuit into a tight spiral around the straw and place on a clean sheet of baking paper, seam side down. Repeat with the second biscuit. Leave these to cool for 2–3 minutes and then carefully pull the straw out of the spiral.

Continued

11. Continue to spread, pipe, bake and roll the biscuits until all of the mixture has been used up. You will need a clean sheet of baking paper each time you bake as it tends to ruckle and crease, making it hard to spread the batter thinly and evenly.

12. Once you have used up all of the batter and the cigarettes are neatly lined up, seam side down, on the lined baking tray, return them to the oven for 1–2 minutes to crisp up further. Leave until cold.

13. Prepare the ganache. Finely chop the 100g chocolate and tip into a bowl. Heat the 100ml cream with the 1 tablespoon of muscovado sugar, drop of vanilla extract and a pinch of salt in a small pan until the sugar has dissolved and the mixture just comes to the boil. Immediately remove from the heat, leave for 30 seconds and then pour over the chopped chocolate. Allow the chocolate to melt in the heat of the cream and then gently stir until smooth. Leave to cool and thicken slightly.

14. Spoon the cooled ganache into a disposable piping bag. Snip the end of the bag into a point and **pipe** the ganache into the middle of each cigarette. Leave until set.

15. **Melt** the 75g white and 75g dark chocolate for the decoration in separate heatproof bowls placed over a pan of barely simmering water (make sure the bottom of the bowl doesn't touch the water). Stir until smooth and leave to cool slightly. Mix together the 2 tablespoons of finely chopped hazelnuts and 2 tablespoons of finely chopped pistachios in a small bowl.

16. **Dip** one end of each filled cigarette into the melted white chocolate and the other end in the melted dark chocolate. Scatter with finely chopped nuts and leave on a clean sheet of baking paper until set.

Chocolate and Vanilla Checkerboard Biscuits

These impressive-looking biscuits require a little precision and care, but once mastered they are easy enough and well worth the effort they take in time and concentration!

For the vanilla dough

125g unsalted butter, at room temperature
75g caster sugar
50g icing sugar
1 teaspoon vanilla extract
1 large egg yolk
200g plain flour, plus extra for rolling out
50g ground almonds (or hazelnuts)
½ teaspoon baking powder
pinch of salt
1 tablespoon milk, plus extra for brushing

For the chocolate dough

125g unsalted butter, at room temperature
75g caster sugar
50g icing sugar
1 teaspoon vanilla extract
1 large egg yolk
175g plain flour
25g cocoa powder
50g ground almonds (or hazelnuts)
½ teaspoon baking powder
pinch of salt
1 tablespoon milk

Up for a challenge

HANDS-ON TIME:
2 hours

BAKING TIME:
12–13 minutes

MAKES:
about 30 biscuits

SPECIAL EQUIPMENT:
3–4 baking sheets, ruler or tape measure, 20cm square cake tin (optional), pizza wheel (optional), palette knife

METHOD USED:
Creamed method, page 25

1. Start by preparing the vanilla dough. Cream the butter with the caster sugar and icing sugar until pale and light. This is easiest and quickest using a free-standing mixer fitted with the creamer/paddle attachment. Scrape down the sides of the bowl, add the vanilla extract and mix again. Add the egg yolk and beat until combined.

2. Tip the flour, ground almonds, baking powder and salt into the bowl, add the milk and mix again until combined. Do not overmix the dough as it could become tough rather than crisp and light. Gather the dough into a ball, flatten into a neat rectangle, cover with clingfilm and pop into the fridge.

3. Prepare the chocolate dough in the same way, adding the cocoa powder with the flour. Chill both the vanilla and chocolate dough for about 2 hours.

4. Divide both the vanilla and the chocolate dough in half as you'll find it easier to work with a smaller amount of dough. Lightly dust the work surface with plain flour and roll one half of the vanilla dough out into a square,
Continued

no more than 2mm thick and about 22cm square.

5. Lay the cake tin on top to use as a guide and, using a long kitchen knife or a pizza wheel, cut out a neat 20cm square. Carefully lift up the square, trying not to stretch it out of shape and place on a sheet of baking paper. Gather the off-cuts into a ball and set aside.

6. Roll one of the chocolate dough halves out in the same way and cut out another 20cm square. Gather the scraps into a ball and set aside. Lightly brush the vanilla square with a little milk and place the chocolate square neatly on top.

7. Using a ruler or tape measure mark the square into five strips, each 4cm wide. Using the knife (or a pizza wheel) cut the square into the five strips. Brush the top of the strip on the right with a little milk and lay the adjacent one on top of it so that it is now four alternate layers of dough.

8. Brush this one with milk and repeat this layering until you have stacked all the strips one on top of each other in alternately coloured layers. Carefully wrap this square log in baking paper and pop into the freezer while you prepare the remaining portions of vanilla and chocolate dough in the same way. Freeze both logs for 15–20 minutes.

9. Unwrap the first log and lay it so that the slices are stacked horizontally. Measure the width of the log and carefully mark it into four even-sized strips down the length – they should each be roughly 1cm wide and 20cm long. Starting on the right-hand side, cut the log into a slice using the marks as a guide. Lay this slice down flat on the parchment and lightly brush the top with milk. Cut the second slice and lay it on a palette knife. Turn this slice around by 180 degrees so that the layers are now the reverse of the first slice and lay the second slice on top of the first.

10. Repeat this slicing and layering, turning the alternate slices so the stack becomes a grid of alternate colours. Wrap in baking paper and freeze again for 20 minutes while you slice and layer the second log.

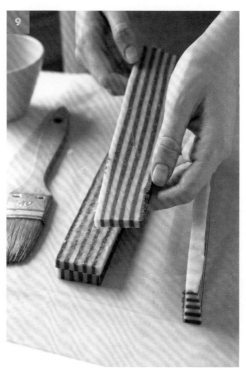

11. Finally, roll the vanilla dough off-cuts out into a rectangle roughly 17 × 20cm and trim one of the longer sides. Brush with milk and lay one of the square logs on top of the dough with the straight edges lined up. Roll the log neatly in vanilla dough as if you were wrapping a Battenberg cake in marzipan. Trim the end to neaten, wrap in baking paper

and freeze for 40 minutes. Roll out the reserved chocolate dough in the same way and use to wrap the second log. Trim to neaten, wrap in baking paper and freeze as before.

12. Preheat the oven to 170°C (150°C fan), Gas 3 and **line** 3–4 baking sheets with baking paper.

13. Unwrap the first log from the baking paper, trim the ends and cut into slices no more than 2–3mm thick. Arrange on the prepared baking sheet, leaving a little space between each one to allow for spreading during cooking. Bake in batches on the middle shelf of the oven for about 12–13 minutes until firm and very pale golden at the edges. Repeat this slicing and baking with the second log. The biscuits will firm and crisp up further on cooling.

Try Something Different

Sandwich the biscuits together with a little chocolate hazelnut spread.

Gingerbread House

Gingerbread houses are fun to make but do require concentration and a little time to get them just right. Pop a night light candle inside as a festive touch to illuminate the stained glass.

For the dough

4 tablespoons golden syrup
2 tablespoons treacle
4 large egg yolks
600g plain flour, plus extra for rolling out
4 teaspoons ground ginger
2 teaspoons ground cinnamon
1 teaspoon mixed spice
1½ teaspoons baking powder
large pinch of salt
300g unsalted butter, chilled and diced
150g light muscovado sugar
75g caster sugar

For the decoration

fruit-flavoured boiled sweets in assorted colours
500g royal icing sugar
sweets, candies and cake decorations

Up for
a challenge

HANDS-ON TIME:
3+ hours,
plus setting

BAKING TIME:
12 minutes for
each panel but
1 hour in total

MAKES:
1 house

SPECIALIST
EQUIPMENT:
several baking sheets,
assorted cutters
(rounds, squares,
hearts),
disposable
piping bags

METHOD USED:
Rubbed-in method,
page 22

1. Heat a measuring tablespoon up in a mug of boiling water for 1 minute – this makes it easy and less messy to measure the golden syrup and treacle. Spoon the golden syrup and treacle into a small bowl, add the egg yolks and mix well to combine.

2. Tip the flour, ginger, cinnamon, mixed spice, baking powder and salt into a large mixing bowl or into the bowl of a free-standing mixer. Add the chilled, diced butter and either **rub** in using your fingertips or by using the creamer/paddle attachment for the mixer. When there are no visible flecks of butter remaining add the light muscovado sugar and caster sugar and mix again to combine.

3. Make a well in the middle of the mixture, add the golden syrup, treacle and egg yolks and mix until the dough starts to come together into clumps. Using your hands, gently knead the dough until smooth but try not to over-work the dough or you will stretch the gluten strands in the flour, resulting in dough that is tough and may shrink and become misshapen during baking. Flatten the dough into a disc, weigh it and divide it in half – you should have two even pieces each weighing just over 700g. Wrap in clingfilm and chill for 2 hours.

4. Meanwhile photocopy the templates for the gingerbread house on page 162 and scale them up by 155 per cent so that they are the correct size; then cut them out.
Continued

5. Unwrap the boiled sweets and divide them into freezer bags so that each bag has just one colour. Double bag them (this will stop them spilling out of the bags) and using either a rolling pin, pestle or the bottom of a pan, lightly bash the sweets to break them up.

6. **Line** three solid baking sheets with baking paper and lightly dust the work surface with flour. Preheat the oven to 170°C (150°C fan), Gas 3.

7. Take one piece of the gingerbread dough and divide it into three portions – one of these portions should be slightly smaller than the other two. Roll out the smaller piece into a neat rectangle just slightly larger than the template for the house side walls. Lay the template on top and using a long, sharp knife or pizza cutter cut out the wall shape. Gather the off-cuts together and put to one side. Carefully lift the wall, trying not to stretch the dough out of shape, and place on a lined baking sheet. Using the cutters stamp out 2–4 window shapes from the wall and fill in the holes with crushed boiled sweets. Do not overfill the holes or the sweets will spill out over the edges of the window shapes as they melt. Chill for 15 minutes while you prepare the next sections.

8. Roll out one of the larger pieces of dough into a large, neat rectangle, this time slightly larger than the roof template. Lay the template on top

and cut around it; reserve any off-cuts. Carefully lift onto a lined baking sheet and using one corner of a square biscuit-cutter stamp out small triangles from the bottom edge of the roof to make a fancy roof tile edge. Chill for 15 minutes.

9. Meanwhile roll the third piece of dough out as before and cut out the end wall, using the template as a guide. Using the knife cut out a door shape and place the door on the baking sheet. Use the cutters to stamp out windows in assorted shapes such as rounds, squares or hearts, fill the windows with crushed boiled sweets and chill as before.

10. Gather the off-cuts together, re-roll and cut out the four chimney sections, using the templates as a guide. If you like you can use any leftover dough to make gingerbread people to complete the scene.

11. Bake the gingerbread sections in batches on the middle shelf of the oven for 10–12 minutes, until firm and slightly darkened at the edges and the sweets have melted. It will still appear soft at this stage but will harden further on cooling. Leave to cool completely on the baking sheets.

12. Repeat with the second half of the dough – you should have two roof sections, two side walls, two end walls, four chimney pieces and one door – plus any optional gingerbread people.

13. Now comes the fun part: decorating and assembling. Choose the board or tray that you plan to display the gingerbread house on, as it will be almost impossible to move it once assembled.

Continued

14. Tip the 500g royal icing sugar into a bowl and gradually add water one tablespoon at a time, beating constantly until the icing is smooth and thick enough to hold a firm ribbon trail. Spoon half of the icing into a disposable **piping** bag (cover the remaining icing with clingfilm) and snip the end into a fine point. Pipe fine lines and dots around the window frames on each wall panel and pipe latticed windowpanes on the stained glass. Stick sweets, candies and cake decorations over the walls, using the royal icing as 'glue'. Be as creative as you like, perhaps enlisting the help of children. Pipe roof tiles over both roof sections and bricks over the chimney pieces. Leave the icing to dry for at least 30 minutes and for up to 1 hour.

15. Take one of the end walls and pipe a line of icing along the bottom edge. Stand this at one end of your board or tray with the best side facing outwards. Hold it in place for 2 minutes to allow the icing to start to set. You can also balance it against a glass for extra stability. Next pipe a line of icing along the bottom and side edges of a side wall section and press this at a right angle up against the end wall. Pipe an extra line of icing inside the join to act as extra 'cement', hold in place and stabilise with a glass on either side. Leave for 10 minutes until firm.

16. Repeat this process of piping and sticking with the remaining two wall sections, remembering to pipe inside the joins for stability. Once you have all

four walls upright leave them to dry and firm up for 1 hour. At this point you can also decorate the outside corners of the house with sweets sticking them on with icing – this not only looks pretty but also hides any untidy joins.

17. Meanwhile assemble the chimney. Take one rectangular section and lay it best-side down on the work surface. Pipe a line of icing along one of the long sides. Pipe icing along one long side of a cut-out chimney section and hold it vertically onto the first section (best side facing outwards) until secure. Repeat with the other cut-out section on the opposite side and finally secure a rectangular piece on top – you should now have a square chimney. Leave until set firm.

18. To secure the roof panels, pipe a line of icing along the upright and sloping roof lines on one side of the house and hold a roof panel in place, so that the top edge lines up with the top of the roof. (You may need a second pair of hands here.) Pipe extra 'cement' underneath the gable ends to secure and prop the bottom of the roof up with a jam jar or mug to hold it in place. Repeat with the second roof panel. Finally pipe a line of icing along the top of the roof and leave to set firm for 30 minutes before attaching the chimney.

19. Stand back and hold your breath.

What biscuits shall I bake today?

Conversion Tables

WEIGHT

Metric	Imperial
25g	1oz
50g	2oz
75g	2½oz
85g	3oz
100g	4oz
125g	4½oz
140g	5oz
175g	6oz
200g	7oz
225g	8oz
250g	9oz
280g	10oz
300g	11oz
350g	12oz
375g	13oz
400g	14oz
425g	15oz
450g	1lb
500g	1lb 2oz
550g	1lb 4oz
600g	1lb 5oz
650g	1lb 7oz
700g	1lb 9oz
750g	1lb 10oz
800g	1lb 12oz
850g	1lb 14oz
900g	2lb
950g	2lb 2oz
1kg	2lb 4oz

VOLUME

Metric	Imperial
30ml	1fl oz
50ml	2fl oz
75ml	3fl oz
125ml	4fl oz
150ml	¼ pint
175ml	6fl oz
200ml	7fl oz
225ml	8fl oz
300ml	½ pint
350ml	12fl oz
400ml	14fl oz
450ml	¾ pint
500ml	18fl oz
600ml	1 pint
725ml	1¼ pints
1 litre	1¾ pints

SPOON MEASURES

Metric	Imperial
5ml	1 teaspoon
10ml	2 teaspoons
15ml	1 tablespoon
30ml	2 tablespoons
45ml	3 tablespoons
60ml	4 tablespoons
75ml	5 tablespoons

LINEAR

Metric	Imperial
2.5cm	1in
3cm	1¼in
4cm	1½in
5cm	2in
5.5cm	2¼in
6cm	2½in
7cm	2¾in
7.5cm	3in
8cm	3¼in
9cm	3½in
9.5cm	3¾in
10cm	4in
11cm	4¼in
12cm	4½in
13cm	5in
14cm	5½in
15cm	6in
16cm	6½in
17cm	6½in
18cm	7in
19cm	7½in
20cm	8in
22cm	8½in
23cm	9in
24cm	9½in
25cm	10in

Templates

Gingerbread House (*see pages 154–159*)

Front and back wall
(x2)

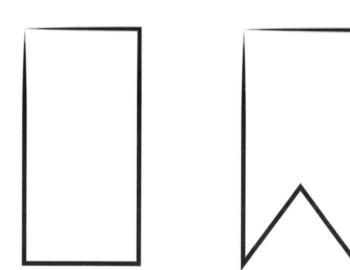

Chimney:
sides and
back/front
(x2 of each)

Side wall (x2)

Continued

Roof (x2)

Index

Acknowledgements

Hodder & Stoughton and Love Productions would like to thank the following people for their contribution to this book:

Annie Rigg, Linda Collister, Laura Herring, Caroline McArthur, Sam Binnie, Helena Caldon, Alasdair Oliver, Kate Brunt, Laura Del Vescovo, Joanna Seaton, Sarah Christie, Anna Heath, Damian Horner, Auriol Bishop, Anna Beattie, Rupert Frisby, Jane Treasure, Sharon Powers.

Continue on your journey to star baker with tips and advice on how to *Bake It Better* from the **GREAT BRITISH BAKE OFF** team.

DON'T JUST BAKE. BAKE IT BETTER.